7 iX. 93

PENGUIN BOOKS

THE NATIONAL TRUS'
BOOK OF THE ENGLISH GA

CW00969833

Richard Bisgrove studied horticultural science and landscape architecture in Britain and the USA and, after a brief period of professional practice, returned to the University of Reading to lecture in landscape and amenity horticulture. He is now a Senior Lecturer and the Course Director of Britain's first degree course in landscape management. He was elected to the Council of the Garden History Society in 1973 and was editor of the Society's *Newsletter* from 1981 to 1983. He is also a member of the National Trust's Gardens Panel and a member of the Institute of Horticulture's Editorial Advisory Committee and Education and Training Committee.

He has written five books on aspects of garden design and garden history, including most recently *Gardens of Gertrude Jekyll*. He was consultant editor of *Colour Schemes for the Flower Garden: The Illustrated Gertrude Jekyll*. He has advised on the restoration and management of several historic gardens and he is particularly aware of the relationship between patron, designer and gardener in the creation of gardens through the ages.

Richard Bisgrove's other research interest is in the development and management of species-rich grassland, a topic closely related to the medieval garden, the Robinsonian 'Wild Garden' and the late-twentieth-century garden.

He lives in Oxfordshire with his wife, four children and a very weedy garden.

horticultural extravaganza.

With love

Lucy

X

THE NATIONAL TRUST
BOOK OF THE
ENGLISH GARDEN

Richard Bisgrove

PENGUIN BOOKS

PENGUIN BOOKS

Published by the Penguin Group
Penguin Books Ltd, 27 Wrights Lane, London W8 5TZ, England
Penguin Books USA Inc., 375 Hudson Street, New York, New York 10014, USA
Penguin Books Australia Ltd, Ringwood, Victoria, Australia
Penguin Books Canada Ltd, 10 Alcorn Avenue, Toronto, Ontario, Canada M4V 3B2
Penguin Books (NZ) Ltd, 182–190 Wairau Road, Auckland 10, New Zealand

Penguin Books Ltd, Registered Offices: Harmondsworth, Middlesex, England

First published by Viking 1990
Published in Penguin Books 1992
1 3 5 7 9 10 8 6 4 2

Printed and bound in Great Britain by
Butler & Tanner Ltd Frome and London

Contents

List of Colour Illustrations

Acknowledgements

Garden history is a subject which has intrigued me for more than a quarter of a century and my first thanks for assistance in writing *The National Trust Book of the English Garden* must go to the many friends in the Garden History Society for feeding that interest. Mavis Batey, Professor W. T. Stearn, Brent Elliott (doubly helpful as Librarian of the Royal Horticultural Society's Lindley Library), John Harvey and many others have provided inspiration by their amiable scholarship. The National Trust, in its unique position as custodian of many of the world's finest historic gardens, has logically been the source of much of my information, both in the gardens themselves and in illustrations used in this book. I am deeply grateful, in particular, to John Sales and his small but dedicated garden advisory team at Cirencester for their continued help and friendship, and to Graham Thomas who has contributed as much to modern gardening through his books as he has to historic gardens in his former role as Gardens Adviser.

The Book of the English Garden has taken a very long time to write, much longer than the publishers would have liked. Often I have felt like an astronomer, trying to map the outer limits of a universe expanding away from him at the speed of light. Eleo Gordon, my editor at Viking/Penguin, nearly succeeded in confining my enthusiasm to within the bounds of realistic production schedules, while Annie Lee (copy editor) and Susan Rose-Smith (illustration research) have greatly eased that production by their efficient and skilful efforts. My sincere thanks must go to all three.

Time is a finite commodity. The thousands of hours it takes to write a book must come from somewhere. My sincere apologies and deepest thanks go to my children, and, in particular, to my long-suffering wife, for their patience, understanding, and sometimes sympathy, on the innumerable occasions when family activities have had to take second place.

R.B.

Introduction

———

Why is England a nation of gardeners? What affects the way we garden as we do? And what will our gardens look like as we enter the next millennium? These are some of the questions asked and answered in the *National Trust Book of the English Garden*.

The great majority of English families have a garden of their own. An increasing number enjoy visiting other people's gardens. The 1,000 gardens open under the National Gardens Scheme in 1932 increased to over 2,200 in 1988, while visitors to the top six National Trust gardens of 1967 almost doubled in number by 1987, from 495,000 to 823,000. The more we know about the origins and development of gardens, their design and contents, the more interesting these activities become. On the wider cultural scene, gardens provide a remarkable indicator of civilization because they require a settled, organized and wealthy society for their creation and continued survival and because they inevitably reflect changes in art and culture, science and technology, politics and society.

This book has been written to provide a concise account of the evolution of gardens in order to foster enjoyment and appreciation of this unique aspect of our heritage. My aim in the pages that follow is to investigate those factors which have influenced the development of English gardens throughout history, to weave these multifarious strands together and to describe the characteristic gardens of each period.

It is very tempting, in trying to present a clear and brief account, to over-emphasize the importance of period styles and to present the history of gardens as a sequence of professional designers and their work. However, developments in art, technology and politics, and the life-spans of great patrons and practitioners, do not fall into neatly synchronized periods. Neither is the relationship between patron and practitioner a constant one. I know from my own experience as a garden designer that clients vary enormously: some need the position of every plant specified down to the last crocus corm; others want help with the general disposition of the garden but are happy to fill in the details themselves, while a few know perfectly well what they are aiming for but like to discuss their ideas with someone equally interested before taking the plunge.

Furthermore, the phenomenon of cultural diffusion of ideas applies as much to gardens as to any other realm of art and craft. Innovations are experimented with by pioneering individuals, perfected and made practicable by professionals, standardized and publicized by the writers of pattern books and, in recent times, watered down and dissolved into a generalized body of gardening practice by glossy magazines and television programmes. In less democratic ages than ours, novel ideas have usually filtered down, with a gradual blurring of intent, from nobility to gentry, to professional and lower classes, over a span of several decades or even generations. An accurately focused snapshot of the nation's gardens at any one moment in history will, therefore, show a great diversity of gardens, pioneering, fashionable and old-hat, maturing and declining.

In the book I have taken the structure offered by the major practitioners – London and Wise, Bridgeman, Kent, Brown, etc. – as the skeleton of the book and have tried to separate out the varied contributions of patrons, practitioners and publishers while weaving together the various changes which have influenced our gardens. Presenting such a cobweb of ideas in a linear way inevitably results in some loose ends and some repetition of key points, but I hope to illustrate both the development and diversity of gardens, to look at the mainstream of garden history and to explore some of the eddies, carefully steering a course between sweeping generalizations and masses of unrelated details.

Throughout the book, including in its title, I have used the word 'English' in a very loose way, as a less pompous-sounding (if slightly less accurate) adjective than 'British'. Partly because of the immense economic and political magnetism which London has exerted for centuries on the populace of our island, the vast majority of British gardens are, in fact, in England. Wales and Scotland have not always been part of Great Britain in a political sense, and any attempt to incorporate Irish gardens into 'British' history in a concise manner without causing offence in some quarter is, sadly, doomed to disaster. I have therefore used 'English' as a vague shorthand alternative to 'British', but have borrowed Welsh, Scottish and Irish examples without hesitation when appropriate, in the earnest hope that this will not cause offence in the other three corners of the UK, for whose landscapes and cultures I have a very deep admiration.

The National Trust Book of the English Garden is self-sufficient in that it paints an overall picture of all aspects of English gardens, but no book on this subject can now honestly claim to be comprehensive. When I first began to think of writing a book of this sort, the only relatively modern book on the subject was Miles Hadfield's *Gardening in Britain*. This remains a treasure trove of information but, since its publication in 1960, interest in gardens and garden history has grown phenomenally. The Garden History Society, founded in 1965, has acted as a focus for research and conservation, while the sixteen volumes of *Garden History* published by the Society, the fruits of innumerable conferences, symposia and other meetings, have produced a mass of detailed information supplemented by a steady flow of books on particular periods or aspects of garden development and by new editions of many books of historical interest in themselves.

It must now be accepted that our current knowledge of gardens in history requires a substantial library rather than a fat volume to accommodate it. The purpose of this book, therefore, is to provide a general description of English garden history, sufficient in itself for those with only a general interest in the subject, and to offer, through footnotes and bibliography, a link to the wider mass of literature for those who wish to follow any specialist topic in greater detail.

The book is published in association with the National Trust. In a country richly endowed with gardens, the 130 gardens of the National Trust represent a resource unique in the whole world, encompassing gardens of almost every age and size, design and purpose, soil and situation. This diversity has been drawn on repeatedly throughout the book to provide examples illustrating particular points, although many other gardens have, of course, been cited where necessary to complete the picture.

The heritage in the care of the National Trust is now of such proportions that it can provide not only wonderful illustrations of past gardens but also seeds of hope for the future. As a repository of gardening skills the Trust is unequalled. New career structures and training schemes for its gardeners carry the potential to reverse nearly a century of decline in skills and to revitalize garden-making in general. Whereas Miles Hadfield saw 1939 as marking the end of garden-making in England, I see the 1990s as an exciting beginning, with many opportunities to provide gardens for a new age.

I

In the Beginning

George Johnson, in his pioneering *History of English Gardening*,[1] reminds us that God first planted a garden and that Noah, only the tenth descendant from Adam, knew enough about gardening to plant a vineyard immediately after the flood and to become intoxicated with the product of its fruit. Whether the Old Testament is taken as an accurate or a figurative account of Man's origins, it indicates very clearly the rapidity with which early Man learned about the cultivation of plants. Physical and spiritual sustenance, religion and ritual, clothing and decoration were inextricably combined, and, from Man's earliest existence, plants have furnished the ingredients of all these facets of life.

The cultivation of plants in gardens, though, requires a settled and organized society, and the making of gardens serves as a barometer of civilization. Since the emergence of the Egyptian Empire some 5,000 years ago, each successive civilization has produced gardens which, in their amalgam of art, craft and science, have reflected the culture of their creators.

A tomb-painting of a high official in the court of Amenhotep III (*c.* 1500 BC) shows rows of palms and sykomor fig trees, a shaded and fragrant grape arbour, pools filled with lotus and bordered by waving papyrus, all within a high-walled enclosure watered by irrigation canals.

Further east, in Assyria and Persia, gardens developed in more favourable conditions. The land was hilly, well watered and thickly wooded. Assyrian nobles, fond of the chase, planted great parks or *pairadaeza* with exotic trees, and stocked them with great herds of wild animals. Tiglath-Pileser I (*c.* 1100 BC) expresses a gardening spirit recognizable in the twentieth century when he boasts of the cedars and box carried off from conquered lands, 'trees that none

Lotus flowers, fish and waterfowl with papyrus around the pool margin, from an Egyptian tomb painting c.1400BC.

of the kings, my forefathers, have possessed, these trees have I taken and planted in mine own country, in the parks of Assyria'.[2]

The Greeks, in their progress across Asia, found many such parks. Xenophon described them in some detail and made his own park at Scillus, dedicated to Artemis, in imitation of them. The Romans in their turn conquered Greece, North Africa and Asia Minor, plundering their palaces and absorbing their cultures. In and around Rome the spoils of war were exhibited in rambling villas and extensive gardens. Perhaps the best known of these was that belonging to the younger Pliny and described by him in a letter to a friend:

In front of the portico is a sort of terrace, embellished with various figures, and bounded with a box hedge, from which you descend by an easy slope, adorned with the representations of divers animals in box. [There] is a very spacious hippodrome, encompassed on every side by plane trees covered with ivy ... behind these bays which blend their shade with that of the plane trees. A semi-circle ... set around with cypress trees, varies the prospect and casts a deeper and more gloomy shade; while inward circular walks enjoying an open exposure, are perfumed with roses, and correct by a very pleasing contrast, the coolness of the shade with the warmth of the sun.[3]

With the expansion of the Roman Empire through Europe, many aspects of their highly organized society moved northwards. The invasion of Britain, beginning in AD 43, had far-reaching consequences in establishing a network of roads for defence and mineral exploitation, in establishing or enlarging many towns to service this network and, perhaps most notably, in establishing London as a centre of national and international importance.

Although a good deal is known about Roman life in Britain, very little is known about their gardens. At home they were knowledgeable cultivators of vegetables and fruits, as well as creators of elaborate pleasure gardens such as Pliny's. Cato mentions turnip, radish, basil, beans, cabbage, garlic and asparagus (150 BC), to which later writers added parsley, lettuce, beet, peas, carrots, parsnips, onions and several others. The Emperor Tiberius even employed hot-beds of manure and thin, translucent sheets of mica to force cucumbers so that he could enjoy them throughout the year. Of fruits, Cato mentions seven varieties of olive, six of grape

An escape from summer heat: the Empress Livia's underground 'garden', painted on the walls in her villa in Rome.

and several apples, pears, nuts, quinces, figs and pomegranates. Cherries, peaches and apricots were introduced later (the cherry by Lucullus, *c.* 73 BC), while strawberries, raspberries, gooseberries and currants grew wild in the hills.

In far-flung corners of the Empire the Romans were forced to live more simply, but they carried with them their native methods of building and gardening wherever possible – and all the plants listed above could be grown with a certain amount of care in southern Britain. Even vineyards were established, with permission from the Emperor Probus, *c.* AD 278.

At Fishbourne, near Chichester, the open courts around which the rooms of a Roman palace were grouped have been revealed by excavation. Because of the very heavy clay of the district the gardeners found it necessary to prepare special trenches for their plants, so it has been possible, in one of the earliest instances of 'garden archaeology', to trace the main outlines of the garden and its neatly trimmed hedges with a completeness seldom possible elsewhere.

It is impossible to say with any accuracy how many of the Roman introductions survived after their departure. However, many of the strategic sites of Roman occupation were soon recolonized by more gentle invaders from the same direction, the Christian monks, and the survival to the present day of *Paeonia mascula* on the monastic island of Steep Holm in the Bristol Channel lends evidence of plant survival over many centuries.

With the collapse of the Roman Empire, Britain was again divided into many small kingdoms. Life became increasingly insecure, and gardens could survive and develop only where security could be ensured – in the monasteries, and later the castles, of medieval Britain.

2

The Medieval Garden

The centuries of invasion and internecine wars which marked the early centuries of Saxon rule well deserve their connotation of 'Dark Ages', and the social turmoil of the period created a fertile environment for the spread of Christianity, which was expanding across Europe from monastic nuclei in Egypt, Persia and Ireland. In 597, less than seventy years after St Benedict had established the first European monastery at Monte Cassino, south of Rome, St Augustine landed in England and founded a monastery at Canterbury. The missionary zeal of the monks, allied to the serene example of their ascetic earthly existence, wielded a powerful influence in a turbulent land and Christianity spread rapidly in the seventh century.

Monastic gardens

Because of their stability and relative freedom from attack, often combined with a code of living which demanded self-sufficiency, the early monasteries provided vitally important reservoirs of classical learning and horticultural practice. For many centuries the monasteries virtually monopolized the skills of reading and writing, law and medicine. Links gradually forged through France and Germany to Rome formed a network for the disseminating of knowledge and the introduction of plants.

Because clerics, with their skills in writing and their knowledge of law, played an important role in the administration of court, monastic growth coincided with (indeed probably assisted) the emergence of three powerful dynasties from the ten or so kingdoms which survived the Dark Ages in England. In 806, with

Northumbria and Mercia crushed by Viking invaders, Egbert of Wessex became in effect King of all England. The relative peace of this fragile unity, the alliance of King and Church and the growth of monasteries both in size and in number ended England's relative isolation from Europe and accelerated the influx of gardening among other skills.

On the European mainland the Frankish Empire paralleled, on a mightier scale, the recurrent phases of invasion, absorption and expansion achieved by the Kings of Northumbria, Mercia and ultimately Wessex. On Christmas Day 800 Charlemagne's imperial coronation took place in Rome, and by his death in 814 his Empire extended from the Pyrenees to Bavaria and from the North Sea to Rome.

From this flowering of the Carolingian Empire three documents have survived more than 1,000 years, to give the clearest picture we have of the contents, form and cultivation of the medieval monastery garden. Although all three emanated from within a few miles of each other near the centre of the Empire, in what is now southern Germany, it is not unreasonable to deduce from them a picture of English monastic life in the same period. Intercourse with European monasteries was increasingly common. Alcuin of York, for example, was a principal adviser to Charlemagne and, only a generation later, England's future King Alfred travelled twice to Rome in his youth and had medical prescriptions from the Patriarch of Jerusalem.

The first of these three documents, the *Capitulare de Villis*, written for Charlemagne himself, describes in fine detail how the Empire was to be managed, even including a list of plants to be cultivated in the monastery gardens. From this list it is obvious that gardens were to be useful. Of eighty-nine plants listed, seventy-three were medicinal. Significantly, though, as throughout the medieval world, two flowers featured first: the rose, symbolizing the blood of Christ and his thorny crown, and the white lily, symbolizing the purity of the Virgin Mary, the Madonna. The list of plants and probable authorship of the *Capitulare* as a whole is attributed to Benedict of Aniome, and although there has been much discussion and doubt concerning the feasibility of growing some of the plants throughout the whole Empire, it is a perfectly credible general-purpose list from which the abbots and gardening obedientiaries could select according to their locale.[1]

Within a few years of the *Capitulare* a plan for an ideal monastery, probably drawn by Abbot Haito of Reichenau, was sent to St Gall, some twenty-five miles away. The plan shows buildings – church,

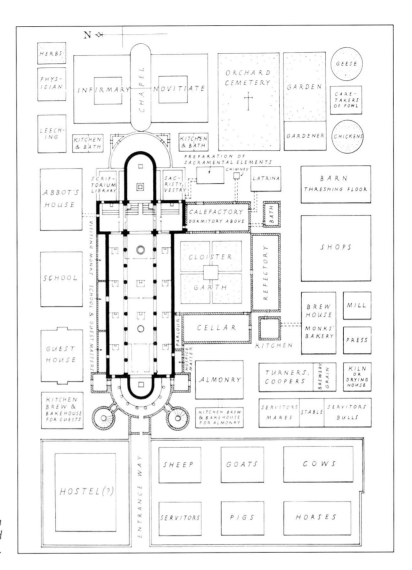

Abbot Haito's idealized plan for a monastery garden, found at St Gall.

school, hospice, stables and farm buildings – grouped around a series of courtyards or cloisters. The cloistered enclosures are shown quartered with a central basin or other feature in the centre, except in the physic garden, adjacent to the physician's house and conveniently near the cemetery. Here the plan shows simply a central path with nine rectangular beds on either side, each devoted to one type of plant. The east side of the garden, behind the high altar, is designated 'paradise' which, with the quartered plan of the cloister garths, is an early indication of Islamic influence. In this earthly paradise one could contemplate the world to come and probably gather flowers for altar decoration.

The 'Little Garden'

Benedict, author of the *Capitulare*, is known to have met Abbot Tatto of Reichenau (whence came the St Gall plan), and Tatto was tutor and master of Walahfrid Strabo, author of the third Carolingian garden source. Walahfrid's *Hortulus* ('Little Garden') was written about 840 but remained undiscovered in the archives of St Gall until 1509. It has since been published several times and, in modern translation, it is one of the most accessible medieval sources as well as one of the most delightful of all garden books.[2]

Hortulus is not as detailed as the great *Capitulare*. It lists only twenty-seven plants, mainly culinary herbs, but Walahfrid's good sense, his practical knowledge, his obvious delight in gardening and his philosophical analogies between the world of plants and the world of man endow his writing with enormous charm.

He begins with the rewards and difficulties of gardening.

> If you do not refuse to harden or dirty your hands ... to spread whole baskets of dung on the sun-parched soil – then, you may rest assured, your soil will not fail you.
> I set to with my mattock ... I tore those nettles though they grew and grew again. I destroyed the tunnels of the moles ... and back to the realms of light I summoned the worms.[3]

When rains and spring sunshine have brought the garden to life Walahfrid lists the contents of his garden. Sage, which needs frequent hard pruning because 'within itself is the germ of civil war; for unless the new growth is cut away, it turns savagely on its parent and chokes to death the older stems';[4] rue and southernwood; gourds which 'aspire to grow high from humble beginnings. They learn to use borrowed strength and, with the swimmer's thrust, climb the steep roofs of the covered cloister';[5] melon, wormwood, horehound and fennel. The iris has many uses:

> ... the beauty of your purple flower ... We dry the shavings of your root, crush them and dissolve them in wine [to] relieve griping pains in the bladder. With your help too the laundryman can stiffen his shining linen and scent it sweetly.[6]

Lovage and chervil are next mentioned, then the lily, poppy, clary and mint in its many varieties.

Walahfrid's description of the lily illustrates its importance as a garden flower and his own close acquaintance with it.

> In this flower lies Chastity, strong in her sacred honour. If no unclean hand disturbs her, if no illicit passion does violence to her, the flower

¶ The quene of fame.   To dame Pallas

Ꝑynces mooſt puſant of hygh pꝛeemynence.
Renoⱳnyd lady aboue the ſterry heuyn.

The rose, pre-eminent of all medieval flowers.

smells sweetly. But should her pride of innocence be lost, the scent turns foul and noisome.[7]

The Madonna lily offers its fragrance freely on the air, but only those who have divided or staked or cut it would be aware of the less desirable odour which it emits when bruised.

Of the common pennyroyal, 'they say that Eastern doctors will pay as much for it as we pay here for a load of Indian pepper', but then 'some things we scorn rich kingdoms pay great prices for and so one hand helps another; so the whole world, through all its parts, makes one family'.[8] Finally comes the rose: '... it well deserves its name "the flower of flowers".'[9]

The *Hortulus*, recreating the sweetness and tranquillity of a medieval monastery garden, also illustrates two less pleasant aspects of medieval life: violence and bad food. While fragrance and beauty are constant virtues of the plants Walahfrid describes, healing of wounds and soothing of stomachs are among their most frequent uses.

Rue has power 'to combat hidden toxin and to expel from the bowels the invading forces of noxious poison'.[10] Fennel 'eases a swollen stomach and quickly loosens sluggish bowels'.[11] Chervil, pennyroyal and poppy leaves make 'a poultice which will prove effective for a stomach that's upset and racked with pain'.[12] Agrimony 'will check the most violent stomach-ache. And if an enemy blade happens to wound us we are recommended to try its aid, pounding the shoots and putting them on the open place.'[13] Catmint 'can cure the hurt of a wound ... renewing the hair which the blood and pus of the gaping sore had eaten away'.[14] Crushed lilies will cure snake-bite or heal dislocated limbs and 'if ever a vicious step-mother mixes in your drink subtle poisons, or makes a treacherous dish of lethal aconite for you, don't waste a moment – take a dose of wholesome horehound; that will counteract the danger you suspect'.[15]

Walahfrid died in 849, drowning as he crossed the river Loire on a mission to his former pupil, Charlemagne's grandson Charles.

In 848, in Britain, Alfred of Wessex was born. A vigorous and victorious fighter against the Danish invaders, Alfred was even more successful in his peaceful pursuits. Many new towns were founded to stimulate trade; foreign scholars and craftsmen brought new skills; schools were established for the sons of nobility, and monasteries and convents were restored and encouraged.

Monastic gardens, too, flourished. England blossomed as never before, but the rich pickings of a prosperous country proved tempting bait. From 1017 to 1042 Danish kings ruled, and in 1066 came the most famous and most significant invasion in England's history, the Norman conquest.

William's coronation had many repercussions. It brought England into closer association with Normandy and into contact with Latin European ideas. It brought stability not only in political terms but also geographically. The nobility were able, indeed were encouraged, to spend much of their lives on their estates instead of travelling to distant battlefields.

In addition to renewed contact with the ancient but moribund culture of classical Europe, the Norman invasion also brought a more vital influence. Norman expansion extended westwards into Islamic Iberia as well as northwards to Britain.

Gardens of Islam

Muhammad's death in 632 had sparked a worldwide expansion of Islam, with dynastic caliphs dedicated to dominating but not destroying the cultures they overran. Arab invaders conquered Persia (642) and Egypt, then crossed from North Africa to Spain (709), Toulouse and the Rhône before their progress was checked by the Franks at Poitiers in 732. In Persia the invaders discovered and absorbed a highly developed culture in which parks and gardens held an important place. Gardens symbolized the source of life, with a central basin feeding four rivers running north, south, east and west to water the earth.

Images of man or animal were forbidden, but this stimulated great ingenuity in the creation of tiled pavilions, complex fountains and elaborate water-engines, tree-shaded walks and fragrant flowers, especially roses. Brilliant colour, heavy fragrance and inner repose merged in a sensuous paradise garden.

The Abbasid dynasty (750–936) saw the highest development of prosperity, building, culture and gardens. When Baghdad was founded in 762, an academy was established to translate into Arabic all the major philosophical and scientific works of the classical world. Fresh research in botany was begun by Abu Hanifah al-Dinawari (c. 820–95), and his *Book of Plants* was taken to Córdoba, the capital of Moorish Spain and the greatest city in Europe. By the tenth century there existed in Spain a flourishing tradition of ornamental gardens with aqueducts, canals and fountains, brilliantly patterned tile-work and plants from as far away as India: a far remove from the beans, onions and starch of European monastic gardens. In the eleventh century scientific botanic gardens were established, 500 years before the Renaissance of European botany, and the Muslims were skilled physicians.[16]

In 1064 William, then Duke of Aquitaine, captured Barbastro in Aragon and sent thousands of Moorish prisoners to Rome, Constantinople, France and later to England, where they practised their skills as linguists, teachers, jewellers, physicians and gardeners.

Enriched by the gradual infusion of new ideas and by the introduction of new plants, the English monasteries continued to expand their gardens. At Winchester, St Albans and Canterbury, for example, gardens and orchards were made and extended. At Ely, too, there were extensive gardens and orchards, and the vineyard planted by Abbot Brithnod in 1107 ranked second only to the Abbey itself among the attractions of Ely. William of Malmesbury considered the wine from these grapes inferior only to that from the Vale of Gloucester. Many more vineyards were planted in the South of England during the twelfth and thirteenth centuries, until a deterioration in the climate and freer trade with France made them increasingly unproductive. (There was a brief resurgence in the sixteenth century, when the mean temperature again rose, and another is evident in the late twentieth century.)

The growth of trade and cities in late medieval times was paralleled by a diversity of monastic orders: Cistercians with great country estates, solitary Carthusians, Dominicans and others. By the early thirteenth century Dominican friars were established on the outskirts of most major cities, settling near the main thoroughfares to minister to the sick and needy of the urban populace. Many of their gardens were managed by and leased to laymen, who produced plants, grafts and seeds for sale to other monasteries and secular gardens. After the Dissolution these nursery gardens often continued to exist, forming the basis of the nursery industry.

Plants – useful and beautiful

Much documentary evidence remains in monastic records to show the contents of these gardens. Apuleius' herbal, unlike most manuscripts which were copied from classical sources, was illustrated from life, using plants growing in the Benedictine monastery garden at Bury St Edmunds. Abbot Neckam (or Necham) was also one of the new generation of scholars who wrote from the experience of his extensive travels rather than plagiarizing debased and often irrelevant classical works. Born in 1157 in St Albans, he was appointed head of the Abbey school in Dunstable. By 1180 he was a distinguished professor at the University of Paris, returning to Dunstable in 1186 and finally to Cirencester where he remained as Abbot until his death in 1217. His poem *De naturis rerum*, in circulation before 1200, had chapters devoted to herbs, trees and flowers in the garden.[17] The longer *De laudibus divinae sapientiae* listed about 140 species of plants, nearly all of which could have been grown in Britain during the exceptionally warm climatic conditions then prevailing, if only, in the case of the most exotic such as citrus and date, as pot plants.[18] Most of the plants he described were common and must have featured in many contemporary gardens.

Neckam recommended:

The garden should be adorned with roses and lilies, turnsole, violets and mandrake; there you should have parsley and cost, and fennel, and southernwood, and coriander, sage, savory, hyssop, mint, rue, dittany, smallage, pellitory, lettuce, garden cress, peonies. There should also be planted beds with onions, leeks, garlick, pumpkins and shalots [*sic*]; cucumber, poppy, daffodil, and acanthus ought to be in a good garden. There should also be pottage herbs, such as beets, herb mercury, orach, sorrel, and mallows.[19]

Fruits included 'medlars, quinces, Wardon pears, peaches, and Pears of St Regula'.

Clearly, as in Carolingian monasteries, gardens were for utility, but this did not prevent them being attractive too. The cloistered setting and simple pattern of quartered plots with a central basin would itself give pleasure. Roses and lilies, enormously important as symbols both of Christ and of the Virgin Mary, also had more prosaic uses. Much later, in 1578, Henry Lyte recorded in his *Niewe Herball* that:

The roote of the white lillie ... pound with hony, joyneth togither sinews that are cut consumeth or scarreth away the ulcers of the head ... and cureth all manner of naughtie scurviness as likewise of the head beard and face and is good to be layed to all dislocations or places out of joint.

White lilies also cured corns and bald patches, while the juice of roses, especially red roses,

purgeth downewarde cholerique humours and openethe the stoppinges of the liver, strenthening and cleansing the same, also it is good agaynst hoate fevers and agaynst the Jaunders. It is also to be used agaynst the shaking, beating and trembling of the hart for it driveth away and dispatcheth all corrupt and evil humours in and about the veynes of the hart.

Of lesser flowers, violets and St Mary golds were eaten in salads; violets, primroses and also roses were cooked and served with milk and honey; scillas, poppy, mallow and dictamnus were used medicinally; celandine was used for healing tired eyes and jaundice and, with mercury and egg yolk, to make gold paint, while the iris, much loved and valued by Walahfrid, had a multitude of uses. The flower provided a juice for removing spots and freckles or for dyeing clothes purple (or green when fixed with alum); ink and orris (an early deodorant) were made from the root, while the leaves were used for strewing, mending roofs and covering chairs.

Sage, rue, rosemary (a late introduction in 1340), parsley, fennel, catmint, cardoon and many other herbs also had excellent foliage, a fact increasingly appreciated in the small, modern-day garden.

The garden plan

The form of these gardens is shown in Utopian symmetry in the plan of St Gall, but the plan of Christchurch, Canterbury, drawn to record the system of water pipes for Abbot Gervase in 1165, is a more convincing illustration of a monastery which had grown over the centuries. The cloister garths are devoted to the Necessarium, the Herbarium and other small gardens. The curved lines on the plan show a network of pipes supplying water to various parts of the monastery. These pipes connect to four scalloped

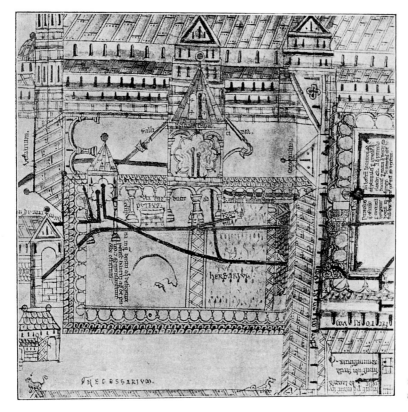

*The Abbey at Canterbury.
The network of pipes supplies
water to the fishpond and
numerous basins.*

circular shapes, which must surely be carved stone basins or fonts
within the buildings, and to a larger fishpond (piscina) by the east
wall. Fish formed an important part of the monks' diet: large ponds
for rearing fish and small stew-ponds in which netted fish could be
stored until required for the table formed an essential part of most
monasteries. These durable and attractive features often survived
secularization and remained an asset much valued by the new
household, as at Chilworth Manor near Guildford, Lacock and
Gunby Hall.

The cloisters formed the heart of the monastery, spiritually and
physically. St Augustine had used his garden for teaching, for
cultivating the human mind as well as the vegetable kingdom. It
symbolized a calm other-worldliness, a paradise only partly
removed from the sense of the Assyrian *pairadaeza*, a perfect
environment in which to transmit ideals of love, purity of heart
and selfless labour. Even in the Carthusian monasteries, where
monks lived a solitary existence in separate cells, the garden and
stream of water connecting the cells created some sense of unity.

These delightful flowery herb gardens, though, illustrate only a small aspect of monastic life. By the thirteenth century the monasteries controlled large estates. The monastic accounts refer almost entirely to field-scale production of staple necessities: it is twentieth-century nostalgia which makes a bushel of onion seed sound attractive. The pipe rolls of the Bishopric of Winchester, complete for the three centuries after 1208, have many entries relating to gardens. Leeks, kale, hedges and fruit feature prominently in the accounts. Peas, beans and onions were also major items in a largely meatless diet. A similar picture emerges at Beaulieu, where thirteenth-century accounts of the Cistercian monastery survive together with substantial remnants of the buildings.

It is perhaps not surprising that the monks, in their ascetic and celibate communities, were unable to respond fully to the influence of Islam with its sensuous, erotic paradise gardens, but the Crusaders could and did. Gradually the impetus for the making of gardens shifted from the monasteries to the King and his noble subjects.

Royal gardens

The Normans loved hunting, so the legends of great Assyrian *pairadaezas*, filled with exotic fruits, flowers, trees and wild beasts, must have held great attraction. William and William Rufus set aside vast tracts of country, royal forests, for the chase, and penalties for infringing forest law were severe. In 1123 Henry I enclosed a park in the ancient manor of Woodstock in Oxfordshire and, in the finest tradition of Assyrian kings, stocked it with rare and exotic animals – lions, leopards, lynx, camels and a porcupine brought from Montpellier, an important multinational city where Moorish physicians later founded a medical school (1221) which became a university in 1289.[20]

Henry II continued to embellish the park at Woodstock, his most notable addition being Rosamond's Bower, where his romance with the fair Rosamond Clifford flourished until Queen Eleanor discovered and killed her rival. The romantic intrigue of Henry and Rosamond became legendary, and 'Rosamond's Bowers' became a feature of many a garden, including some in the unlikely confines of monasteries. Henry also made gardens and herbers at Winchester Castle (1178), Nottingham (1183) and Arundel (1186–8).

In the fifty-six-year reign of Henry III, with his marriage to Eleanor of Provence and the court filled with her French relatives, a new taste for luxurious living developed and gardens flourished. Henry himself developed and embellished nine major gardens, beginning at Windsor, which he continued to improve from 1222 until his death fifty years later. At Nottingham Castle a herber was walled in 1238. In 1243 two lawns and a garden were made at Kempton in Middlesex and 330 feet of wall was built around the Queen's herber, which was estimated to cover two or three acres. Three years later the gardener's house at Windsor was removed to make way for a pleasure garden, then work resumed in earnest at Woodstock. From 1248 to 1260 walls were made around the Queen's garden and hedges planted around the King's garden. Two new gardens, one with a stew-pond, were made on either side of the King's chamber, covered walks were repaired, and at both Woodstock and neighbouring Everswell springs were harnessed to create ornamental pools and fountains. In 1252 a lawn was made at Winchester Castle. In 1256 a marble-pillared cloister was added to the King's garden at Guilford Manor, Surrey, where a Queen's herber was made in 1268. At Winchester, where Henry rebuilt the Abbey in the new Gothic style, the palace garden was levelled and turfed in 1259, and in 1263 the huge sum of ten pounds was spent on plants including pears, other fruits and lilies – for the garden on Tower Hill.

All this work resulted in the regular appointment of master gardeners, the name of at least one – Fulk le Provincial – proclaiming the Queen's influence in the import of foreign skills.

Henry's son, Edward I, spent much of his early life in the Holy Land, finally returning from the Crusades through Italy and France. His extensive travelling and his marriage to Eleanor of Castile made him the arbiter of taste in Europe.[21] Perhaps because of prolonged attempts to subdue the Welsh and Scots from bleak border castles, he chose to concentrate on London for his garden-making – at Westminster and especially on Tower Hill. At the Tower 9,000 turves were laid in 1277 and large numbers of pears, peaches, roses, lilies and vines were planted. At Westminster a new garden was made beneath the Queen's window, with a lead-lined pool. From 1278 an even more distinctly Moorish influence could be detected in the garden of Leeds Castle in Kent, where an island was made in the large lake around the castle and a pavilion built on it.

The Queen also took an active interest in garden-making. She leased King's Langley, near Hemel Hempstead, Hertfordshire, from the Earl of Cornwall in 1279 and, with her Moorish gardener, imported apple grafts from Aquitaine and planted extensive orchards and a vineyard.

Noble gardens

By the end of the thirteenth century royal palaces and gardens were numerous, but so were those of the nobility, the archbishops and bishops. William Fitzstephen's *Description of London, c.* 1180, praises the streets lined with fine houses and large, tree-shaded gardens. Neckam also praised the spacious houses and gardens of Holborn, the finest of the suburbs. The Earl of Lincoln's garden (now Lincoln's Inn) with its vineyard, orchards and nursery produced an income of £8–9 per year, comparable with the income from a large monastery garden. Lord Grey of Wilton rented thirty acres (now Gray's Inn Fields) from St Paul's Cathedral. The Archbishop of Canterbury's London palace at Lambeth had fifty acres of park and garden.

Further from the city, the Earl of Kent had fine gardens at Kempton in Middlesex before they became royal property. The Earl of Cornwall leased his house and gardens at King's Langley to Eleanor of Castile, and from 1270 to 1306 Earl Marshall developed his garden at Hampstead Marshall, near Newbury, to include a cloister garden, an east garden with fish-ponds and a west garden.

A lively trade in seeds and plants developed during Edward I's reign, and by the end of the thirteenth century there were commercial gardens in London, Oxford, Norwich and York in addition to the output from numerous essentially private gardens.[22] In 1345 the Mayor of London was petitioned to stop the unseemly bustle and foul language of gardeners selling their produce opposite the church of St Austin in Watling Street near the gate of St Paul's churchyard.[23] The gardeners counter-petitioned, pointing to the loss of income which their noble employers would sustain.

By the fourteenth century many of the colleges, too, had fine gardens: the vineyard planted in New College, Oxford, in 1390 survived at least until 1576. Another very important type of garden arose from the separation of the church from the other professions (another largely Moorish influence). Physicians and surgeons were no longer necessarily clerics depending on the long-established resources of the monastery garden. They started their own gardens, established their own professional links and enormously stimulated the science of botany and the interchange and introduction of plants.

Henry Daniel, an old man in 1379, translated many medical works into English and grew 252 plants in his garden at Stepney, east of London. John Bray (d. 1381) was another noted botanist/physician. John Arderne (1307–78) was a surgeon and author of several botanical works, the illustration of which marked the beginning of accurate botanical draughtsmanship. During these fruitful decades Master Ion Gardener wrote his *Feate of Gardening*, the first entirely original, practical and English manual of gardening, with eight divisions: 'Of settyng and reryng of Treys', 'Of graff-yng of Treys', 'Of cuttyng and settyng of Vynys', 'Of settyng and sowyng of Sedys', 'Of sowyng and settyng of Wurtys', 'Of the kynd of Perselye', 'Of other maner Herbys' and 'Of the kynde of Saferowne'.[24]

Garden features

By 1400 Hubert van Eyck's calendars in the *Hours of Turin* show garden features in some detail, while illuminations of the *Très riches heures du Duc de Berry* portray precisely the gardens of the Duc's country château and his palace in Paris. From fifteenth-century illuminated manuscripts it becomes possible to describe not only the contents but the accurate form of gardens.

The first essential was enclosure. Garth (plural 'garthen' – hence 'garden'), geard or yard meant simply an enclosed space. A yard used for the cultivation of plants was a 'wort yard', or 'ort yard' – a term which, finally corrupted to 'orchard', took on the more restrictive meaning of a fruit garden.

In the Dark Ages and for centuries after, noble families and their retainers lived, ate and sometimes slept in one great hall with an open fire in the centre. Before chimneys were developed in the thirteenth century, smoke drifted out through holes in the roof. In an age when washing was uncommon the stench was overpower-ing, and two important uses for plants were as strewing herbs for the floor and as fragrant nosegays to be pressed closely to the nostrils to mask other smells. Enclosure offered privacy, an opportunity to relax away from prying eyes. An enclosure filled with fragrant and aromatic plants created a veritable heaven. The fashion for frequent bathing introduced by Eleanor of Castile, wife of Edward I, created an even more obvious reason for privacy: medieval illuminations frequently portray bathers, amorous couples and strolling musicians in the secluded gardens.

Arbours were also important features of the garden although, as in the case of orchards, the origins of the arbour in the modern sense of the word are obscured by changes in meaning. The 'herber' mentioned so frequently in accounts of early gardens was undoubt-edly a herb-garden in some instances, whereas in other cases it possibly indicates a shelter or 'harbour'. To further complicate matters, the word 'arbour' in some contexts is a corruption of 'arbre', the French word for 'tree'. The first arbours in the modern sense of the word were simple structures of poles over which vines, honeysuckle or clematis might ramble. Such structures would create privacy and shelter, and would provide the scent, shade and buzzing insect life associated with the forest fringe, all within the safe confines of the garden. In later gardens trees were planted on either side of a seat and the branches were plaited overhead to make a living roof. Later still the shelters became more elaborate, more architectural and more numerous, from light exotic tents inspired by the Crusades to substantial banqueting houses, but such elaboration belongs to the sixteenth and seventeenth centuries and not to early medieval gardens. It is possible that Rosamond's Bower at Woodstock was an arbour but equally probable that it was a labyrinth of some description.

Labyrinths and mazes became widespread from the twelfth century. They first appeared in cathedrals as patterns in the floor, symbolizing the complicated folds of man's sin, but in Britain they soon became popular out of doors. Turf mazes were cut out of pasture, often quite temporarily at local fairs, but a few have survived to the present – at Hilton, near Cambridge, for example. Mazes with low divisions of wattle hurdles or clipped evergreens also appeared frequently in gardens, re-establishing a feature popular in Roman and earlier gardens, but they were ephemeral in construction and none have survived to modern times. (Mazes enclosed by high hedges are relatively modern developments, of the seventeenth or, more commonly, the nineteenth century.) The medieval maze had symbolic and religious significance but, in gardens, it also had the advantage of being intricate, interesting, playful, offering the maximum diversion in a minimum space.

Water was another essential of the new garden of pleasure. It had long been a useful and ornamental adjunct of the house as a stew-pond, fish-pond or well, but more decorative treatment of tanks, fountains and baths increased as the garden took on its new role as a resort of pleasure.

In their planting these new gardens were very similar to the old monastery gardens to which they owed their origin. Plants were grown in small rectangular beds and served many culinary and medicinal purposes as well as being attractive to the eye and the nose. The beds were raised by means of low walls or planks, unlike Moorish gardens where beds were sunken to create a flat carpet and presumably also to facilitate irrigation. Crisp, who shows many

illustrations of medieval gardens, can suggest no reason for this practice, but one reason is undoubtedly that offered by Walahfrid: 'That it [my small patch of ground] should not be washed away we faced it with planks and raised it in oblong beds a little above the level ground.'[25]

It is interesting to note than the raising of beds and borders continues in the old colonial gardens ('yards') of the United States of America. It also survives in part among old-fashioned British gardeners who take out deep edges to separate grass and soil and heap up the soil ostensibly to improve drainage and display their plants to better advantage.

In later gardens the beds were edged with box, rosemary, hyssop or other low evergreen to emphasize their pattern as well as their contents. Such edgings also served as fragrant surfaces on which linen could be spread to dry in the sun. Later still the evergreens were used alone as patterns on a sand or gravel background, but again such ideas belong to the sixteenth and seventeenth centuries.

Raised beds and a fine-textured tapestry of flowers in an enclosed garden by Hans Weiditz, 1542.

The flowery mead

Other raised beds were covered with turf, fine turf richly sprinkled with thyme, self-heal, chamomile and other bright or fragrant plants. Sitting on these plants released their fragrance and added to the pleasure of the garden, but some illustrations show pointed supports for the seats in positions which would demand the greatest care from those about to sit on them. As the turf dried out and died it could be replaced with little effort.

The use of turf in medieval gardens is very interesting, as it appears either to be entirely absent, with the exception perhaps of

The Madonna on a turf seat with a flowery mead at her feet.

a turf seat or two, or to cover the whole garden. In the first case the garden might consist of a central water feature, with raised beds of plants surrounded by low clipped hedges and separated by paths of sand or fine gravel. In the second type, of which there are many illustrations, the garden is depicted as an enclosed area carpeted with grass, among which are many wild flowers.

This 'flowery mead' was neither accidental nor taken for granted. Its construction was described in detail by Petrus de Crescentiis, an eminent and widely travelled Bolognese lawyer, in his *Liber Ruralium Commodorum* (1305), but Crescentiis borrowed freely from ancient sources and plundered large sections of Albertus Magnus's *On vegetables and plants* (1260), so his advice was far from original in 1305. He advised scalding the soil with boiling water to kill weed seeds, then laying turves upside down and beating them firmly into place with wooden mallets. Such punishment and soil compaction would have the effect of encouraging the finer grasses and some wild flowers while discouraging coarse grasses and rank weeds.

The turf was not cut frequently. Interestingly, of the many illustrations in Crisp's *Mediaeval Gardens* showing gardeners at work, only one crudely drawn picture shows a gardener with a scythe. In 1457 the cloister garth at Westminster was scythed three times. The Norwich accounts of 1484 show that the garth there was mown twice. A payment was also made that year for removing moss. Usually the whole garden was returfed every two or three years, by which time stronger grasses and weeds would be invading.

The effect of the fine turf sprinkled with wild flowers is beautifully described by Chaucer in his English version of the *Romaunt of the Rose*:

> Ful gay was al the ground, and queynt
> And poudred, as men had it peynt,
> With many a fresh and sondry flour,
> That casten up a ful good savour.

Medieval gardens remained recognizable as orchards or herb gardens, as places of utility, but they could also be very attractive. From the thirteenth century onwards the emphasis was directed to achieving use and beauty in equal proportions. (In this respect they serve as excellent models for the shrinking gardens of the twentieth century.) Of all the features of medieval gardens, the arbour and the flowery mead best typify the efforts of the early gardeners to bring the delights of the countryside – shade, greenery, colour, shelter and softness – into the safe confines of the garden, but to

these two essentially medieval ideas must be added a third: a love
of birds and other animal life.

To illustrate this and other aspects of the medieval garden one
can do no better than to paraphrase again Petrus de Crescentiis.
There should be fragrant herbs and flowers, trees and vines for
shade – not too thickly planted. The centre of the garden should
be open to avoid spiders' webs, and the garden should be open to
the bracing air of the north and east but sheltered from the strong
south-westerly winds (good advice for Bologna, perhaps, but often
repeated in English manuscripts). For people of moderate means
one-and-a-half to two acres of garden should suffice, with rows of
trees 'constantly weeded from every base and worthless weed'. For
kings and other illustrious persons the garden might be twelve acres
or more, with a palace to the south, a grove of trees to the north
for wild creatures and ponds for fish. Hares, stags, rabbits and the
like harmless beasts may be put among the bushes, with singing
birds along the rows of trees which must run north to south (from
the palace to the grove) so that the animals may be more easily
seen.

That such gardens were not confined to southern climes is
delightfully illustrated by James I of Scotland, imprisoned in the
tower of Windsor Castle and describing the garden below his prison
window:

> Now was there made, fast by the Towris wall,
> A garden fair; – and in the corners set
> An arbour green, with wandis long and small
> Railèd about, and so with treès set
> Was all the place, and Hawthorne hedges knet
> That lyf was none walking there forebye
> That might within scarce any wight espy.
>
> So thick the boughs and the leaves green
> Beshaded all the alleys that there were,
> And mids of every arbour might be seen
> The sharpe greene sweet Juniper
> Growing so fair with branches here and there,
> That as it seemed to a lyf without,
> The boughes spread the arbour all about.
>
> And on the smalle greene twistis sat
> The little sweet nightingale, and sung
> So loud and clear, the hymnis consecrat

> Of loris use, now soft, now lowd, among,
> That all the gardens and the wallis rung
> Right of their song.[26]

Edward I, whose queen, Eleanor of Castile, has been referred to as a skilful gardener, was succeeded by his son, the ineffectual Edward II, then his grandson Edward III. Like his grandfather, Edward III married an enthusiastic gardener. Philippa of Hainault received cuttings of rosemary from her mother in Antwerp in 1340, together with a text on its virtues and cultivation translated into English by Henry Daniel.[27] Rather more significantly, Edward III began the Hundred Years War with France, an act which confirmed England's position as a distinct and unified country. Through the fifteenth century the country was again divided as the Houses of York and Lancaster struggled for supremacy with only their badges – the red and the white rose – signifying any interest in gardens.

With the victory of Henry Tudor of Richmond at Bosworth in 1485, followed by his coronation and his marriage in 1486 to Elizabeth of York, the two factions were united. Henry VII became the first of the Tudor kings. Peace, prosperity and gardens were restored.

3
Tudor Gardens

Even before Henry VII's accession there were signs of a new style of building and gardening, a style in which allegiance to Rome and familiarity with the coherent symmetry of early Italian Renaissance architecture were clearly evident. In 1456 Thomas Bourchier, Archbishop of Canterbury, bought the rambling medieval pile of Knole in Kent from William Fiennes and encased it in a series of elegant and orderly courtyards. Defensive towers and machicolations were reduced to merely decorative devices, and large, glazed windows illuminated spacious interiors.

Pitched upon by Pleasure

During Henry VIII's long reign, as in his father's, ostentation was regarded as an outward sign of power and an undesirable threat to the throne. Whether this threat was manifested by an individual or by the Church, the result was the same. In 1511 Edward Stafford, 3rd Duke of Buckingham, began Thornbury Castle in Gloucestershire, one of the last and most splendid fortified baronial houses. Ten years later he was executed and his estates were forfeited to the Crown. Knole, too, inhabited by successive Archbishops of Canterbury, was seized by Henry in 1538.

In 1514 Thomas Wolsey, Archbishop of York, began an even more magnificent but more modern palace at Hampton Court. In 1529 Wolsey, now Cardinal and Lord Chancellor of England, gave the palace to Henry in a last, but unsuccessful, attempt to regain the King's favour. Wolsey's personal fate was soon to be shared by the Church as a whole when the monasteries were dissolved, its

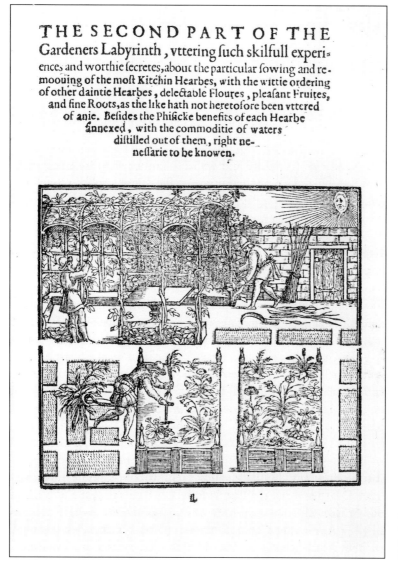

THE SECOND PART OF THE
Gardeners Labyrinth, vttering fuch skilfull experience, and worthie fecretes, about the particular fowing and re-
moouing of the moft Kitchin Hearbes, with the wittie ordering
of other daintie Hearbes, deleátable Floures, pleafant Fruites,
and fine Roots, as the like hath not heretofore been vttered
of anie. Befides the Phificke benefits of each Hearbe
annexed, with the commoditie of waters
diftilled out of them, right ne-
neffarie to be knowen.

*Raised beds with carved finials
and an elegant arbour
('Didymus Mountain',
Gardener's Labyrinth).*

properties confiscated and its wealth redistributed to supporters of
the King.

Henry kept Hampton Court and began immediately to enlarge
and elaborate upon Wolsey's already splendid palace. Gardens were
extended and new ones made. In 1533 Henry Blankeston received
nearly £30 for painting 96 poles and 960 yards of wooden rail
around the flower beds of the King's garden. Clipped greens were
introduced; gilded carved beasts decorated the garden; a great
mount was constructed with 256,000 bricks and planted with 12,000

quicksets to hold the mound of soil in place. On top of the mount was a lofty 'arbour' or banqueting house, two storeys in height and glazed with forty-eight lights.

From Hampton Court Henry turned his attention to Nonsuch, a fairy-tale castle surrounded by extensive pleasure grounds near Ewell in Surrey. He did not live to see its completion, which was left to the Earl of Arundel, but Paul Hetzner, describing Nonsuch in 1598 (some fifty years later), described it as 'so encompassed with parks full of deer, delicious gardens, groves ornamented with trellis-work, cabinets of verdure and walks so embrowned by trees, that it seems to be a place pitched upon by Pleasure herself, to dwell in along with Health'.[1]

Henry's influence was not confined to buildings and pleasure gardens. He was a giant of a man both in body and in character, and his delight in conspicuous extravagance affected the arts and crafts in general. His taste for fruits and vegetables as supplements to meat dishes stimulated commercial horticulture. Richard Harris, the King's fruiterer, imported many grafts and trees of the best apples, pears, cherries and other fruits from continental nurseries, and established orchards extending over 100 acres near Sittingbourne in Kent. Acting as a nurseryman as well as a fruiterer, he distributed his plants widely. By 1596 Lambard described Kent as being full of flourishing orchards.[2]

Advances made during the long reign of Henry VIII were continued and accelerated, after the reversals of Mary's rule, by Elizabeth I. A vigorous merchant fleet, protected by a powerful navy, carried cloth and grain overseas and brought back wines, spices, fruits, silks, tobacco and other valuable commodities on which many fortunes were built. Such was the strength and popularity of the Queen that her admirers vied with each other to provide magnificent houses and gardens in which she might be induced to stay as she journeyed about her realm, palaces and gardens literally fit for a Queen.

Fit for a queen

Elizabeth's reign brought a new respectability to ostentation, as it could be regarded, genuinely, as a symbol of loyalty and admiration. At Theobalds, Hardwick, Montacute, and on the Northamptonshire estates of Holdenby, Newton and Lyveden, new and elegant mansions arose. At Burghley, Haddon Hall and Longleat older houses were greatly enlarged, with formal façades, composed seemingly more of glass than of masonry, enveloping more solid interiors and accommodating new galleries and state-rooms. In 1579 William Cecil wrote from Burghley to Sir Christopher Hatton at Holdenby: 'God send us both long to enjoy Her, for whom we both mean to exceed our purses in these buildings.'[3]

Whether new or remodelled, these magnificent buildings were mirrored by gardens of equal formality and grandeur of scale. 'Mirrored' is a particularly appropriate term to identify the gardens of Elizabethan England as distinct from those of the earlier Tudors, as it emphasizes a new relationship between house and garden.

In the fifteenth century there were basically two types of house. The smaller type evolved from the manorial hall, the larger from fortified castles. Originally the hall had only one principal room, in which the household lived and slept together. By the fifteenth century separate family rooms had been introduced; servants were banished to the other side of the partitioned hall, and as family fortunes grew, new kitchens, withdrawing rooms and other extensions were added around the old hall. Because of the relatively humble origins of such houses, their gardens, if any, were limited to small orchards and yards. Larger houses were defended not only by strong outer walls and often by moats but by their arrangement around an inner court. To gain access to the great hall, the hub of the castle, it was necessary to pass first through a fortified gatehouse, with perhaps a drawbridge and barbican as further defences, then across the central court before reaching the strong door of the great hall. Bodiam Castle illustrates this ground-plan perfectly and indicates the inward-looking character of such buildings, deliberately cut off from their environs.

Ightham Mote, Oxburgh and Knole show how the introvert castle plan was progressively modified as the need for defensive walls and arrow-slit windows diminished. Ill-fated Thornbury and Hampton Court, Hatfield (built in 1497 by the Bishop of Ely and also appropriated by Henry VIII during the Dissolution), and Wilton, an entirely peaceful palace started in 1540, were all of this pattern. Haddon Hall is a more complicated example which grew slowly from the eleventh to the sixteenth century, but its main court, finally enclosed by Sir George Vernon c. 1550, captures the spirit of this type of building perhaps better than any other.

Once large private armies were dispersed the inner courtyards would serve more peaceful purposes, of course. The court at Thornbury, about forty yards square, had a garden on the south side with a covered gallery leading through it from the main rooms to the chapel.

Other gardens could be added by enclosure beyond the house. On the east side of Thornbury was a large garden enclosed by high walls, again reached by covered galleries. Alongside were an orchard 'full of newly planted fruit trees well-laden with fruit' and a park. At Hampton Court there were

> ... gardens sweet, enclosed with walls strong,
> Embanked with benches to sit and take my rest;
> ... with arbours and alleys so pleasant and so dulce,
> The pestilent airs with flavours to repulse.[4]

Such houses were, however, essentially introvert, turning their backs to a hostile world. By the latter half of the sixteenth century, when Elizabeth ruled England, a more open ground plan prevailed: the new houses of the age extended welcoming arms to visitors instead of presenting hostile fortifications. Montacute and North Mymms were linear rather than quadrangular houses. Eventually even Hatfield itself, where Elizabeth spent her childhood, had three sides of the old quadrangle torn down to leave only a linear block, while at Longleat, where the old pattern apparently survived, the main entrance, the hall and principal rooms were at the front of the building rather than sheltering within the court.

The open approach, the formal and symmetrical façades of the house and the garden beyond were now conceived as a single idea. The garden literally mirrored the house in its symmetry and proportions, and the close relationship was emphasized by fenestration, terraces, paths and the design of garden walls and buildings.

Florist flowers

The increasing display of wealth which characterized Tudor gardens was to be measured not only in financial terms but also in wealth of skills and new plants. Persecution of Protestants in Europe drove many refugees to England from 1540 onwards, culminating in the Huguenot influx of 1571. Flemish clothworkers and French silk-weavers settled near the ports through which they entered or migrated gradually towards London, bringing with them not only their weaving skills but their traditional love of flowers.

Settling in self-contained communities, they established florist societies, groups of enthusiasts dedicated to the perfection (as defined by elaborate and rigid rules of colour, shape and proportion) of particular flowers. The plants which particularly attracted them were small hardy plants, so that a great number could be grown in a small garden, with flowers of circular shape and variable colouring. Hyacinth, anemone, ranunculus, tulip, carnation, polyanthus, auricula, sweet william and pansy were the most important flowers. Hundreds, sometimes thousands of named varieties were raised, exhibited and exchanged, often at high prices; a month's wages might be asked for a particularly fine introduction. Plants were treasured and cosseted – there are accounts of lives being lost by sacrificing a blanket to keep the plants warm in severe weather[5] – and gave great pleasure to their owners in return. These florist societies eventually disappeared as the settlers were absorbed into the rapidly growing populace, and their houses and gardens were lost beneath factories and terraced houses as the industrial revolution gained momentum in the nineteenth century, but love of flowers and of meeting to discuss and show them still forms a recognizable part of the character of English gardeners.

In addition to cloth-workers and other artisans to stimulate English manufacturing, there were many skilled gardeners among the refugees. Like the cloth-workers, some settled where they entered the country, around Yarmouth, Harwich, Dover and Sand-wich. By 1572 immigrants constituted half the population of Sand-wich, and some established themselves as commercial growers of vegetables and fruits for the burgeoning towns, a trade scarcely known in England before their arrival. Market gardening became widespread on suitable soils in the district, establishing Kent's repu-tation as the garden of England. Many gardeners moved nearer to London, to Wandsworth, Battersea and Bermondsey, the better able to supply the city with perishable produce. Others found employment in large private gardens.

Born in Lille, Mathias l'Obel came to England c. 1584 and eventually became superintendent of Lord Zouche's garden at Hackney, famed for its extensive plant collections. From Hackney l'Obel (or Lobelius) undertook surveys of the flora of England and built up the plant collection still further. The garden became a focus for London gardeners and botanists and a link with continental ideas. In 1607 l'Obel was appointed King's Botanist to James I, who was himself an enthusiastic gardener.

The European flora

By their example and their contacts with European nurseries and botanists – and thus with southern and eastern sources of plants – the gardening fraternity gave a great boost to plant culture in England. With few exceptions, the plants coming into English gardens were native to Europe, including native English plants producing different coloured flowers or double forms, or simple larger flowers than the species.

Acanthus mollis and *Anchusa italica* came from southern Europe. *Anemone appenina* joined our native wood anemone in its varied forms, and the Pasque flower (*Anemone pulsatilla, Pulsatilla vulgaris*), still to be found wild in a few chalk meadows. Thrift, double daisies and lady's smock or cuckoo flower (*Cardamine pratensis*), cornflowers, *Trollius europaeus* and heartsease (*Viola tricolor*) were all brought into gardens from English woods, meadows and shores to be cultivated and selected.

Europe also furnished cyclamen, gentians, *Iris xiphium* and *I. xiphoides*, martagon lilies and several species of narcissus to add to our own *N. pseudonarcissus*. Also from Europe came the first species of gladiolus, *G. illyricus,* in fact a native of Hampshire but so rare that it was introduced from Europe before native colonies were discovered.

Shrubs native to England are by no means numerous. Most popular by far is the rose, a flower which is so universally cherished that, unlike most other native flowers, it has been brought into gardens from the earliest times. In addition to our native briars and the dog-rose, the red-flowered *R. gallica* of France has probably been grown here since the seventh century, possibly even from Roman times. Other roses were brought back by Crusaders, including the semi-double *R. gallica* var. *officinalis*, the Apothecary's Rose. The climbing *R. moschata*, the repeat-flowering autumn damask (from Damascus, an ancient hybrid between *R. gallica* and *R. moschata*), *Rosa alba* (a cross between the damask rose and a white sport of the dog-rose) and the very double *R. centifolia* were all known in Tudor gardens, although the last named, a complicated garden hybrid, appears only *c.* 1580.[6]

Returning to natives, the elder in its cut-leaved and white-berried forms has long been grown in gardens. *Daphne mezereum* may be native or a garden escape. *Clematis vitalba*, the old man's beard of hedgerows, is too vigorous to be admitted into most gardens, but the more slender and more decorative *C. viticella*, the sweetly scented *C. flammula* and the winter-flowering *C. cirrhosa*

Trifolium &cctosum flore albo. Rola Damascena flore pleno. Trifolium fiectosum flore flavo.

The flat, many-petalled flowers of a damask rose.

were introduced from southern Europe in Tudor times. *Quercus ilex, Phillyrea decora* and *P. latifolia, Viburnum tinus* and the more tender *Myrtus communis* are also southern European, and were particularly favoured for their cheering bright evergreen foliage, whether grown as clipped greens in pots to be moved to heated 'green-houses' or grown outside in the garden. Many species of *Cistus,* also rather tender, were welcomed for their aromatic ever-green foliage as well as for their delightful flowers. The alpenrose (*Rhododendron hirsutum*) is a surprising latecomer known to, but not grown by, Gerard.[7]

From 1550 onwards a new and exciting source of plants was opened up as ambassadors were dispatched to Istanbul to develop diplomatic links with the Ottoman Empire, which had spread to control the holiest places of Christendom. The most important

figure in this new era was Augerius de Busbecq, sent by the
Habsburg emperor Ferdinand I to the court of Suleiman the Magnificent in 1554. De Busbecq, in common with other travellers,
was astonished at the floral wealth of Constantinople: tulips, crown
imperials, iris, hyacinths, anemones, ranunculus, narcissus and lilies
were grown in great quantities, already as highly developed garden
plants. He is particularly associated with the introduction of tulips
to Vienna, from whence the botanist Charles l'Écluse (Clusius) took
some to Holland on his appointment as Professor of Botany at
Leyden in 1593. It was bulbs stolen from Clusius – he asked too
high a price to encourage legitimate exchange – which formed the
nucleus of the Dutch bulb industry and the subject of ruinous
speculation in the 'tulip mania' of the 1630s.

De Busbecq also introduced two much-confused garden shrubs
to European, and hence to English, gardens. *Philadelphus coronarius*
(mock orange) and *Syringa vulgaris* (lilac) could hardly be confused
as plants, but both have hollow stems, both were used by the Turks
for making musical pipes, and both therefore came to Europe with
the common name of 'pipe tree' or 'syringa' (syringe). Gerard
distinguished them as White Pipe and Blew Pipe. Although the
White Pipe was given its botanical name of *Philadelphus* in 1623 it
is still, in the twentieth century, commonly known as 'syringa' and
therefore confused with lilac.

Constantinople, a bridge between East and West, also served as
a station for the introduction of the few Middle and Far Eastern
plants which found their way into Europe at this time: the
mulberry, horse chestnut, peach, apricot and cherry laurel, for
example.

The Americas

With the discovery of the Americas at the end of the fifteenth
century it might be thought that these vast lands would contribute
much to the floral wealth of Tudor gardens. However, the early
Atlantic crossings were few and perilous, hardly suited to the
introduction of live plants, so it was not until the mid seventeenth
century that the Americas contributed much to English gardens.
The exceptions were few but exceedingly important.

The potato was introduced from Central America to Spain in
1569 and it was soon distributed throughout Europe but grown as
a flowering plant only. Gerard is shown in the frontispiece of his
Herbal holding a spray of potato flowers. The tomato was introduced from Mexico, again via Spain, even earlier, in 1544. Its

irregular, ribbed fruits were also regarded with suspicion and considered variously as potent drugs, carcinogens or aphrodisiacs. It was commonly known as the 'love apple'.

The Jerusalem artichoke was also introduced from America in the late sixteenth century. Parkinson said of it: 'We in England, from some ignorant and idle heads, have called them artichokes of Jerusalem, only because the root being boiled is in taste like the bottom of an artichoke head. This plant has no similitude with any artichoke, neither came it from Jerusalem, but out of America.'[8] Parkinson would have preferred its other widely-used name, potatoes of Canada. Like the potato, Jerusalem artichokes were first regarded as a delicacy and then, as they became common, despised and considered fit only for animals. Whether from England, Europe, the East or the New World, the collecting, listing and enumeration of plants had a great fascination. In 1580 William Harrison reported in his *Description of England:*

How art also helpeth in the daily colouring, doubling and enlarging the proportion of our flowers it is incredible to behold ... there is not almost one noble gentleman or merchant that hath not great store of these flowers ... in so much as I have seen in some one garden to the number of three or four hundred of them if not more, the half of those names within forty years past we had no manner of knowledge.[9]

The herbals

The interest of noble gentlemen and merchants of Tudor England in gathering new and rare plants was fostered in no small degree by the herbals and garden books beginning to appear from the new printing presses. Although the science of botany was still inextricably bound with medicine, and botanists were concerned as much with the medicinal uses of plants as with the plants themselves, the painstaking gathering and growing and describing of plants which physicians and apothecaries undertook in the sixteenth century laid the foundation for major scientific advances in pure botany in the seventeenth and eighteenth centuries.

The first Chair of Botany was established in Padua in 1535 and the first botanic garden was laid out there ten years later. It still survives, remarkably unaltered after 400 years. Similar gardens were established elsewhere in Europe and eventually, in 1621, at Oxford.

The first English herbal was written by William Turner, the first part of *A new Herball* appearing in 1551 with an illustration of Nonsuch Palace and its gardens on the title page. Turner, a Protestant, fled to Europe during Mary's reign, studying botany and medicine in Italy, but the second and third parts of the *Herball*, dedicated to Elizabeth, were published in 1562 and 1568. Henry Lyte, of Lyte's Cary, published his *Newe Herball* in 1578, and Gerard's famous – or infamous – *Herball* appeared in 1597. The fact that Gerard had 'borrowed' large tracts of Doden's *Cruydeboek* (1554) was not acknowledged until the second edition of Gerard's *Herball* was published, edited by Thomas Johnson and corrected by Mathias de l'Obel, in 1633.

Lupins from Gerard's Herball *or General Historie of Plantes, the most famous of all the herbals.*

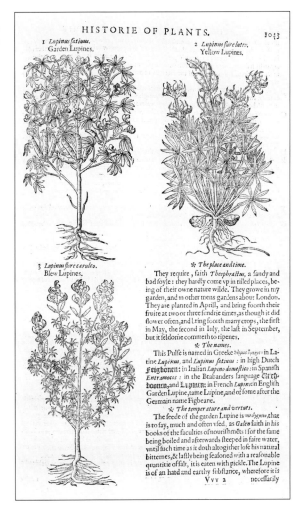

All these works were botanical in scope: lists of plants, their origins and their uses. More practical works came rather later, on the whole, but were not completely lacking.

Andrew Borde's *The boke for to lerne a man to be wyse in buylding of his house* (1540) did not confine its attention to the house alone: 'in the garden may be a poole or two fysshe, yf the pooles be clere kept' and 'it is a commodious and a pleasant thing in a mansyon to have an orcharde of syndreye fruites', it advised. Thomas Tusser's *A hundreth pointes of good husbandrie* (1557) and the expanded *Five hundreth points of good husbandry united to as many of good huswiferie* (1573) combined common sense and old wives' tales with advice on which plants to grow for various purposes, when to sow, plant and harvest, all in jogging rhyme. It was immensely popular and *Five hundreth points* ... was reprinted on innumerable occasions. Thomas Hill's *A most briefe and pleasaunt treatyse, teachyinge howe to dress, sowe, and set a garden*, published in 1563, reappeared five years later as *The proffitable Arte of Gardening*, with subsequent additions including expanded sections in grafting and planting of fruit trees. Under the pseudonym 'Didymus Mountain' Hill also wrote *The Gardener's Labyrinth* (1577). Like many more botanical authors, he borrowed freely from classical and other sources including Borde, but the woodcuts of garden plans, knots and mazes in *The Gardener's Labyrinth* make it as interesting now as it was popular in its day.[10]

It is interesting, too, in demonstrating that even in the early years of Elizabeth I's reign there existed a demand for gardening books, as men from all stations in life sought to improve their surroundings.

The Elizabethan garden

A list of features in these great Elizabethan gardens would read very similarly to the contents of a medieval garden, but the scale and degree of elaboration were very different.

Enclosure was still essential. A garden was literally an enclosed space. However, the embattled walls of Thornbury (Avon) had given way to lighter, more decorative walls at Montacute, or hedges of thorn or roses, or decorative fences intertwined with climbing plants. At Harrington and Wakerley, both in North-amptonshire, walls disappeared and enclosure was achieved by low raised walks on three sides of the garden, enclosing, with the house on the fourth side, rectangular gardens of one and two acres respectively.

The crude rustic arbours of the medieval garden had evolved into elegant trellis shelters set into the boundary fence or standing in the centre of the garden. Larger structures of a similar sort were frequently erected, especially for festive occasions, serving as banqueting houses. At Theobalds one circular summer house was on two levels, with statues of the twelve Roman emperors around the lower level and tanks of water filled with fish on the upper. At Lyveden, Northamptonshire, the upper garden, around the handsome New Bield begun in 1597, had eight large arbours on its periphery, the whole being surrounded by a sunken alley some 10–12 feet wide and 4 feet deep. Kenilworth had a terrace walk with arbours at either end 'redolent by sweet trees and flowers'. The banqueting house at Hampton Court, which perhaps inspired many of these later examples, was a more substantial brick structure on a large, raised platform.

Arbours and summer houses might be connected by galleries arched over with trellis interlaced with ivy and other greens, or framed by pleached lime or elm. At Theobalds 'one might walk twoe myle in the walks'.[11]

Labyrinths and mazes, so popular in medieval gardens, were also enjoyed throughout Tudor times. By the late sixteenth century the enthusiasm for labyrinths and the enjoyment of shady galleries and covered walks began to combine to produce a labyrinth with higher divisions, but it was a century more before the solidly hedged maze by which we usually understand the word today appeared.

Water had always been enjoyed in gardens. The moat and the fish-pond had long served as defensive and utilitarian features and they continued to decorate Elizabethan gardens. 'They would afford you fish, fence and moysture to your trees and pleasure also, if they be so great and deep that you may have swans and other winter birds, good for devouring of vermin, and a boat for many good uses.'[12] At Theobalds the garden was 'encompassed with a ditch full of water, large enough to have the pleasure of going in a boat, and rowing between the shrubs'.[13] At Harrington ponds were made symmetrically on the terraces descending from the road. Between 1580 and 1587 six new ponds were made and an old one enlarged at Holdenby, a garden modelled on Theobalds. Water was conduited a quarter of a mile across the fields from an old well to supply the upper pond.[14]

Increasingly the water was ornamented by fountains and sculpture. In the centre of the garden at Kenilworth was a white marble fountain in an octagonal basin full of carp, tench, bream, perch and

The mechanical owl and twittering birds at Villa d'Este, from Salomon de Caus, Les raisons des forces mouvantes.

eel. Francis Bacon preferred the fountains to the pools themselves, which 'mar all, and make the garden unwholesome, and full of flies and froggs'[15] but, probably because of our cooler summers and greyer skies, fountains were not enjoyed so much or carried to such degrees of inventiveness as in Italy and France. At Villa d'Este, forty miles from Rome, the water jets played music and activated mechanical singing birds until they were silenced briefly by the water-powered appearance of an equally mechanical owl. Water jokes, which soaked unsuspecting guests, were also popular on the Continent. Henry VIII gave a lead in England with surprise fountains at Hampton Court, Whitehall and Nonsuch, and a few were constructed even into the eighteenth century, such as the one at Dyrham Park, Gloucester, described by Stephen Switzer.[16]

At the bottom of the steps are planted two thorns encompass'd with seats, which are arriv'd to a large stature, and being kept of a round regular form with frequent clippings, make a very good figure: There are small pipes which twine round the bodies of the trees, and appear more like ivy on the rough bark (being painted green), than leaden pipes, which on the turn of a cock discharge water from a vast number of small nosils in the head of the trees, all round as natural as if it rain'd; and in a cloudy day I have been inform'd, spectators setting down here to rest themselves, the more these pipes have play'd, the closer they have embrac'd the tree for shelter, supposing it had really rain'd, 'till the gardener has convinc'd them of their error, after they had partaken of a sufficient sprinkling to imprint in their memories the pleasurable mistake.

Because of the dubious pleasure of these 'pleasurable mistakes', water jokes were never very popular in England: English guests dried out too slowly.

In the beds and borders of Tudor gardens, the virtues of plants continued to have considerable importance, but many of the new plants were enjoyed mainly or entirely for the pleasure they gave. The whole garden, too, took on a more decorative appearance. Simple rectangular beds of the physic garden were raised more formally with brick or wooden edgings and railed about. Rails or edgings of low evergreens provided a framework for the garden, a framework which was emphasized by clipped columns or pyramids of greens or carved and painted figures. Eventually the regular pattern of rectangles gave way to more elaborate patterns, with diagonals and circles introduced.

Knots and other delights

In *The Gardener's Labyrinth*, Thomas Hill shows a very typical garden pattern incorporating these simple variations, but quite early in the sixteenth century the patterns became so complicated that they were termed 'knots'. In 1502 the Duke of Buckingham paid 3s 4d to 'John Wynde, gardener, for diligence in making knottes in the Duke's garden',[17] while for the Earl of Northumberland a gardener was required 'to attend hourly in the garden for setting of erbis, and clypping of knottes'[18]. Wolsey's garden at Hampton Court had 'the knots so enknotted it cannot be expressed'.[19] In most gardens the pattern was loosely defined with an edging of santolina, box, thrift or other low greens, over which spilled a great variety of colourful flowers, a mildly disciplined 'flowery mead'. In some, however, the pattern was all-important. The informal masses of flowers and their unendearing habit of dying after flowering could not be tolerated. Instead their place was taken by coloured

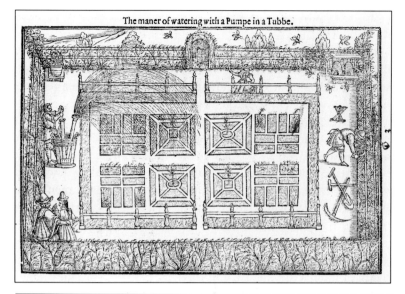

The maner of watering with a Pumpe in a Tubbe.

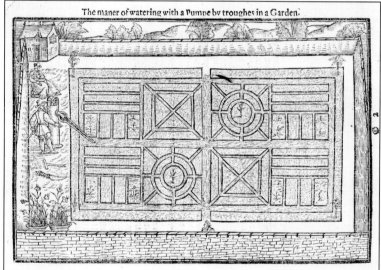

The maner of watering with a Pumpe by troughes in a Garden.

Two methods of watering the garden (Gardener's Labyrinth). *Garden beds are gradually becoming more complex in shape.*

gravel or minerals. Even in 1597 Francis Bacon complained that this style of gardening was childish, the patterns more suited to decorating tarts than gardens, thus pre-dating William Robinson's protestations against 'pastry-cutter gardening' by nearly 300 years.

Orchards and kitchen gardens were equally important. Along with the many varieties of apple, pear and peach introduced into England in the sixteenth century came the apricot ('abre praecox' or 'early tree') *c.* 1524 and, with winter protection, the orange *c.* 1560. These orchards were enjoyed in flower as well as in fruit.

Although the flowery mead, so important in medieval gardens, did not appear to survive as such into Elizabethan gardens, it evolved into two very important garden features. The simpler knots of the medieval garden were fundamentally flowery meads without the grass, a patchwork of bright flowers. Removing the flowers left grass alone, and this was appreciated in two respects: as green grass, closely shorn, the best setting for any garden (to paraphrase Bacon), and as a playing surface for bowls. By 1541 the game of bowls was so popular that a law was passed to forbid its being played other than in private gardens. Gambling associated with the game and fear that it might distract young men from practising their archery had brought it into disrepute. Most gardens had greens for bowling and it was not very long before grass as a purely decorative surface was introduced into the garden proper, serving as a soft path, as a foil to the flowers and later to achieve much needed economy of effort as gardens in general became larger, more complex and prohibitively expensive.

A third, and perhaps a minor, offshoot of the flowery mead was the wilderness. Francis Bacon's ideal garden was in three parts: a green approach, a main garden bordered by alleys and covered walks, and a heath or wilderness. In its published description Bacon's wilderness sounds surprisingly modern, but one must bear in mind that this was a solitary description not echoed in other contemporary works. Much later 'wildernesses' of which plans survive, such as the late seventeenth-century one at Hampton Court, were stiffly formal in character despite verbal descriptions which might suggest that they were very natural. Their character is splendidly represented in the wilderness at Ham House, restored by the National Trust in 1976/7.

Bacon's wilderness serves to remind us again, however, that there were many parts to the Elizabethan garden. The bright, easily recognizable and (especially in the early days of printing) easily reproduced patterns of the flower garden tend exclusively to occupy our attention, but orchards and vegetable gardens flourished and the deer parks within which the house and gardens were set continued to be very important. It was the orchard and park in the hazy background of Elizabethan illustrations that fired men's imaginations and came to the fore in the eighteenth century.

Ups . . . and downs

Thus far the list of garden features is recognizably medieval in origin, but two features set the Tudor garden aside from being merely an expanded and elaborate garth: the introduction of the mount and the treatment of the garden as a whole instead of as a series of unrelated parts.

The mount is perhaps medieval in the sense of existing in or near older gardens. In monasteries a mount symbolized the Hill of Calvary, while in secular gardens a rough mound often remained from old defences. It was in Tudor times, however, that the mount was introduced as a deliberate garden feature. At first it was a rough mound in the centre of the garden planted thickly, perhaps with thorn or raspberry, to prevent erosion. Very soon it became a more architectural circular or square structure built of brick or stone and surmounted, as at Hampton Court, by a banqueting house or shelter.

Leland, antiquary to Henry VIII, described a mount at Wressel Castle with paths 'writhen about in degrees like turnings of cokil-shells to come to the top without payne'.[20] William Lawson's plan of a garden with a mount at each corner in *A new Orchard and Garden* (1618) might well have been patterned on the garden of exactly this idea begun by Sir Thomas Tresham at Lyveden New Bield in 1597.[21] Bacon would undoubtedly have approved of the mount at New College, Oxford, as it was ascended by a series of steps and terraces. This was shown in Loggan's *Oxonia Illustrata* of 1675 but is typical of earlier designs. In other instances the mount was placed at the edge of the garden, sometimes transformed into a long raised walk. The Privy Garden at Hampton Court still has a mount of this type. Raised walks were also extended around two or three sides of the garden, connecting with the terrace of the house to enclose a sunken garden.

As gardens expanded from small yards to cover tens of acres they had to take account of variations in topography, so terracing was often necessary. With the abandonment of defensive moats it was possible to build anew on higher and healthier land, and terracing became a feature of the garden, in the two great terraces flanking the house at Holdenby for example, or the flight of six terraces known as the Falls at Harrington.[22]

Sometimes terraces and mounts were combined. At Harrington the lowest of the six terraces was wrapped around three sides of the main garden, with the manor house making the fourth side of a sunken rectangle.

Remains of the great formal garden of Harrington. The six terraces or 'falls' descending to the forecourt with its central basin are still clearly discernible.

Mounts served a variety of purposes. Switzer pointed out that the foundations could usefully consume vast quantities of rubble resulting from the alteration or demolition of an old house (a favourite Tudor occupation). Olivier de Sèvres suggested a mount as the basis for a physic garden: it has a larger surface area than the flat plot which it covers, and the four different aspects could be utilized by the flora of quite different regions. Lawson, whose four mounts were conveniently sited by a river, saw them as places where 'you might sit . . . and angle a peckled trout or weightie eele' or possibly shoot at deer or other game from a safe vantage point. Most significantly, the mount was an ideal place from which to look into the surrounding country, not to watch for approaching enemies, but for pleasure. For centuries the garden wall had been a means of shutting out a hostile world: now the world was sufficiently peaceful that its contemplation brought added pleasure to the garden.

The mount could equally well be used for looking inwards to the garden. This raised viewpoint from a mount, from a terrace or raised walk, or from the windows of the new galleries, gave a strong stimulus to order the garden in a more regular pattern, a stimulus reinforced by the symmetrical façades of splendid new houses. The random collection of beds and fountains, statues and arbours, seats and mazes which characterized the medieval garden gradually gave way to elegant symmetry, with features organized at regular intervals along wide sanded paths, or forthrights, emanating from the windows and platform of the house. At Montacute, Holdenby, Harrington, Wakerley and many other Elizabethan houses the main garden is rectangular, quartered with a central circular feature, probably a pond.

The embroidered garden

The relationship is well illustrated in Elizabethan embroidery. Examples now in the Victoria and Albert Museum show garden scenes with arbours, covered galleries, fountains, patterned flower-beds and above all people: people on horseback, people talking, people strolling or sitting in arbours or asleep among the flowers.[23] Their clothes are as richly embroidered as are the flower-beds bright with colour. John Parkinson described beds of tulips with 'one colour answering and setting off another that the place where they stand may resemble a piece of needlework', and crocuses in various colours which 'will give such grace to the garden'. The later Stoke

Knots from Gervase Markham's Country Hous-wifes Garden.

The stately proportions of the Tudor garden at Canons Ashby survive beneath centuries of later planting.

Edith hangings, now at Montacute, show a stiffer, more formal garden layout, but it is still bright with colour and lively with people, fountains and carved figures. It is not difficult to imagine the ladies of an Elizabethan household gathering in the fine new galleries in inclement weather and looking from the windows to gain inspiration from the garden for their needlework, thus bringing the garden inside to cheer them through the winter, and sauntering in the garden in summer with equal pleasure. The garden was no longer an escape from a dark, crowded and malodorous house and a refuge from a hostile world. House and garden together were expressions of the joy of living. Just as the garden inspired embroideries, so embroidery later inspired gardens, and the increasingly ornate flower-beds were conceived as brightly coloured ribbons of richly patterned scrollwork. Such devices are more characteristic of the seventeenth than of the sixteenth century, however, and are dealt with in the next chapter.

Most Elizabethan gardens have long since disappeared. The great expense involved in their making and the changing political fortunes of many of their makers caused many of them to disappear almost as quickly as they were made. Those families which managed to survive political turmoil and retain their wealth and influence in succeeding generations were, of course, in the vanguard of later changes in taste and themselves destroyed their great formal gardens to replace them by landscaped parks. Paradoxically it is those gardens which disappeared first of which we now have the most substantial remains. In Northamptonshire, the county known in 1610 as the 'Herrald's Garden' as 'no shire within this lande is so plentifully stocked with gentry', remains of many of the great houses and their gardens may be traced in the terracing and slight depressions or moundings of land which has since remained as permanent pasture. Harrington, Holdenby, Lyveden and Wakerley have been referred to on several occasions in preceding paragraphs and have been expertly mapped and described by John Steane and others.[24] Lyveden New Bield, on the eastern edge of North-amptonshire, fell into ruin after the death of Sir Thomas Tresham and the implication of his son in the Gunpowder Plot. A happier fate befell Canons Ashby in the west of the county. Successive generations of the Dryden family have lived at Canons Ashby from their acquisition of the estate during the Reformation until the present day. Acquired by the National Trust in 1980, the manor house and gardens retain much of their Elizabethan grandeur.

4
Stuart Gardens

Thanks to the careful preparation by Lord Burghley and his son Robert Cecil, James VI of Scotland's accession to the throne of England on the death of his cousin Elizabeth was accomplished smoothly. Life continued much as before and, to a substantial degree, early Stuart gardens embodied many Elizabethan ideas. Of the growing number of garden books published during the reigns of James I and Charles I many were conceived, even substantially written, during Elizabeth's reign and show a continued interest in the making and cultivating of gardens.

A bounty of books

Sir Hugh Platt's *Floraes Paradise* (1608), reprinted posthumously in 1653 as *The Garden of Eden*, was a supplement to *The Jewell House of Art and Nature*, in which he dealt with soils and manures. *The Garden of Eden* is important for its accounts of early plant houses and for Platt's suggestion of using waste heat from laundries, distilleries and similar buildings to protect tender plants through the winter.

Gervase Markham's *The English Husbandman* (1613) contained information on soils, planting and grafting. *The Second Booke ...* (1614) dealt with the kitchen garden. These were the first of Markham's many books. His *Covntrie Farme* (1616) was taken from Richard Surflet's translation of *Maison Rustique*, a general agricultural treatise written originally by Charles Estienne and published by his son-in-law Jean Liebault. Markham's *A way to get wealthe* (1638), a compilation of his earlier agricultural works, not

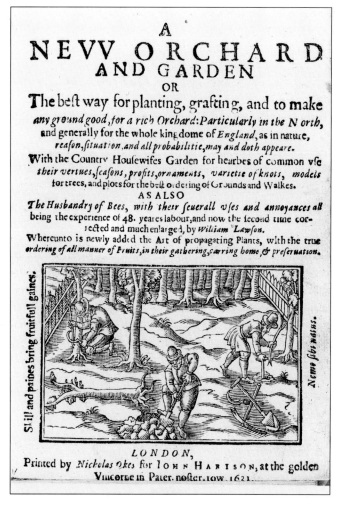

'Skill and paines bring fruitful gaines': sound advice from the title page of Lawson's New Orchard and Garden.

only contained long passages from William Lawson's *New Orchard* but even the title was borrowed from Bernard Palissy's *Le moyen de devenir riche* (1593).

William Lawson's *A new orchard and garden* bound together with *The Country Housewife's garden* appeared in 1618 and again in 1623. Reference to Lawson has already been made in Chapter 3 in connection with the use of mounts, but his practical outlook is also shown in other aspects of garden planning. Referring to the recent popularity of topiary, he suggests that the gardener could be instructed 'to trim small trees into the shapes of men at arms, or swift running grey hounds to chase the deare, or hunt the hare. This kind of hunting shall not waste your corne, nor much your coyne.'[1] In the protection of plants against pests and diseases he was not in favour of new-fangled remedies: of the practice of lighting bonfires in the orchard to suffocate caterpillars he wrote: 'I like nothing of smoake among my trees. Unnaturall heates are nothing good for naturall trees.'[2] Worries about pesticide pollution are not, perhaps, as new as one might imagine.

One of the most significant suggestions made by Lawson, undoubtedly chronicling contemporary events rather than publishing a new idea, is that the garden should be compartmented, separating the pleasure garden from vegetables and fruit so that the appreciation of flowers is not marred by the odours of onions and cabbages. This separation was a major feature of late Tudor gardens.

Lawson and, more especially, Markham were concerned with farms as well as gardens, and dealt with a whole spectrum of situations from cottage gardening to estate management. Their interests were essentially practical. Not so Francis Bacon, Lord Verulam. His *Essay on Gardens*, printed in 1625, the year before his death, but probably written *c.* 1600, was a visionary essay rather than a practical description. Bacon was not concerned with salads, pot herbs and plants for the still. To him a garden 'is the purest of humane pleasures . . . the greatest refreshment to the spirits of man'. To enable it to fulfil these roles it should have plants for all seasons and plants to perfume the air, covered walks for shade in the heat of summer and a main garden more open for the temperate parts of the year. By such means Bacon hoped to create a *ver perpetuum*, a perpetual spring to refresh the soul as much as the body. This idea of a philosopher's garden, held for ever in the unchanging freshness of springtime, grew in importance as the seventeenth and eighteenth centuries progressed.

Bacon's idea of a garden was reflected, too, by John Parkinson (1567–1650). His *Paradisi in Sole, Paradisus Terrestris*, published in 1629,[3] was the first book to deal mainly with ornamental plants and with their enjoyment rather than their uses. The humour apparent in its title, 'Park in Sun's Earthly Paradise', a pun on his own name, was matched by the freshness of his writing. The *Paradisi* was followed in 1640 by the more traditional *Theatrum Botanicum: A Herball of a Large Extent*, in which Parkinson described nearly 4,000 plants, four times as many as Gerard grew and listed in his *Catalogus arborum* of 1596.

News of the forthcoming publication of Parkinson's enormous work prompted Gerard's editors to produce a new edition of the *Herball* in 1633. The banana was among the many exotic plants illustrated for the first time in the second edition.

With these new books to describe plants and gardens and to inspire gardeners, it is not surprising that the momentum of

Exotic flowers adorn Parkinson's 'earthly paradise'.

Elizabethan garden-making continued into the seventeenth century. James I himself took a keen interest in gardens, as in other arts and sciences. In 1605 he issued a royal charter incorporating the Companie of Gardiners in London, giving it powers to stop bad practices among persons living within six miles of the capital. A second charter, issued in 1616, increased these powers, limiting trade in plants to those who had served a seven-year apprenticeship and giving freemen of the company power to search out and destroy inferior or illegal produce. In 1617 James also issued a charter to the 'Society of the Art and Mistery of Apothecaries of the City of London', separating the makers of medicines from spicers, peppers and other members of the Grocers' Company. He established vineyards and mulberries in the lower parts of St James's Park, and, in 1609, ordered 1,000 mulberry trees to be sent to each county town, to be sold at six shillings the 100 in an attempt

High walls, turf seat, roses, lilies and small beds of simple flowers: the
private paradise of a medieval garden (P. de Crescens, *'Le Rustican'*, c.1460).

Needlework hangings from Stoke Edith in Herefordshire (*c*.1720) show how closely gardens mirrored architecture in the seventeenth century. Balustrades define the garden boundary but no longer exclude the landscape beyond.

Despite its exotic animals, the Soho tapestry of 'Africa' at Packwood House (*c*.1733) has a distinctly English character.

The flat, riverside site of the royal palace at Hampton Court provided ideal terrain for the creation of a garden in the grand manner, influenced by both France and Holland.

The apparently simple lines of Maynard Colchester's garden at Westbury Court
conceal the tantalizingly maze-like quality of the Dutch-inspired design.

Rigaud's view of the Rotunda and Queen's Temple at Stowe shows the garden in
transition: classical formality extends into an increasingly natural landscape.

At Studley Royal the symmetry of a canalized river, cascades and twin pavilions is
subordinate to the genius of the place.

The mausoleum at Castle Howard. Vanbrugh's theatrical experience is clearly
evident in this dramatic building and its landscape setting.

(Opposite above) Lancelot Brown's sublime composition of landform, trees and water at Blenheim, in scale with the grandeur of Vanbrugh's great palace and bridge, brilliantly exploits the capabilities of the place.

(Opposite below) In contrast to Brown's professionalism at Blenheim, Henry Hoare's Stourhead shows the work of a gifted amateur. The landscape is more intimate and eventful.

(Above) Bridges and temples, tents and galleons, a rock arch and hilltop mausoleum embellish the remarkable landscape at West Wycombe, but the main ornament of the scene was the house itself.

(Right) Banksias painted by Sidney Parkinson, Joseph Banks's botanical artist on Cook's voyage to Australia.

Before and after at Wimpole: Repton used his watercolours to enchant
patrons with instant transformations of their estates.

to establish an English silk industry. Although James had many palaces at his disposal, he preferred Robert Cecil's Theobalds above all, and in 1607 he persuaded Cecil to exchange Theobalds for Hatfield. By the following year Cecil had pulled down three sides of the old Tudor palace at Hatfield and was using the bricks to build a splendid new house only 100 yards away. Many names are connected with the new palace and gardens at Hatfield, but the presiding genius was Cecil himself: there is a tradition that he commissioned 'front' and 'back' elevations for the building, then used estate craftsmen and his own ingenuity to connect the two. The garden was largely the work of Mountain Jennings, his gardener brought from Theobalds, with water features planned by Salomon de Caus (or de Caux).

The Tradescants

The most famous name connected with the gardens at Hatfield, and at the Cecils' Dorset estate at Cranborne, is the elder John Tradescant. Tradescant, the son of a Huguenot who had settled in East Anglia, was married at Meopham, Kent, in 1607 while working at Shorne for Robert Cecil.[4] Cecil sent him on extensive tours through Europe to buy fruit trees and other plants for the new garden at Hatfield. Limes, mulberries (possibly the four which survived until recently in the West Garden), cherries and other trees were bought, together with tulips, anemones, and other unusual flowers. Tradescant also accompanied Lord Digges to Russia in 1618, compiling the first flora of that vast country and bringing back many plants. In 1620 he went to Algeria, ostensibly to worry pirates but in fact to bring back a particularly fine variety of apricot. In 1625 he became gardener to the Duke of Buckingham and finally, in 1629, he was made gardener to Charles I.

On his appointment as royal gardener (in the year that Parkinson became King's Botanist), he moved to Lambeth to form a collection of plants and curiosities brought back from his extensive travels. On his death in 1638 the royal appointment was transferred to his son, also John, who was in Virginia at the time collecting plants and seeds. The tulip tree *Liriodendron tulipifera*, the swamp cypress *Taxodium distichum*, Virginia creeper, phlox, Michaelmas daisy and of course the spiderwort *Tradescantia virginiana* are but a few of his introductions. John junior added to the collections at Lambeth, already so well known in his father's day that the house was dubbed 'The Ark', and on his death in 1662 he bequeathed the contents of

*John Tradescant, carved in the
newel post at Hatfield House.*

The Ark to Elias Ashmole, who in turn left them to Oxford
University as the nucleus of the Ashmolean Museum. Two lists
published by the Tradescants, in 1634 and 1656 (as part of the
catalogue of the Museum Tradescantium), are important in indicating the plants known to them.

Further and much closer links between Tradescant and Oxford
would have developed had the Earl of Danby been successful in his
attempt to appoint Tradescant as the Keeper of Oxford Physic
Garden. Danby founded the Physic Garden, the first in Britain, in
1621, but after four years of importing dung to raise the garden
sufficiently above the River Cherwell, and another seven years in
which the handsome surrounding walls and Inigo Jones's gateway
were erected, there was little left of the endowment to attract
Tradescant. Instead the keeper of the local inn, Jacob Bobart, was
appointed Keeper (with a capital K) of the new Botanic Garden as
well. He fulfilled his duties admirably and his son, also Jacob,
became both Keeper and Professor of Botany until his death in
1719, almost a century after the foundation.

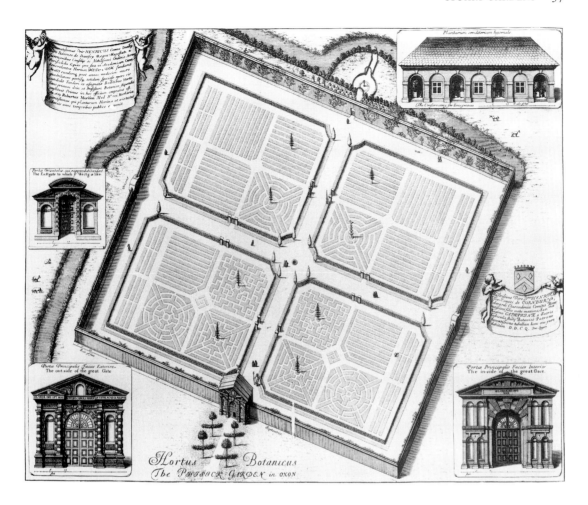

The Oxford Physic Garden (now the Botanic Garden) from Loggan's Oxonia Illustrata – *an ordered world of plants.*

The Tradescants, father and son, were buried in their parish church of St Mary-at-Lambeth, at the gates of Lambeth Palace, and there they might have lain in increasing neglect had not the present Church Commissioners, faced with problems of soaring costs and dwindling congregations, declared the church redundant and proposed its demolition. There ensued a vigorous campaign, ably led by Mr and Mrs Nicholson, to save the church and to designate it as the Tradescant Centre and Museum of Garden History. The Tradescant Trust was founded in 1977, and the churchyard garden was stocked with plants introduced by or contemporary with the Tradescants to a design by the present Marchioness of Salisbury (of Hatfield and Cranborne).

The stage is set

Tradescant was not the only notable person connected with the garden at Hatfield, and the garden was not only a collection of new and exciting flowers and fruits. Like other new gardens of the early seventeenth century it was conceived primarily as a setting for the great new house and as a stage for courtly display. Salomon de Caus, who designed the elaborate waterworks, was the author of *Les raisons des forces mouvantes* (1615), one of the first and most important of the books on hydraulics which appeared during the seventeenth century, marking the transition from the empirical and innovative fountains of sixteenth-century Italy to the more solidly reasoned and calculated effects of France. It was the French rationale which prevailed as a model in England.

Blickling has much in common with Hatfield. When Sir Henry Hobart acquired the estate in 1616 he chose Robert Lyminge, who had been involved in the building of Hatfield, as architect for the new house. The formal approach to the south front flanked by low wings of outbuildings, the moat of the earlier house and the long vista extending northwards into the gentle slope remain characteristic of the seventeenth-century scale although, like Hatfield, the garden was extensively altered, restored and remodelled, especially in the eighteenth and early twentieth centuries.

Wilton was built in the 1550s around a quadrangle, but William Herbert, 3rd Earl of Pembroke, and his brother Philip, the 4th Earl, both generous patrons of the arts, shared a desire to improve and alter their home. Although their plans to alter the house were not completed until a terrible fire in 1647 prompted Philip Herbert to consult Inigo Jones, the great formal garden designed by Isaac de Caus *c.* 1630 did materialize. De Caus's engraving[5] shows the garden over 1,000 feet long and 400 feet wide, divided into three main compartments; the first a parterre of great complexity, the second filled with formal groves of trees and bordered by shady galleries, the third a simpler, more airy space, with tree-lined paths around the statue of a gladiator. A wide central path bisected the compartments and terminated in a splendid grotto filled with waterworks.

William Herbert did not confine his improvements to Wilton. In 1626 he bought Moor Park in Hertfordshire and laid out a garden which might well have been the precursor of the Wilton garden. Sir William Temple spent his honeymoon at Moor Park in 1655 and, thirty years later, described it in his essay *Upon the*

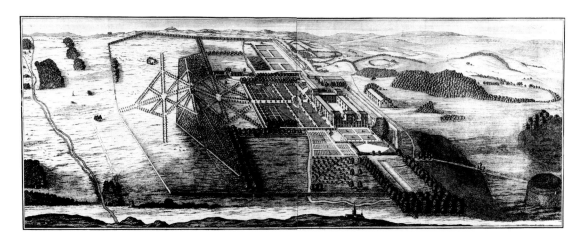

Kip's view of the Earl of
Pembroke's house and garden
at Wilton.

Garden of Epicurus as 'the perfectest figure of a garden I ever saw,
either at home or abroad'.

Commonwealth and Restoration

Civil war brought the development of gardens to an abrupt halt.
With the execution of Charles I, the nobility and gentry joined
forces with the Parliamentarians or left England to join the young
Prince Charles in exile or simply tried to remain neutral in their
country estates. The Puritan Commonwealth was not a suitable
environment for the creation of splendid new houses or gardens,
but exile abroad brought some compensations.

John Evelyn travelled through France and Italy observing and
describing the gardens, farms and other aspects of the two cultures.
Christopher Hatton, in exile from his Northamptonshire home of
Kirby from 1648 to 1656, sent back trees and flowers for his garden
from French nurseries. Sir Thomas Hanmer retired to Bettisfield
in Flintshire to devote himself to his garden and to the writing of
his *Garden Book*. Completed in 1659, the manuscript was lost and
not rediscovered until 1933, when it was published, so it is readily
accessible today, a very charming and informative book. In it
Hanmer described the gardens of his day and the great improvement
brought about by the influence of French and Dutch gardeners.

Cromwell's interregnum brought not only a chance to reflect
but also a much closer relationship between the English nobility
and the mainstream of European culture.

The return of Charles II from France in 1660, where much of
his time had been spent at the great palace of Versailles, heralded a

new age in gardening and the lead was given by the King himself. As if to acknowledge his debt to France, he appointed two brothers, André and Gabriel Mollet, trained by le Nôtre at Versailles, as royal gardeners. At Hampton Court a vast canal was dug and 758 lime trees were imported to create a semicircular walk and avenues, all aligned on a newly gilded balcony in the apartments of Charles's new queen, Catherine of Braganza. The flat, well-watered site at Hampton Court lent itself admirably to grand gardening in the French manner.

Similar grandeur was achieved in a very different setting at Cliveden in Buckinghamshire by George Villiers, 2nd Duke of Buckingham. His father, the favourite of James I and Charles I, was assassinated, and young Villiers travelled to France and Italy to escape a similar fate. Soon after the Restoration his vast fortunes were restored by Charles II, and he bought Cliveden in 1666. With William Winde as architect, he began the great red brick terrace astride the chalk spur, falling steeply to the Thames, thus establishing the main axis of the layout which has developed in the succeeding three centuries.

Another garden in which French influence is very direct, in a most unlikely setting, is at Levens Hall, Cumbria. When James II was forced to flee the country in 1688, Colonel Graham, Privy Purse and Keeper of the Buckhounds to the King, retired to Levens and employed Guillaume Beaumont, who had also worked for James II, to plan and create a new garden. The box-edged parterres decorated with clipped greens formed a French garden in miniature, and despite vicissitudes the layout has been preserved in a remarkably intact state, although the clipped greens have grown to enormous proportions and now dominate the plan. Two features on the plan, made for Graham's son-in-law c. 1730, are of great significance. First, the deer park with its splendid oak avenue is shown complete with ancient stag-headed trees instead of being made entirely new and orderly. Second, the west side of the garden has a sunken boundary with a semicircular bastion, so the garden ceases to be a complete enclosure and offers uninterrupted views through the surrounding landscape. The sunken boundary or 'ha-ha' was depicted in Dezallier d'Argenville's *Théorie et Pratique du Jardinage*, translated as *Practice of Gardening* by John James in 1712, and its employment at Levens, to forge a closer link between the garden and its surroundings, marked an important change in English gardens.

French influence in post-Restoration England was undoubtedly strong, but it must not be forgotten that Sir Thomas Hanmer

The formal garden at Levens Hall survives, with its clipped greens now grown to enormous size.

attributed the 'recent' improvements in gardening jointly to the French and to the Dutch. Dutch nurseries had developed rapidly in the sixteenth century, and it was Holland which provided many of the fruits, the flowers and especially the greens to fill the gardens of seventeenth-century England. The smaller scale, less assertive nature and more complex planting of the Dutch garden also found more sympathy among the English gentry than did the grand and plainer schemes of France.

This Dutch influence is nowhere more clearly seen than in the delightful restoration of Westbury Court, Gloucester, by the National Trust.[6] Maynard Colchester inherited Westbury Court in 1694, and during the next ten years constructed a long canal with a summer house at one end and a fountain at the other, the whole enclosed within a high wall pierced only by a wrought-iron screen on the axis of the canal.

The canal was bordered by hedges of yew, holly and thorn, with bay, laurel, laurustinus, phillyrea, pines and spruce used for topiary.

On the walls were apples, pears, peaches, apricots, cherries and nectarines, while the beds of the parterre laid out south of the house in 1700 were filled with tulips, iris, jonquils, hyacinths, ranunculi, crocus and other bulbs imported by the hundreds from Holland. The garden was developed further by Maynard Colchester's nephew, also Maynard, from 1715 to 1756, quite against the prevailing fashion, and was maintained for another 150 years before becoming increasingly ruined as the twentieth century progressed.

Restoration by the National Trust from 1967 was simplified by the discovery of the elder Maynard's meticulously kept notebook, and although the plan of the garden has had to be tailored to twentieth-century financial constraints, it is in some ways more interesting – even more authentic – than the overgrown remains of an untouched seventeenth-century garden: it shows the garden in its youth much as its creators must have enjoyed it rather than overlaid with centuries of romantic growth and decay.

Westbury Court by Kip. The house and part of the garden have been built on but the gazebo and canal garden were rescued by the National Trust in 1967.

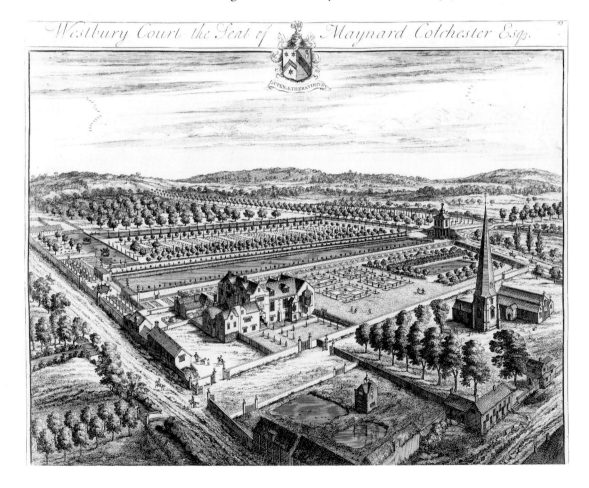

Sudbury by Jan Griffier, 1681:
post-Restoration grandeur.

A French connection?

In the decades after the Commonwealth, during the reigns of
Charles II, James II and William and Mary, artistic allegiance
to France was tempered by English restraint and by the English
environment. Omnipotence, and even the desire for omnipotence,
so important in shaping the gardens of France, was lacking in
England. The rolling topography of much of England made it
difficult to plan on an impressive scale. Avenues simply disappeared
over the next hill. Even at Hampton Court, where the flat meadows
and high water table were ideally suited to the grand manner, the
misty atmosphere softened, often obscured, the reflections of the
palace in the grand canal.

Parterres, avenues, canals and clipped greens, the components of
late Stuart gardens, might justifiably be attributed to French and
Dutch influence, but the gardens themselves were essentially
English: accretions of garden compartments each grand and symmetrical in itself but stubbornly refusing to conform to an overall
scheme.

Boughton in Northamptonshire was thought to be the finest
garden in England. From 1684 to 1709 Ralph Montagu, who had
been Charles II's ambassador at Versailles, laid out 100 acres with

the aid of his Dutch gardener Van de Meulen. Even in 1694 Charles Hatton wrote that 'my lord Montagu is very much concerned that ye water with wch he hoped to make so fine fountains hath failed his expectations',[7] but in 1712 John Morton described three parterres below the west front of the house, 'the Parterre of Statues, the Parterre of Basins and the Water Parterre', in the last of which an 80-foot high jet rose from the centre of an octagonal basin 216 yards in circumference. On the north side was a wilderness 'nobly adorned with basins, jet d'eaux, statues, with the platanus, lime tree, beech, bays etc., all in exquisite form and order', and the River Ise was canalized to enclose the parterres on two sides.

For all the elaborate features and the obvious connections with France and Holland, Braisier's survey of Boughton made in 1715 shows an inward-looking collection of gardens rather loosely connected one with another and standing conspicuously separate from the park through which the second Duke 'John the Planter' drove his numerous avenues.

On a lesser scale, at Kirby in Northamptonshire, the garden developed partly from exile by Christopher Hatton III was extended westward by his son, also Christopher. In 1686 £59 7s 4d was spent on levelling, on 'digging of borders and bringing of moulde and dunge in' and 'to the masons seting of the bordring stones and the statuse up'.[8] Although the estate was neglected within thirty years of this new work, the 'bordring stones' remained *in situ* to enable a partial restoration by the Department of the Environment.[9] The quartered pattern of the west garden, half enclosed by raised walks, is re-established, and the canalized stream bounding the south side of the garden remains, but the shady wilderness, noted for its collection of trees, and the great avenues have disappeared.

The garden at Ham House shows many similarities to Kirby, particularly in the quartered parterre leading to a wilderness, and at Ham the entire scheme has been reconstructed by the National Trust. An even more remarkable restoration is the garden at Erddig in North Wales. Entirely encompassed within a high brick wall, the garden has a central canal and a second smaller rectangular pool, walks bordered by pleached limes and by Irish yews, a shady wilderness, orchards, beehives in a sculpted yew hedge and, on the walls, old varieties of fruit, many of them recorded in the gardener's original lists because very little at Erddig was ever thrown away.

The steeply terraced garden of Powis Castle, necessarily Italian in inspiration.

Italian inspiration

Less than thirty miles from Erddig is Powis Castle, another late Stuart garden but of a very different mould. The steeply terraced garden below and around the castle is essentially – and of necessity – Italian in character, thus coming nearer in inspiration to the source of the classical garden. In Italy, the fount of the Renaissance, gardens epitomized more than any other art the admiration of classical ideals. As Plato taught in the tree-shaded Academy, so the members of de Medici's Platonic Academy gathered in their own villas and gardens modelled on descriptions of Pliny's villas and embodying ideas of Varro and Palladio. A garden was the essential background to the social, commercial and intellectual life of Renaissance Italy.

John Evelyn, probably more than any other individual, was responsible for translating this Italian model to English soil. In 1651 he designed the garden of his brother's house at Wotton in Surrey.[10] The hillside was terraced and, on the axis of the house, pierced by a grotto with a classical portico. The courtyard had a central fountain fed by a stream led along the terrace. It was a substantially architectural scheme reflecting Evelyn's own interest in art and architecture, but planting was of course necessary and, perhaps to prepare himself for that part of the garden's design, in 1650 Evelyn bought a copy of Parkinson's *Paradisi*. He became inspired by the ideology of paradise, by the idea of a perfect place of everlasting spring, and sought the evergreen plants by which this state could be created on earth. These he collected in his own garden at Sayes Court, south of London, acquiring simultaneously all the newest publications on husbandry and the natural sciences to assist in their cultivation. Evelyn claimed to be the first to recommend the yew for topiary, and his holly hedges at Sayes Court were renowned.

He also created a philosopher's garden at Albury in Surrey for Henry Howard in 1667, drawing up detailed plans which Howard followed to the letter.[11] The main axis of the house continued to an alcove in the terraced hillside and thence via a tunnel through the hill to a pine walk through the fields. There were elaborate waterworks, vineyards on the slopes below the terrace and fruit trees trained on the terrace wall, all features combining classical precedent with modern husbandry. The tunnel was inspired by the 'noble, and altogether wonderful, Crypta' seen in Italy in 1645, cut through Mount Pausilippe and with Virgil's sepulchre at its mouth; the vineyards below were enclosed against animals as advised by Virgil in the *Georgics*.

Evelyn was consulted on the gardens at Cornbury in Oxfordshire and Clarendon House in London by the Chancellor, Lord Clarendon, at Euston, Suffolk, by the Earl of Arlington and at Cassiobury, Hertfordshire, by the Earl of Essex. He collected his wealth of knowledge on gardening in *Elysium Britannicum*, but the manuscript was never published. A third of it was recently discovered in the library of Christ Church, Oxford, and is being transcribed for publication. It is an immensely detailed account and will be a delightful addition to the literature of garden history.

Evelyn is most widely known, however, for his authorship of *Sylva: a discourse on forest trees*, published by the Royal Society in 1664. Concerned by the loss of tree cover in Britain, especially during the Commonwealth, and by the shortage of timber and fuel which this threatened, the Royal Society sought to stimulate interest in tree planting. *Sylva*, a fusion of practical estate management, gardening and philosophy, promoted the idea that gardening was an activity worthy of gentlemen and that the planting of woods created both material and spiritual wealth, thus stimulating the surge of 'improvements' which continued into the eighteenth century.

The Green House

With improvements taking place in every estate and garden of note, the demand for plants was enormous. England had very few native trees and even fewer of the cherished 'greens'. There were Scots pine, yew, holly, box and ivy, but these did not bear comparison with the more exciting exotics. The beauty, fragrance and fruitfulness of the orange had a special appeal, and it was attempts to cultivate the orange in England which led to the development of glasshouses, thus making possible the cultivation of many other tender plants introduced from the late eighteenth century onwards.

The orange had been grown in England since at least 1580 by the Carews of Beddington in Surrey[12] but, being planted outside and given only makeshift protection in the winter, they were not very fruitful. Parkinson advised growing the trees in large boxes, to be manhandled into protective structures for the winter; throughout the seventeenth century these structures improved in light and elegance, though more for architectural effect than horticultural necessity, as the importance of light for plant growth was not generally realized. Poor growth in these dark but impressive buildings was attributed to harmful vapours arising from the open fires used to heat the buildings, and not entirely without reason. John Evelyn wrote to the Earl of Sandwich on the dangers of burning sulphurous coal, commenting that, at the Chelsea Physic Garden, the doors and windows were left open to obviate the danger!

In 1670 the freestanding iron stove was developed in Holland and the stove house took a major step forward. John Field, gardener to the Earl of Bedford, acquired a Dutch stove, procured for him by George London of Brompton Park Nurseries, and others soon followed his example. By 1685, the year in which Mansart completed the great orangery at Versailles to accommodate 1,200 orange trees, Sir William Temple had orange trees as large as any he had seen as a youth in France and with a flavour to match all but the very best from Seville or Portugal. At Chatsworth in 1694 the 1st Duke of Devonshire built a handsome greenhouse, shown in the engraving of the garden by Johannes Kip, and from 1694–1703 Celia Fiennes described in her journal many such structures in the gardens she had visited. In 1691 Dr Robert Uvedale was described not only as master of Enfield Grammar School but also as 'master of the greatest and choicest collection of exotic greens . . . anywhere in the land'.[13] Of the six or seven houses in his garden, the largest was filled with oranges and large myrtles, the next with smaller myrtles and the remainder with other choice and tender plants.

Oranges, lemons, myrtle, pomegranate, laurustine (*Viburnum tinus*) and other tender (and supposedly tender) plants were almost universally imported from French and Dutch nurseries, together with fruits, forest trees, bulbs and flowers, as the nursery industry in England was rudimentary in comparison with its continental counterparts.

Early nurseries

After the dissolution of the monasteries, many orchards and gardens were leased by new owners to tenant farmers and the orchards and market gardens supplied plants and seeds, occasionally in substantial quantities, as a sideline. Specialist seedsmen also appeared, selling mainly vegetable seeds and bulbs, and by 1688 London had three major seed firms with a few more widely scattered in the provinces. The royal gardeners, the Tradescants and later Captain Leonard Gurle (chief gardener to Charles II from 1677 to 1685), collected and propagated plants which were distributed to other gardens, in the case of the Tradescants from Lambeth and by Gurle from one of the first general nurseries, about twelve acres of land between Whitechapel and Spitalfields.

For the most part, landowners obtained seeds where they could and raised them in private nurseries to plant out or exchange with friends. In this respect some were more fortunately placed than others. William Blathwayt, who made the great formal garden at Dyrham in the closing years of the seventeenth century, was an administrator of the American colonies and brought back seeds for the nursery at Dyrham: Virginian pine, sassafras, tulip tree and many oaks were raised. John Evelyn asked his friend Samuel Pepys, as Secretary to the Admiralty, to persuade officers in the colonies to bring back seeds on their return to England.

Even more important was Henry Compton (1632–1713), Bishop of London from 1675 until his death nearly forty years later. Compton was a keen gardener, and filled the garden of the Bishop's Palace at Fulham with more than 1,000 varieties of rare plants which he cultivated with great skill and distributed generously among his friends. As head of the Church for the American colonies he received a steady flow of seeds and plants. John Baptist Banister, sent by Compton as a missionary to the West Indies and thence to Virginia, was instructed to collect plants as well as to save souls. He dispatched the first of the American azaleas, *Magnolia virginica* and the beautiful *Dodecatheon meadia* before earning the dubious distinction of being the first plant-hunter to lose his life in the search for plants. He lost his footing while collecting, and fell to his death in 1692 at the age of thirty-eight.

Brompton Park

In the seventeenth century there was no universally recognized system of naming plants, and certainly no means of standardizing the names of new varieties, so the purchase of plants was fraught with difficulty. In an attempt to produce some order out of the chaos, four gardeners took the lease of Brompton Park in Kensington in 1681 and founded a nursery intended to provide correctly named plants and seeds of good quality and to lay out gardens. The initiative came from Joseph Lucre (or Looker), gardener to the Queen at Somerset House, with Moses Cook (Cooke), chief gardener to the Earl of Essex at Cassiobury, and John Field, chief gardener to the Earl of Bedford at Bedford House as senior partners. The fourth and youngest partner was George London, Bishop Compton's gardener at Fulham and subsequently gardener to Queen Mary. In such experienced hands the venture was an immediate success and quickly became the principal nursery in the country.

The first major commission came within a year, the four partners spending one month each in rotation at Longleat in Wiltshire, the seat of the first Viscount Weymouth, supervising the construction and planting of the great parterres, basins, groves and allées spanning the leat, or stream, and terminating in an amphitheatre-like wilderness of radiating walks on the hillside opposite the great house.

Lucre died in 1685, Field soon after, and Moses Cook retired, so George London took on a new partner, Henry Wise, trained under John Rose, the royal gardener, and in France. In 1686 Bishop Compton was suspended for refusing to restrain anti-Roman-Catholic preaching, and he gave his gardener permission 'to wait upon other gentlemen' while he himself turned enthusiastically to his own garden at Fulham.

For nearly two decades, until London died in 1713, the nursery of London and Wise was without parallel. The partnership appears to have been rather a loose one, with each man working on different commissions, but this had its advantages. George London had been appointed royal gardener to Queen Mary. When Anne succeeded to the throne in 1702, London was quickly dismissed, but, as Henry

Wise was appointed to replace him, Brompton Park flourished as before. For one of the improvements at Windsor, Brompton Park supplied 238 spruces clipped into pyramids nine feet high and hundreds of fruit trees and vines, together with 41,150 whitethorn for hedges.[14] At Hampton Court 400 thirty-year-old lime trees were moved to make an avenue.

In 1688 London signed a contract with the 4th Earl (later the 1st Duke) of Devonshire to make a parterre west of the remodelled house at Chatsworth in Derbyshire. In 1694 another contract was made for the great south parterre, 473 feet long and 227 feet wide, and although little other documentary evidence remains, it is probable that most of the enormous garden at Chatsworth emanated from Brompton Park.

On quite a different scale, both London and Wise contributed to the garden at Melbourne in Derbyshire. When Thomas Coke inherited Melbourne in 1696 he immediately set about improvements. Wise sent two plans, of which Coke selected one for implementation. In 1699 further expansion was contemplated and Coke sent his own plan to Wise, who in turn passed it to George London, newly returned from a second visit to France, for approval. Within a month 1,000 elms, 600 limes, 2,000 hornbeams, hundreds of shrubs and thousands of bulbs were on their way from Brompton Park for the new garden. In 1701 London fitted in a visit to Melbourne while at Chatsworth to examine the improvements, and the garden expanded yet again in 1704 with a further six acres taken in for the delightful *patte d'oie*. With its terraced parterres, formal pool and hedged walks radiating through a diminutive woodland, the garden was a Versailles in miniature.

At Chatsworth, Dyrham, Chicheley (Buckinghamshire), Stonyhurst (Lancashire), Winslow (Buckinghamshire) and many other places of greater and lesser extent, London and Wise planted fruit gardens, dug canals, made fountains and cascades, and planted parterres, wildernesses and woods, but their greatest work, for which Henry Wise was chiefly responsible, was at Blenheim. Together with Hampton Court, Blenheim came nearest of all English gardens to the grandeur of Versailles.

The old royal park of Woodstock was given to the Duke of Marlborough by the nation after his victory at Blenheim. In 1704 Henry Wise surveyed the 2,000-acre estate, in June 1705 the men arrived from Brompton Park, and by October the great bastioned parterre was complete. Plants came by barge and by wagon. Half a million bricks enclosed the eight-acre kitchen garden, and in 1707 Wise wrote to the Duke expressing his satisfaction with the work:

only thirty of 1,600 large elms planted in the avenues had died and the kitchen garden was already the finest in England, probably the finest in the world. Blenheim's glory was short-lived, however. In 1708 the Duchess quarrelled with Sir John Vanbrugh, the architect, and later with the Queen. In 1710 the Queen withdrew her favour and work came to a halt. Within fifty years most of Wise's work was obliterated by change of fashion.

While Wise worked at Blenheim, George London attended to other major gardens: 100 acres, for example, at Wanstead, Essex, from 1706 for Josiah Child, newly wealthy from his East India Company trading. Canons at Edgware, for James Brydges, later Duke of Chandos, Earl of Caernarvon and Viscount Wilton, was still being made when George London died at the end of 1713.

Stephen Switzer, himself trained as a foreman at Brompton Park, said of George London:

Badminton by Kip: the house and gardens in the middle of a web of radiating avenues.

. . . it will perhaps be hardly believed in time to come that this one person actually saw and gave directions once or twice a year in most of the noblemen's and gentlemen's gardens in England. And since it was common for him to ride fifty or sixty miles in a day he made his northern circuit

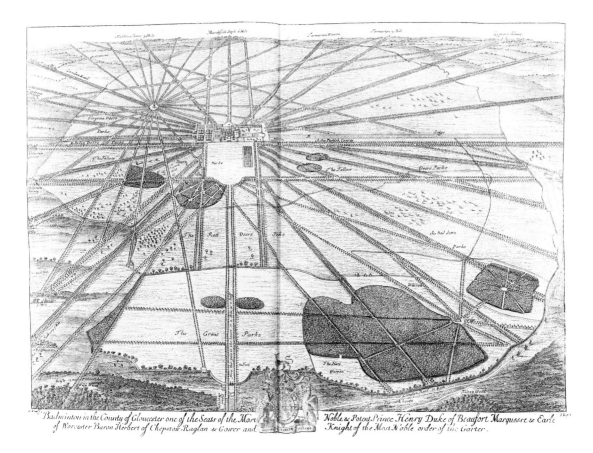

Badminton in the County of Gloucester one of the Seats of the Most Noble & Potent Prince Henry Duke of Beaufort Marquesse & Earle of Worcester Baron Herbert of Chepstow Raglan & Gower and Knight of the Most Noble order of the Garter.

in five or six weeks and sometimes less, and his western in as little time: as for the south and east they were but three or four days work for him; most times twice a year visiting all the country seats conversing with gentlemen and forwarding the business of gardening in such a degree as is almost impossible to describe.[15]

That the 'business of gardening' revolved around Brompton Park is beyond dispute. By 1700 there were fifteen nurseries in and about London with a handful more in the provinces, but Brompton Park remained pre-eminent. Bishop Compton maintained contact with his former gardener until his death; John Evelyn was a frequent visitor to the nursery and sang its praises at every opportunity. Thomas Hurnall, the head gardener at Dyrham, visited George London to obtain seeds whenever the latter was at Longleat, and would certainly have brought with him plants raised in the nursery at Dyrham or seeds obtained through his employer's colonial interests; in 1704 when London supplied a new gardener for Lord Weymouth, he sent him first to Bishop Compton for roots and

Ham House with its broad terrace, grass plats and stiffly formal 'wilderness'.

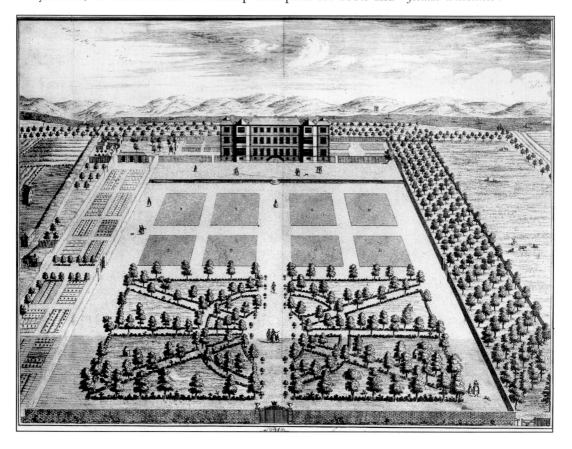

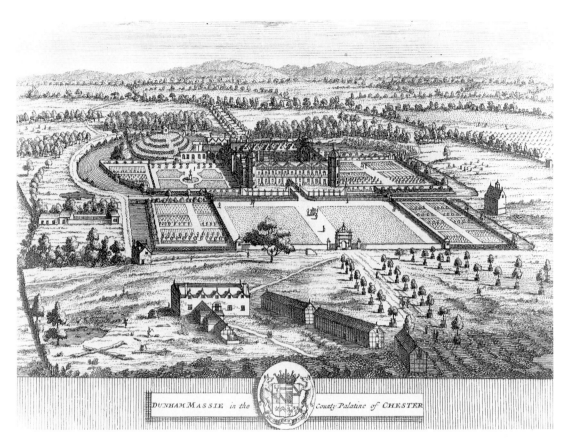

DUNHAM MASSIE in the County Palatine of CHESTER

Dunham Massey by Kip, 1688. The multi-tiered mount overlooks the deer park and garden.

plants to present to his new employer. By virtue of the enormous practice organized from Brompton Park, the nursery acted almost fortuitously as a clearing-house and hub for the prestigious gardening fraternity of the whole nation.

Garden portraits

Such was the interest in gardens that many proud owners had them depicted by a new generation of topographic artists. Foremost of the painters was Leendert Knyff, whose bird's-eye views of many country seats were engraved by Jan Kip for *Britannia Illustrata* (1709) and *Nouveau Théâtre de la Grande Bretagne* (1770). Among the eighty plates in *Britannia Illustrata* are three showing Lord Burlington's houses: his London house in Piccadilly, the suburban retreat of Chiswick and his country seat of Londesborough in Yorkshire. Of the Duke of Beaufort's Badminton there are three plates, the third showing the house and formal gardens as a tiny postage stamp in the centre of a huge web of radiating avenues. Knole, Wimpole and Uppark are shown, and at Dunham Massey the multi-tiered mount is a conspicuous feature overlooking the deer park. The tiny hunting lodge of Ashdown House in Berkshire, built by Lord Craven for Elizabeth of Bohemia, sister of Charles I, contrasts sharply with Lord Craven's own seat at Hampstead Marshall.

In most of the plates the countryside is very open, the avenues newly planted. Already, however, there was an important distinction to be seen in gardens. London and Wise were men of enormous practical experience, considerable ability and sound business sense, but they were not innovators. Their gardens, made around the year 1700, were no more than competent adaptations of garden styles current for more than half a century. They were dated, a part of the establishment and therefore fair targets for a new generation of garden-makers: John Evelyn had shown that a garden was more than a theatrical stage. It could be an earthly paradise, a Garden of Eden, an experiment in the philosophical relationship between man and nature. The question was – how?

5

The English Landscape Garden

The first indications of a new era came with criticisms of the old style of gardening. Even as early as 1681 John Worlidge (or Woolridge), author of *The Art of Gardening*, complained bitterly that the desire for rigid formality in parterres had led to the banishment of many beautiful flowers – a cry to be repeated almost word for word two centuries later by William Robinson. The pedantic symmetry of London and Wise's gardens was rejected as stiff and autocratic. At Longleat, especially, 'grove nods at grove, each alley has a brother, and half the platform just reflects the other'. Sometimes the criticism was as amusing as it was pointed: Alexander Pope's satirical 'Catalogue of Greens to be disposed of by an eminent Town-Gardiner', published in the *Guardian* in 1713,[1] includes:

Adam and Eve in Yew; Adam a little shatter'd by the fall of the Tree of Knowledge in the great Storm; Eve and the Serpent very flourishing.

St George in Box; his Arm scarce long enough, but will be in a Condition to stick the Dragon by next April.

A green Dragon of the same, with a Tail of Ground-Ivy for the present.

A pair of Giants, stunted, to be sold cheap.

Divers eminent Modern Poets in Bays, somewhat blighted, to be disposed of a pennyworth.

A Quick-set Hog shot up into a Porcupine, by its being forgot one Week in rainy weather.

Noah's Ark in Holly, standing on the Mount; the Ribs a little damaged for want of Water.

The garden liberated

There was rejection, too, of the old order from which such gardens arose. Prolonged wars with France fostered distaste for the autocracy symbolized in Le Nôtre's extensive parterres and endless vistas, which were characterized by Lord Shaftesbury as 'the formal mockery of princely gardens'. Liberty was the mood of the new order: liberty in politics, in the arts, even in the freedom for a tree to grow unhindered by the gardener's shears.

In 1712 Addison wrote in the *Spectator*:

I do not know whether I am singular in my opinion, but, for my own part, I would rather look upon a Tree in all its Luxuriancy and Diffusion of Boughs and Branches, than when it is thus cut and trimmed into a Mathematical Figure; and cannot but fancy that an Orchard in Flower looks infinitely more delightful, than all the little labyrinths of the most finished Parterre.[2]

In the second decade of the eighteenth century the old order was changing rapidly. Henry Compton, Bishop of London, died in 1713. George London, for many years his gardener, died at the end of the same year and Henry Wise retired from Brompton Park in 1714, leasing it to Joseph Carpenter and William Smith, in whose less capable hands it soon lost its hitherto unrivalled position. Queen Anne also died in 1714 and with the accession of George I of Hanover, scarcely able to speak a word of English, the gradually diminishing power of the throne was further dissipated among the new King's ministers.

Nature improved

The early eighteenth century was also a time of widespread agricultural improvement. Jethro Tull's seed drill, introduced in 1701, the use of root crops such as turnip for winter feed, selection of superior types of cattle and grasses and the use of clover and marl for the improvement of light soils all led to an increase of agricultural productivity and to the enlargement of estates on light soils.

The destruction of forests for fuel created additional farmland. In the 1695 edition of *Britannia*, Gibson noted that 'the ironworks in the counties around destroyed such prodigious quantities of wood that they quickly lay the country, a little open, and by degrees made room for the plough'. Before Evelyn's death the extensive Forest of Arden in Warwickshire had virtually disappeared; much of the country faced fuel famine unless waterborne supplies of coal were within reach. Coal extraction increased more than tenfold during the seventeenth century, providing added wealth for landowners to invest in their estates, and the hammer ponds initially created to provide power for the iron works often formed the beginnings of an ornamental landscape.[3]

Long before the Parliamentary enclosures of 1760 to 1815, substantial areas of the landscape were reorganized into larger, more efficient parcels of woodland and meadow, mainly as a result of economic forces.

The most important change manifest in the early eighteenth century, though, was a radically altered attitude to nature. During medieval times the walled garden epitomized a generally defensive outlook. In the early seventeenth century Lawson saw the mount as a place from which wild animals might be shot from safe vantage points. Half a century later the walls of Stuart gardens had become light, decorative, pierced by clairvoies, but the diarist Celia Fiennes and the several painters of gardens still depicted their subjects in meticulous contrast to the surrounding wilderness. By the eighteenth century, though, nature was being tamed, 'improved' and increasingly understood.

Plants collected from all corners of a rapidly expanding world and scrutinized in the new botanic gardens showed many affinities; the universe, whether examined through a telescope or a microscope or with the aid of the new chemistry of Sir Robert Boyle, revealed more and more an underlying organization. Lord Shaftesbury wrote in 1711 there is 'Idea of Sense, Order and Proportion everywhere'.

The Grand Tour

This new attitude to nature was apparent as the Grand Tour became an essential part of the education of every young man of means or of literary or artistic pretentions. Young impressionable travellers made their journeys of discovery through scenery of a grandeur and savagery hitherto unimagined. Terror and elation combined. When the excited and exhausted travellers reached Italy and saw the sylvan scenes of Claude and the rugged majesty of Salvator Rosa's paintings expressing their innermost emotions on canvas, the result was electrifying. Correspondence, diaries, sketchbooks were filled with new sensations: thundering waterfalls, towering

peaks, limitless views across the *campagna* and the realities of the classical world set in dramatic surroundings. A new word emerged – 'prospect' – not simply the view but the effect of what the eye saw on highly educated and highly excited minds.

'Clifden [Cliveden], that stupendious prospect…' by Tanleims, c. 1760.

John Evelyn's journeys through France and Italy were prompted by the civil war. When he later visited the Duke of Buckingham's newly completed house at Cliveden in 1679, he wrote in his diary:

> Clifden that stupendious natural Rock, Wood, & Prospect … 'tis a romantic object & the place alltogether answers the most poetical descriptions that can be made of a solitude, precipice, prospects & whatever can contribute to a thing so very like their imaginations … on the platforme is a circular view to the utmost verge of the Horizon, which with the serpentining of the Thames is admirably surprising.[4]

Stephen Switzer described the garden at Dyrham, a product of Brompton Park, in 1718. Although he paid due attention to the parterres, the fountains, the greenhouses and the canal 'where two swans continually waft themselves with grandeur', he was clearly more interested in their setting. 'To describe the Situation of the

Seat ... 'tis a beautiful Irregularity, here a Dale, there a Mount, here a winding Valley, there a parting Stream &c.' His description continued through the gardens, past 'thundering cascades' and up a series of terraces to finish above the roof of the house.

From this Terras you have a prospect from you of about eight or ten Miles over a rich and fertile Vale, which, by Variety of Woods, Groves, and Meadows, appears like a *Rural Garden* to this stately Mansion.[5]

Joseph Addison reminded his fellow Englishmen that the great formal gardens of France and Italy were always set in large and less rigid parks:

... our English gardens are not so entertaining to the Fancy as those in France or Italy, where we see a large Extent of Ground covered over with an agreeable mixture of Garden and Forest, which represents everywhere an artificial Rudeness, much more charming than the Neatness and Elegancy which we meet with in those of our own Country.[6]

A pretty landskip

Although Addison advised against following the French and Italian example here (the making of large forests in a densely settled country would withdraw too much land from agriculture), he saw no reason why a whole estate might not

be thrown into a kind of Garden by frequent Plantations, that may turn as much to the Profit, as the Pleasure of the Owner. Fields of Corn make a pleasant Prospect, and if the Walks were a little taken care of that lie between them, if the natural Embroidery of the Meadows were helpt and improved by some small Additions or Art, and the several Rows of Hedges set off by Trees and Flowers, that the Soil was capable of receiving, a Man might make a pretty Landskip of his own Possessions.[7]

The lack of 'artificial rudeness' was clearly felt by the Italians themselves, for when Adelaide, daughter of the Marquis Paleotti of Bologna, married Charles Talbot, 1st Duke of Shrewsbury, in 1704 and settled at Heythrop, Oxfordshire, the garden was extended with winding walks through shady groves of trees complete with cold bath and bath-house so that she could live in the manner to which she was accustomed in Italy. How much use was made of the cold bath is not recorded, but Switzer heard of the new garden while working at the nearby estate of Blenheim and described it in his *Nobleman, Gentleman and Gardener's Recreation* of 1715.[8]

Switzer, too, considered that 'those large sums of money that have been buried within the narrow limits of a high wall upon the trifling and diminutive beauties of greens and flowers [would be employed to better advantage] lightly spread over great and extensive parks and forests.'[9]

By 1715, when this was published, excitement in the gardening world was intense. Farming had turned much of the English landscape into a garden: cultivated, productive and entirely pleasurable to behold. Forestry provided an investment, a wise use of agriculturally worthless land, and had been shown to be a noble activity worthy of the finest minds. From farm and forest 'a Man might make a pretty Landskip of his own Possessions', and if that landskip were enlivened by buildings it could be charged with recollections of the classical world. After all, had Virgil himself not seen a simple, rural life as civilized man's worthiest achievement?

One of the first to realize the dramatic potential of buildings in the landscape was the soldier/dramatist/architect Sir John Vanbrugh. In 1709, ten years after his triumphant architectural composition at Castle Howard, Vanbrugh wrote to Sarah, Duchess of Marlborough, at Blenheim, urging her to keep the old Woodstock Manor to enliven the park, for the development of which he advised her to send for a landscape painter. The relationship between Vanbrugh and the Duchess had rarely been anything but stormy, so it is scarcely surprising that the garden and park at Blenheim were strictly regular, Henry Wise's greatest achievement, but Vanbrugh's advice did not fail entirely to bear fruit: two of Wise's foremen, Charles Bridgeman and Stephen Switzer, played major roles in the later development of the English landscape garden.

Stephen Switzer's *The Nobleman, Gentleman and Gardener's Recreation* of 1715, enlarged as *Ichnographia Rustica* in 1718, his ideas of rural or extensive gardening and his description of Dyrham, have already been referred to.

Charles Bridgeman was a practitioner, not a writer, and emerged as natural successor to Henry Wise. He joined Wise at Blenheim in 1709, and became his partner in the royal gardens in 1726 and sole royal gardener after Wise's death in 1728.[10] His signed drawing of Blenheim in 1709 must be a depiction of someone else's ideas, presumably Vanbrugh or Wise, as Bridgeman was too young to have been entrusted with so important a task, but within a few years he had produced drawings for Eastbury (Dorset), Claremont (Surrey), Stowe (Buckinghamshire) and other new gardens, at all of which Vanbrugh was also consulted. The extent to which the designs were conceived by Bridgeman or merely penned by him

Claremont, anon., c. 1740.
Formal features set informally
in the landscape.

remains uncertain. It seems probable, however, that he arrived at Blenheim under Henry Wise's wing, possibly as surveyor/draughtsman, and, having found a like mind in Vanbrugh, developed an informal partnership in which the older man undertook architectural work while Bridgeman laid out the general lines of the garden.

Eastbury has the forceful lines of a military parade. It is comparable in this respect to Blenheim, and was probably attributable largely to Vanbrugh. Claremont is freer in its parts: the bowling green, amphitheatre and round pond reflect more the natural arrangement of hill and hollow than the preconceived lines of an overriding idea. At Stowe, the angle chosen for Bridgeman's bird's-eye view c. 1720[11] seems deliberately chosen to reduce the forcefulness of the central axis, and to dwell instead on the complex network of walks and vistas which laced the garden together, suggesting the increasing importance of the younger man.

Bridgeman was employed at Stowe from 1714, two years before Vanbrugh. Lord Percival, after a visit to Stowe in 1724, recorded that 'Bridgeman laid out the ground and plann'd the whole'. Vertue in 1735 noted that Bridgeman 'had the direction and disposition of the Gardens' while Vanbrugh was concerned with the buildings.

Over the garden wall

Lord Percival also added, in his comments from Stowe, that the garden 'is not bounded by walls, but by a ha-Hah, which leaves you the sight of the beautiful woody country and makes you ignorant how far the high planted walks extend'.[12]

This ha-ha, or sunken boundary wall, was Bridgeman's most notable and most lasting contribution to English gardens. It was not the first ha-ha. Beaumont had one at Levens in 1689 (see page 60); John James's translation of d'Argenville in 1712 implies that the ha-ha was an established feature. But Stowe was already becoming a garden of considerable note; the ha-ha was a key feature in its development and it underlined here the changing role of the garden in the early decades of the eighteenth century. At Blenheim the garden was walled: it stands out clearly in Bridgeman's plans from the park around it. At Eastbury the distinction is blurred: the specific garden near the house was larger in scale, simpler in detail and the garden and park are as one. At Stowe the parterres dissolved imperceptibly into the wider landscape of buildings, pools and tree-lined vistas. Gradually the garden had become not something to look at but something to look through, and because of the encompassing ha-ha at Stowe one could look still further to surrounding woods and fields.

Bridgeman's work extended through much of southern England: at Amesbury, Hampshire, for the Duke and Duchess of Queensberry; at Woburn, Bedfordshire, where he worked for the Duchess of Kent, granddaughter of Sarah, Duchess of Marlborough; at Boughton, Northamptonshire, for the 2nd Duke of Montagu, son-in-law of the Duchess of Marlborough and nicknamed John the Planter. Wimpole in Cambridgeshire was one of Bridgeman's largest schemes. When Edward Harley, second Earl of Oxford, married Henrietta Cavendish Holles he married into one of the richest families in the country and acquired the Wimpole estate. There he set about expanding his father's already extensive library and cultivated a household filled with artists, poets and cognoscenti. Bridgeman was a frequent visitor between 1720 and 1724, not only planting avenues and forests to add interest to the flat landscape but joining in the general life of the house and making much use of the library.

Other commissions were much smaller by comparison. At Purley in Berkshire the house was not enlarged, as shown in a view which hangs in a drawing-room, but the T-shaped canal terminated by a flint temple was made and is still recognizable.[13] At Rousham in

Allées and avenues at Cliveden adapting to the 'genius of the place', by James Andrews, 1762.

Oxfordshire, Bridgeman's formal woodland layout was sandwiched in a small triangle between the high ground on which the house stands and a bend of the River Cherwell. At Cliveden the recently discovered Bridgeman plan is for a small part of the garden as a whole, but the network of allées and round points characteristic of his designs translates effectively as a series of gentle ramps zigzagging down the steep slope by the Thames and framing views of the river, of statues, urns and the tiny amphitheatre.

On his royal appointment in 1728 Bridgeman began extensive alterations in the parks and gardens, especially at Kensington and Richmond, in the latter of which Horace Walpole later reported that he 'dared to introduce cultivated fields', cornfields for the benefit of game which formed a major attraction of Richmond.

The amateurs

In many instances Bridgeman worked with, rather than for, his patron, acting as adviser, consultant, approver, and usually leaving the building and planting to estate staff. It is not surprising, therefore, that many gardens were laid out, without the assistance of a professional, by the owner of an estate immersing himself in improvements and alterations in the new taste. By 1739 *Common Sense* declared that 'Every Man Now, be his fortune what it will, is to be *doing something at his Place*, as the fashionable Phrase is; and you hardly meet with any Body, who, after the first Compliments, does not inform you, that he is *in Mortar* and *moving of Earth*; the modest terms for Building and Gardening.'[14] Horace Walpole was less flattering. 'There is not a citizen who does not take more pains to torture his acre and a half into irregularities, than he formerly would have employed to make it as formal as his cravat.' There were many instances, however, in which a landowner of wide education and good taste produced results to match or outshine professional efforts.

At Shotover in Oxfordshire James Tyrell, who had fought under Marlborough at Blenheim, started a new house and garden in 1715 but barely finished the house before his death in 1718. His son developed the garden, with an obelisk and Gothic temple, representing respectively pure classical geometry and rude simplicity, at opposite ends of the axis through the centre of the cubic house. Each feature was reflected in a canal, while allées and round points dissected the woodland wilderness on either side.

St Paul's Walden Bury in Hertfordshire was laid out from 1725 by Edward Gilbert. Three hedged allées radiated from the house through a formal woodland. The central allée focused on a statue of Hercules 600 yards from the house. One lateral allée ended with a small rotunda while the other was directed at a church tower, not within the garden but beyond the ha-ha and across the fields.

When John Aislabie resigned as Chancellor in 1721 as a result of his implication in the South Sea Bubble, he retired to his Yorkshire estate of Studley Royal to create the now famed garden. The long terraced walk gave distant prospects of Ripon and closer views of the lake from various angles, while the whole scene was enlivened with canals, cascades, temples, a Gothic tower, a Chinese house, statues and thick woods to frame innumerable views.

The development of Wentworth Castle, also in Yorkshire, was due in part to less aesthetic motives.[15] Thomas Wentworth, who had fought under Marlborough, received none of the estate of his great-uncle, the Earl of Strafford, and it passed instead to a grandson, Thomas Watson. In an effort to match Watson, Wentworth acquired Stainborough Hall in 1708, changed its name to Wentworth Castle, managed to revive the title of Earl of Strafford in 1711 and even, in 1723, bought the neighbouring estate of Rockley anonymously from his detested relative. Soon the estate vied in splendour with the ancestral seat of Wentworth Woodhouse, only five miles away. In the formal woodlands were a sham Gothic castle, a menagerie, an obelisk to Queen Anne, a lodge disguised as a church and classical temples.

The most famous amateur of the day was undoubtedly Alexander Pope. His garden at Twickenham, begun in 1719, became an almost legendary place of pilgrimage. Although his garden was limited to a few acres of land separated from the Thames by a main road, Pope contrived a landscape full of variety and crammed with classical allusions.[16] In the main garden, a broad expanse of grass terminated by an obelisk was flanked by regular groves of trees which thickened into woodland in which were walks, pools, temples and statues. Uninhibited by the boundary, he made a grotto studded with minerals and passing under the road to emerge in another grassy plot overlooking the Thames. The garden, the buildings framed by unclipped trees and the inscriptions ancient and modern which embellished many of the features demonstrated forcefully the unity which Walpole later saw in painting, poetry and gardening, 'the three Sisters or three new Graces who dress and adorn Nature'.

Pope's advice to other garden makers in his voluminous writings can be distilled in two lines from the poem 'On Taste', published in 1731: 'In all let nature never be forgot./Consult the genius of the place in all.'

Kent: the painter

Pope's villa was the natural meeting place for the new artistic fraternity, a hotbed of new ideas to be disseminated by word and by example, the latter particularly by Bridgeman's friend and successor William Kent. If Bridgeman marked a break with tradition by separating design of gardens from the nursery business, Kent marked an even great departure: his training was not in gardening at all but in painting.

In 1710, at the age of twenty-four, Kent travelled to Italy to study painting. As a resident English artist in Rome he met many of the young noblemen on their tours, among them Lord Burlington in 1716 and Thomas Coke, later Earl of Leicester, between 1714 and 1718.

Kent returned to England in 1719 to become the leading figure in a group of artists gathered around Lord Burlington, the leading disciple and evangelist of the restrained Palladian order. Initially he practised as a painter, enriching the interior of many eighteenth-century houses with allegorical 'histories'. He also designed furniture, and eventually turned his hand to architecture. Holkham in Norfolk, built to house Thomas Coke's vast collection of Italian works of art, remains Kent's most distinguished building.

More important by far than his major buildings were the designs for innumerable smaller buildings, and his creation of landscapes of which these buildings formed an inseparable part.

Kent's wide experience and versatility made him the ideal person to weld together the many elements of the new English landscape garden. In 1734 Sir Thomas Robinson wrote to Lord Carlisle:

There is a new taste in gardening just arisen, which has been practised with so great success at the Prince's garden in Town [Frederick, Prince of Wales at Carlton House], that a general alteration of some of the most notable gardens in the Kingdom is begun, after Mr Kent's notion of gardening, viz. to lay them out, and work without either level or line ... The celebrated gardens of Claremont, Chiswick, and Stowe are now full of labourers, to modernise the expensive works finished in them, even since every one's memory.[17]

At Claremont, Bridgeman's circular basin was irregularized and terminated by a rustic grotto, in sharp contrast to the elegant temple which Kent designed for the island. At Chiswick, Kent 'serpentized' the great canal into a majestic winding river, broke the lawns with clumps of trees, loosened formality and engineered distant prospects to evoke sensations of grandeur, gaiety, tranquillity, sublimity and the newly discovered melancholy. Kent was so overcome by melancholy while sitting under the obelisk at Chiswick that he remained all night, transfixed until released by the morning sun.

At Stowe the Temple of Venus was the first building by Kent, adding to the Lake Pavilions, Rotunda, Pyramid and other features designed by Vanbrugh. It was sited at the southern extremity of the garden, on an outlying bastion of Bridgeman's ha-ha, but Kent soon began to concentrate his efforts on a small valley to the east of Bridgeman's main vista, creating an immortal landscape, the Elysian Fields. Here a Temple of Ancient Virtue (c. 1734) adjoined the Temple of Modern Virtue built as a ruin to indicate distaste for the government of the day. A robust and stolid Temple of British Worthies answered the classical perfection of Ancient Virtue across the mythical River Styx, an artificial stream emerging from the upper end of the valley beneath a mysterious grotto and tumbling through the Shell Bridge before winding around the lower temples

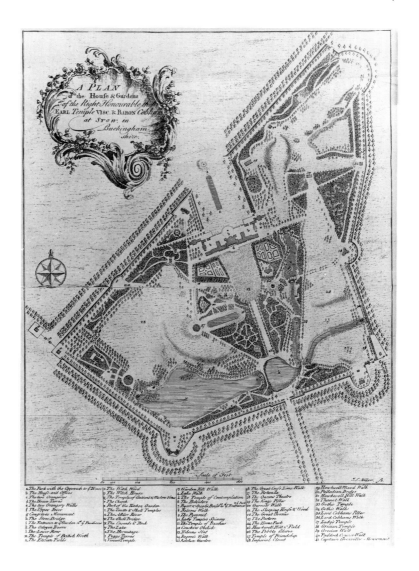

Kent's irregular landscape at Stowe within the geometry of Bridgeman's ha-ha.

to join the main lake. Groves of trees on the valley slopes gave diversity of colouring, light and shade answering to the chiaroscuro of a painter's canvas.

By 1742 the Octagon Lake, loosened from its stone edge to form a broad river, was terminated by a Palladian bridge, a copy, like the later one at Prior Park near Bath, of the Wilton original designed in 1737 by Lord Pembroke and Roger Morris. Over the bridge could be seen the battlements of 'Stowe Castle', a farmhouse decorated to create the required effect.

Rousham, in Oxfordshire, was not among the 'celebrated gardens' mentioned by Sir Thomas Robinson but here, too, Kent

Rousham, Venus's Vale by Kent.

overlaid Bridgeman's axial plan with a series of set pieces. A Gothic eyecatcher enlivened the distant scene beyond Scheemaker's statue of a lion attacking a horse. A path from the house paralleled the ha-ha and passed the statue of the Dying Gladiator to descend into the shaded Vale of Venus, with its three arched cascades descending the grassy slope to the river. Beneath the Gladiator lay the dark arcades of the Praeneste, a hallowed Roman memory, thinly concealed by trees from an amphitheatre ringed by statues. Beyond this sylvan scene and the contrasting openness of the smooth, grassy slope below the house and Scheemaker's statue was a more ancient relic still, the pyramidal Egyptian temple. To the other side of Venus's Vale a serpentine path meandered through the trees to reveal a stone bath-house and octagonal bath linked to the vale by a winding stream.

With the death of the owner, General Dormer, in 1741, improvements at Rousham came to an abrupt halt. The younger generation chose to spend their time in London. In 1750 their gardener, John Macclary, wrote plaintively to his employers, describing the many delights of the garden and pleading with them to come and enjoy it − or at least to send his wages![18] The letter, which describes in great detail the correct route for viewing the garden and the many features to be seen, did not have the required effect, but the garden has survived to the present day, changed only by the relentless growth and decay of its many large trees.

Kent's great contribution to the English garden was in the softening of outlines, the opening of distant prospects and the creation, with the help of many and varied buildings, of an idealized landscape in which the garden and park were indistinguishable. Walpole saw Kent as a genius,

... painter enough to taste the charms of landscape, bold and opinionative enough to dare and to dictate, and born with the genius to strike out a great system from the twilight of imperfect essays. He leaped the fence, and saw that all nature was a garden.

That Bridgeman had lowered the fence to make it easier for Kent's somewhat corpulent figure to manage was also recognized. Walpole saw the ha-ha as 'the capital stroke, the leading step to all that followed'.

The inspiration for the 'new taste' practised by Kent has long been attributed, with ample justification, to Italian painting and the Italian landscape. It is, though, a remarkable coincidence that he struck out on his new system just at the time that Lord Burlington acquired an album of engravings of Chinese gardens brought to Europe by Father Matheo Ripa. In Kent's meandering paths, winding rivers, scattered trees and borrowed scenery one can detect the first tentative experiments in Anglo-Chinese gardening, the studied irregularity or 'Sharawady' which Sir William Temple warned in 1685 would be 'too hard an achievement for any common hands'.

The ferme ornée

A further factor in the development of the landscape garden, in addition to classical and possibly oriental influences, was the economic improvement of the native English landscape. Addison's suggestion that 'a Man might make a pretty Landskip of his own Possessions' was eagerly seized upon, and Switzer's system of 'rural or extensive gardening' was used increasingly to highlight the beauties of the English scene. The most famous, and quite probably the first, example of the complete combination of farm and garden was that at Wooburn (or Woburn) on the outskirts of Weybridge.[19]

Philip Southcote, the creator of Wooburn, had lived for long periods in France and travelled in Italy. In 1732, at the age of thirty-five, he married the Dowager Duchess of Cleveland, a woman nearly twice his age. The marriage hardly promised romance and long happiness, but the couple moved into the duchess's house in St James's Square and in 1734 bought Wooburn Farm. Deprived of public office by his religion, Philip Southcote developed the

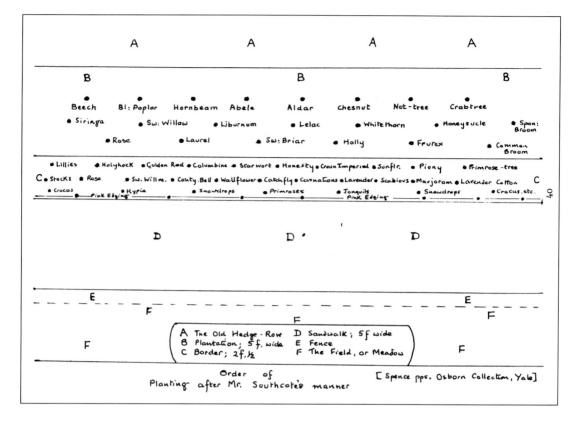

farm – a low-lying stretch with one low hill – into a private paradise.

The main element of the plan was the boundary walk, emanating near the house and winding through the farm to display it and its surroundings as a succession of varied scenes. The approach was purely pictorial. Light and shade were carefully balanced. Banks of the excavated river were carefully shaped, and the boundaries were concealed by flowers, shrubs and trees rising one above another. Great pains were taken to achieve the desired effect: 'I believe I walked the ground above a hundred different times before I could fix the whole line of the walk from the Temple to the Octagon,' he wrote to Spence.[20] The peripheral walk combined beauty and utility. It was shut out from the country '... by a thick and lofty hedgerow, which is enriched with woodbine, jessamine and every odoriferous plant ... the turf on either hand is diversified with little groups of shrubs, or firs, or of the smallest trees, and often with beds of flowers.' There were beech, alder and black poplar, laurel, holly, sweetbriar and broom, hollyhocks, golden rod, stocks, Canterbury bells, wallflowers and scabious, so that 'every gale was full

Philip Southcote's flower-fringed walk around the fields of his ferme ornée at Wooburn.

of fragrancy'. It was no coincidence that Southcote was related to Lord Petre, one of England's most distinguished cultivators of rare plants, whom he greatly admired.

The lawns were grazed by sheep, the lowing of cattle could be heard throughout the grounds, and even a small serpentine river was made for waterfowl. This combination of farm and garden Southcote called his *ferme ornée*.

There were many visitors to Wooburn. Some daubed the buildings with anti-Catholic slogans and Southcote was obliged to close the garden for a time, but most were ecstatic in their praise and many borrowed his ideas freely for the improvement of their own estates. The poet William Shenstone developed a *ferme ornée* at Leasowes, Halesowen, West Midlands, although he admitted that he would rather have had a less practical and more elaborate garden had finances permitted. His landscape, with its circuit walk and numerous cross-views, was much admired.

The partnership of farm and garden was a difficult one to weld satisfactorily. The *ferme ornée* scarcely outlived Southcote, but he had reintroduced flowers into the extensive garden – he claimed to have taught Kent 'to resume flowers in the natural way of gardening' – and had shown convincingly that a man might make 'a pretty landskip' of his *own* possessions. Walpole's later words fitted admirably:

In general it is probably true, that the possessor, if he has any taste, must be the best designer of his own improvements. He sees his situation in all seasons of the year, at all times of the day. He knows where beauty will not clash with convenience, and observes in his silent walks or accidental rides a thousand hints that must escape a person who in a few days sketches out a pretty picture, but has not had leisure to examine the details and relations of every part.[21]

A possessor of taste

It is not surprising, then, that the most famous and probably best-loved survivor from the eighteenth century was the work of a 'possessor' with taste, Henry Hoare.

Henry Hoare inherited Stourhead in Wiltshire in 1743, having spent nearly twenty years travelling in Italy. He carved a path from the classical garden, made by his father, down the slope of the adjacent valley and around the hillside. The Temple of Ceres (now Flora) was built in 1745, the grotto in 1748 and the Temple of

Hercules (the Pantheon) in 1754 with the help of Henry Flitcroft, an associate of William Kent. The dam was also completed *c.* 1754, allowing several natural springs to fill a lake in which the buildings were reflected. The two temples exactly answered each other across the water, while the deep gloom of the grotto contrasted deliciously with the classical splendour of Hercules' Temple. From the inner-most depths of the grotto one had a framed view of Stourton church, a view supplemented by the turf bridge (1762) and the Bristol Cross brought to Stourhead in 1765 to complete an essen-tially English scene. Many more perishable features were added and have long since disappeared, but the containment of the valley, the rich and varied greens of beech and pine and the stone buildings remain as a sublime landscape now in the care of the National Trust. The exotic trees and shrubs planted by Hoare's grandson Henry Colt Hoare and by his successors have added an extra dimension to the garden, and sometimes compete with the original idea, but for those who can appreciate the carefully calculated placement of temples, bridges and viewpoints, the subtly changing

Stourhead: English incidents in a classical landscape.

mood of open lawn and shady grove, the garden remains a magical place. As the National Trust's management plan for the garden gradually takes effect the original concept and later additions should be increasingly reconciled.[22]

Other gardens were also made by amateurs. At Studley Royal John Aislabie's son succeeded, where his father had failed, in acquiring from his neighbour the small valley in which lay the majestic ruins of Fountains Abbey, a fitting climax to the view from the long terrace. At Painshill, Surrey, Charles Hamilton made a broad lake filled by a cast-iron waterwheel, a grotto studded with minerals, temples Gothic and classical, and bridges all set within a savage 'Salvator Rosa' landscape of pines and firs.[23] At West Wycombe in Buckinghamshire Sir Francis Dashwood, a founder member of the Society of Dilettanti in 1732, created the strange hybrid of formal and landscape garden. From 1737 to 1752 lodges, temples, a cascade and other features were placed to terminate vistas. From 1755 the house itself was embellished with colonnades and porticos, the west portico modelled on the newly available measured drawings of the Temple of Bacchus at Telos. Suitably framed by trees, the various façades of the house became, in effect, a series of garden temples rather than one house.

Rather than attempt to improve the surroundings of his ancestral home at Stanton Harcourt in Oxfordshire, the 1st Earl Harcourt abandoned the old house in 1756 and sought out an eminence commanding a fine prospect over the Thames at Nuneham. Here, despite his wife's qualms that they were to live in a villa, not a seat, he built an elegant Palladian villa to command and decorate the landscape. The village of Nuneham Courtenay was removed to the turnpike, a mile away. The terrace curving round the hillside created Claudian views of the new temple and then recurved to reveal the distant spires of Oxford, a worthy substitute for Rome.

For improvers of lesser means, unable to afford architects or Grand Tours, pattern books and manuals of instruction were published and widely read. Castell's *Villas of the Ancients Illustrated* appeared in 1728, as did Batty Langley's *New Principles of Gardening*, filled with extravagant illustrations and helpful advice: 'There is nothing more shocking than a stiff and regular garden.' The Halfpenny brothers provided clear examples of cottages, Gothic summer houses, bridges and ruins, for those who neither could afford a purpose-built ruin such as Sanderson Miller provided at Wimpole, nor had the good fortune to acquire a genuine ruin as at Studley Royal.

Capability Brown

By the middle of the eighteenth century much new ground had been broken, and new ideas tested and established. Charles Bridgeman died in 1738, Kent in 1748, a year before Lord Cobham at Stowe. The time was ripe for a new professional to provide ready-made landscape gardens in much the same way as London and Wise had created the great formal gardens of the late seventeenth century. The man who filled this new role was the much praised, much maligned and much misunderstood Lancelot Brown.

Brown was born the fifth of six children in Kirkharle, Northumberland, in 1716, and on completing his schooling in 1732 began working for Sir William Loraine, the principal landowner of Kirkharle. Loraine, then seventy-three, had been improving his estate since his inheritance at the age of sixty, removing the old village, creating extensive lawns over the old parterre and planting more than half a million trees. Brown gained experience in land reclamation, husbandry, forestry, horticulture and building, and within a few years was entrusted with major landscape improvements. The work was completed in 1738 and Brown left for the south in the following year, staying with Lady Loraine's father, Richard Smith, until he moved to Kiddington Hall near Woodstock in 1740.

In February 1741 Brown was appointed head gardener at Stowe, and for ten years he carried out the improvements planned by Lord Cobham and William Kent. Kent was unreliable: important plans would arrive weeks or months late, and so with a competent, tactful, eager-to-learn head gardener on hand it is not difficult to imagine how Brown's importance increased. The Grecian Valley to the north of the Elysian Fields was reputedly planned by Cobham and Brown together, and shaped by Brown acting as head gardener and clerk of works.

In 1742 Brown received small payments from Cobham's nephew Richard Grenville of nearby Wotton for improvements to the newly enlarged park, and other small commissions continued throughout his employment at Stowe.

Lord Cobham died in 1749 and Brown, after tidying his affairs at Stowe, moved in 1751 to the riverside hamlet of Hammersmith, where several notable nurserymen and horticulturists were already established. Here he set up an architectural practice. Croome, on low-lying land between the Severn and the Avon, was an early commission on a recommendation by Sanderson Miller to Lord Coventry. Much reclamation work was necessary, but by 1752

Lord Coventry wrote to Miller, obviously very pleased, that 'Mr Brown has done very well by me and indeed I think he has studied both my Place and my Pocket, which are not always conjunctively the Object of Prospectors.'[24]

With no apparent effort on Brown's part commissions began to pour in, and he was obliged to apologize repeatedly when ill health (he was asthmatic) prevented him from coping promptly with the pressure of work. Petworth, Sussex, for Lord Egremont (related by marriage to Richard Grenville of Wotton), was one of his first and most celebrated works. At Moor Park in Hertfordshire, Admiral Lord Anson spent £5,000 shaving away a hill. At Lord Egremont's recommendation Lancelot Brown was consulted, and scooped away still more of the hill to open up views below it, using the spoil to raise hillocks to vary the skyline. Horace Walpole later chided Brown for 'making molehills out of mountains'.

At Burghley, Cambridgeshire, Brown was a regular visitor for almost thirty years, altering the house and reshaping the surrounding landscape for the 9th Earl of Exeter. In 1758 he was called in by the Marchioness de Grey at Wrest, Bedfordshire, on his way to Burghley, and there made a sinuous river winding around the formal canal garden which, at the insistence of Lady Grey, was kept almost intact.

While working at Burghley, Wrest and the nearby Cambridgeshire property of Madingley Hall, Lancelot Brown was also planning and supervising major alterations at Longleat and Bowood in Wiltshire. At Longleat the enormous formal garden made by George London was swept away, the central canal of the parterres was converted into a cascading river which widened below the house into a curving lake, and the stiff wilderness was loosened into the now majestic hanging woods crowning the hills.

There soon followed commissions at Ashridge, Hertfordshire, for the Duke of Bridgewater, Alnwick for the Duke of Northumberland, Chatsworth for the Duke of Devonshire, Harewood (Yorkshire), Castle Ashby (Northamptonshire) and, in 1762, Holkham (Norfolk), where he smoothed the rough edges of William Kent's landscape.

In 1764 came the twin culminations of Brown's career, the royal appointment to the gardens of Hampton Court, Richmond and St James and his commission at Blenheim for the 4th Duke of Marlborough. At Hampton Court he resisted George III's wish to alter the great formal layout, perhaps realizing that such a scheme was ideally suited to its flat, watery site, but at Blenheim, Henry Wise's parterres were swept away and grassed over, the avenues

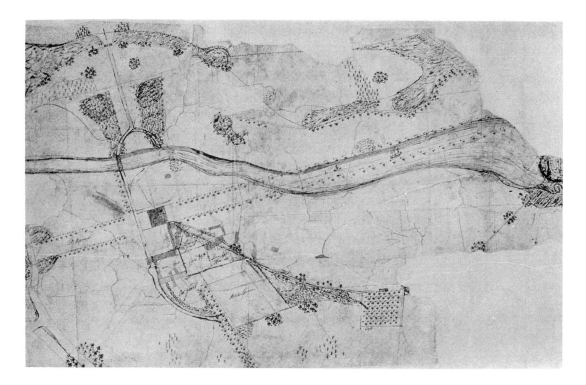

thinned and the trees regrouped to give a softer effect in the rolling landscape, and the cascade was made near the southern end of the park, damming the Glyme and flooding its steep-sided valley to create the two great lakes.

Brown continued on an ever-widening scale for nearly twenty years after his royal appointment, until his death at the age of sixty-six, in 1783. His method of working varied from place to place. Sometimes he started afresh, as at Croome and at Longleat. Frequently he followed where Bridgeman and Kent had led, thinning, regrouping and supplementing earlier tree planting. Sometimes he made a single visit, outlining a scheme which the owner and his estate staff could digest and implement at their leisure, as at Highclere in Hampshire for the Earl of Caernarvon. For other patrons he returned repeatedly, enlarging and revising both house and landscape, over ten, twenty or more years. François de la Rochefoucauld wrote that Brown conceived a design in an hour and that half a day more sufficed for marking it out, indicating not a skimped approach but a keen, experienced and inspired eye for the 'capabilities' of the place.

(Above) preliminary scheme for Packington, Warwickshire; (Right) the finished plan. Brown carefully incorporated the vista of the old avenue into his new landscape.

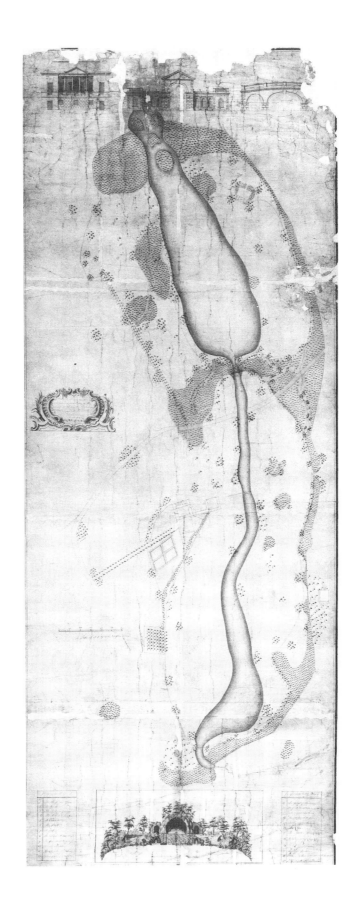

Brown's sketch for the cascade at Blenheim.

Dammed by the cascade, the narrow River Glyme spread into broad sheets of water embracing Vanbrugh's bridge.

THE ENGLISH LANDSCAPE GARDEN · 99

A literary man

The landscapes Brown created were entirely English in character, to be enjoyed in themselves rather than as reminders of a classical past. He had never experienced the Grand Tour, had not immersed himself in painting and classical literature and, although his approach has been described as literary, it was literary in the sense of rules of composition rather than in alluding to classical literature. 'Now there, said he [to Hannah More], pointing his finger, I make a comma, and there, pointing to another part [where an interruption is desirable to break the view?] a parenthesis – now a full stop, and then begin another subject.'[25]

Of course, his works have changed in the course of two centuries: surviving plans reveal a much more complex picture than the rolling parkland with its large trees normally thought of as typifying Brown's work. At Longleat he laid out a new flower garden a little way from the house, concealed by a gate. At Petworth there was a gravel path through a menagerie and a list of shrubs and flowers for the garden. Such ephemeral features have long since disappeared, but were probably characteristic of his work.

His influence was enormous. In thirty years he worked on over 200 commissions, many of them extending to thousands of acres. Much of what we now accept as the 'natural' landscape of lowland England is the work of Capability Brown and his followers.

He was not universally admired, however. Owen Cambridge declared that he hoped to die before Brown so that he could see heaven before it was 'improved'. To many, Brown symbolized oppression of the poor, displacing humble villagers from their homes in order to create his vast landscapes. To others he was the father of all 'landscape gardeners' and therefore responsible for all the evils of sham naturalism typical of less able designers. In 1892, Reginald Blomfield wrote that Brown 'began as a kitchen gardener, but took the judicious line that knowledge hampered originality. He accordingly dispensed with any training in design, and rapidly rose to eminence.'[26] Christopher Tunnard, in 1938, considered that 'because improvements were the fashion ... the literary and grammatical allusions with which [Brown] invariably illustrated his ideas no doubt helped to produce, in a gullible public, the sense of a competence which he was in fact far from possessing'.[27] And in the otherwise splendid exhibition of *The Garden* at the Victoria and Albert Museum in 1979, Brown was not included. A small plaque indicated that his work was 'an aberration lasting only half a century, depriving the English of the sort of complicated flowery gardens that they love. *Le jardin anglais* . . . refers to the time, when the English lost their heads and scrapped their gardens.'

Nothing can rival, though, the ferocity of the attack which Brown faced from the venomous pen of his contemporary, Sir William Chambers. More than once Chambers had submitted plans for improvements only to have lost the commission because of his patron's preference for Lancelot Brown's designs. In 1769 the first Lord Clive sought plans for his new house at Claremont from William Chambers and from Lancelot Brown, choosing Brown's plans to build. In 1770 Lord Milton obtained plans for his house and for a new village, Milton Abbas, from Chambers, but chose instead James Wyatt's designs for the house and Brown's for the village. Two years later Chambers published *A Dissertation on Oriental Gardening*, which was received with amazement.

The Chinese challenge

Despite a thin oriental disguise Chambers's *Dissertation* was transparently an attack on Lancelot Brown. The criticism of English gardens 'in which no appearance of art is tolerated . . . and which differ very little from common fields, so closely is nature copied' might have applied, if over-harshly, to a great many gardens made by amateurs and less able professionals, but his accusations that 'in this island [gardening] is abandoned to kitchen gardeners, well skilled in the culture of sallads, but little acquainted with the principles of Ornamental Gardening', and his assurance that in China gardeners were skilled in botany, painting and philosophy, not 'as in another famous country, where peasants emerge from the melon grounds to commence professors', were attacks directed specifically at Brown.

Chambers's thesis was that, while nature and its materials formed the basis for a garden, too close an adherence to nature was insipid, an idea which already had wide support. However, it was difficult to see, in his more reasonable descriptions of 'Chinese' gardens, any difference from their English counterparts. It is difficult to imagine, in the more outrageous descriptions, how one might usefully learn from them!

The Chinese introduced statues, carved inscriptions, memorials, 'every production of the chisel' to ornament and enrich the landscape with ideas and associations. The scenes within the gardens, arranged for different seasons and even for different times of day 'range in three separate classes ... the pleasing, the terrible, and the surprising'. Among the pleasing scenes were 'rare shrubs, flowers and trees from the torrid zone' covered with heated glass temples, verges of hyacinths, wallflowers and daffodils, menageries, dairies and pavilions for more voluptuous pastimes. In a terrible scene the trees were

... seemingly torn to pieces by the violence of tempests; the buildings are in ruins; or half consumed by fire, ... bats, owls, vultures and every bird of prey flutter in the groves; wolves, tigers and jackalls howl in the forests; half-famished animals wander upon the plains; gibbets, crosses, wheels and the whole apparatus of torture, are seen from the roads ... and to add both to the horror and sublimity of these scenes, they sometimes conceal in cavities, on the summits of the highest mountains, founderies, lime-kilns, and glassworks; which send forth large volumes of flame, and continued columns of thick smoke, that give to these mountains the appearance of volcanoes.

To surprise the visitor there were

... preparations that yield a constant flame; from time to time he is surprised with repeated shocks of electrical impulse, with showers of artificial rain, or sudden violent gusts of wind, and instantaneous explosions of fire; the earth trembles under him ... and his ears are successively struck with many different sounds ... some resembling the cries of men in torment; others the roaring of bulls, and howl of ferocious animals ... the mixed croaking of ravenous birds ... and all the noise of war.

Most English gardeners would surely have fled to dull green fields with their boundary walks.

Many of Chambers's ideas would have fallen upon sympathetic ears, but his criticism of Brown could only result in ridicule:

... the ax has often, in one day, laid waste the growth of several ages; and thousands of venerable plants, whole woods of them, have been swept away, to make room for a little grass, and a few American weeds. Our virtuosi have scarcely left an acre of shade, nor three trees growing in a line, from the Land's-end to the Tweed ... and if their humour for devastation continues to rage much longer, there will not be a forest tree left standing in the whole kingdom.

Brown's supporters rallied even more loyally. Encouraged by Horace Walpole, William Mason countered the *Dissertation* in 1774 with *An Heroic Epistle to Sir William Chambers*.

... at our magic call,
Monkies shall climb our trees, and lizards crawl;
Huge dogs of Tibet bark in yonder grove,
Here parrots prate, there cats make cruel love;
In some fair island we will turn to grass
(With the Queen's leave) her elephant and ass.
Giants from Africa shall guard the glades,
Where hiss our snakes, where sport our Tartar Maids ...

For forty years Lancelot or 'Capability' Brown was pre-eminent in his profession. Hearing of his death in 1783, Walpole wrote to the Countess of Upper Ossory, 'Your dryads must go into black gloves madam, their father-in-law, Lady Nature's second husband, is dead.' More soberly, he said in Brown's memory: 'Such was the effect of his genius that when he was the happiest man he will be least remembered, so closely did he copy nature that his works will be mistaken.'

Poetic justice

This same thought was expressed in verse by William Whitehead, describing a supposed confrontation between Lancelot Brown and Dame Nature at Nuneham, where the house had been built on a grassy knoll above the Thames by the 1st Lord Harcourt in 1756 to take advantage of a naturally beautiful situation. The 2nd Lord Harcourt inherited in 1777 and immediately called in Lancelot Brown to reshape the newly enlarged park, already heavily wooded.

Whitehead's description of the confrontation between an outraged Dame Nature and the upstart Brown is amusing but also illustrates very perceptively the way in which Brown worked and the effects which he hoped to create.

Dame Nature, the Goddess, one very bright day
In strolling thro' Nuneham, met Brown in her way;
And bless me, she said, with an insolent sneer,
I wonder that fellow will dare to come here.
What more than *I* did has your impudence plann'd!
The lawn, wood, and water, are all of my hand;
In my very best manner, with Themis's scales,
I lifted the hills, and I scoop'd out the vales;
With Sylvan's own umbrage I grac'd ev'ry brow,

And pour'd the rich Thames thro' the meadows below.
I grant it, he cry'd; to your Sov'reign command
I bow, as I ought – Gentle Lady, your hand:
The weather's inviting, so let us move on;
You know what you did, and now see what I've done.
I with gratitude own you have reason to plead
That to these happy scenes you were bounteous indeed:
My lovely materials were many and great!
(For sometimes, you know, I'm obliged to create)
But say in return, my adorable dame,
To all you see here can you lay a just claim?
Were there no slighter Parts, which you finish'd in haste,
Or left, like a friend, to give scope to my taste.
Who drew o'er the surface, did you, or did I
The smooth flowing outline, that steals from the eye,
The soft undulations, both distant and near,
That heave from the lawns, and yet scarcely appear?
(So bends the ripe harvest the breezes beneath,
As if earth was in slumber and gently took breath)
Who thinn'd, and who group'd, and who scattered those trees,
Who bade the slopes fall with that delicate ease,
Who cast them in shade, and who plac'd them in light,
Who bade them divide, and who bade them unite?
The ridges are melted, the boundaries gone:
Observe all these changes, and candidly own
I have cloth'd you when naked, and, when o'erdrest
I have stripp'd you again to your boddice and vest;
Conceal'd ev'ry blemish, each beauty display'd,
As Reynolds would picture some exquisite maid,
Each spirited feature would happily place,
And shed o'er the whole inexpressible grace.

One question remains, Up the green of yon steep
Who threw the bold walk with that elegant sweep?
– There is little to see, till the summit we gain –
Nay, never draw back, you may climb without pain,
And I hope, will perceive how each object is caught,
And is lost, in exactly the point where it ought.
That ground of your moulding is certainly fine,
But the swell of that knoll, and those openings, are mine.
The prospect, wherever beheld, must be good,
But has ten times its charm when you burst from this wood,
A wood of my planting. The Goddess cried, Hold!

'Tis grown very hot, and 'tis grown very cold.
She fann'd, and she shudder'd, she cough'd and she sneez'd,
Inclin'd to be angry, inclin'd to be pleased;
Half smil'd, and half pouted – then turn'd from the view,
And dropp'd him a curtsie, and blushing withdrew.

Yet soon recollecting her thoughts, as she pass'd,
'I may have my revenge on this fellow at last;
For a lucky conjecture comes into my head,
That, whate'er he has done, and whate'er he has said,
The world's little malice will balk his design:
Each fault they'll call his, and each excellence mine.'

In the last third of the eighteenth century the English landscape garden entered a new phase. In the 1730s and '40s William Kent had 'struck out a system from a twilight of imperfect essays', the first phase of adventurous innovation and sometimes outrageous mistakes. In the 1750s and '60s Lancelot Brown had perfected his own interpretation of the landscape garden, mature and thoroughly reliable, the second phase of professional expertise. From 1770 there appeared a series of essays describing and analysing the landscape garden and prescribing methods whereby the amateur could try his hand at this 'new' style.

Thomas Whately's *Observations on Modern Gardening*, published in 1770, included many references to Brown's work. Horace Walpole's *History of the Modern Taste in Gardening* followed in 1771. It was written while Walpole was working on his villa at Strawberry Hill but, to avoid hurting people criticized in the text, it was not published until 1780.

Walpole praised Kent as 'born with a genius to strike out a great system', but the praise was not unbounded. 'Kent's ideas were rarely great . . . Kent's landscapes were seldom majestic. His clumps were puny.' Walpole disapproved of hermitages in particular: '. . . the ornament whose merit soonest fades, is the hermitage or scene adapted to contemplation. It is almost comic to set aside a quarter of one's garden to be melancholy in.' Of Lancelot Brown he would say only that 'it was fortunate for the country and Mr Kent, that he was succeeded by a very able master; and did living artists come within my plan, I should be glad to do justice to Mr Brown; but he may be a gainer, by being reserved for some abler pen'.

In 1772, the year of Chambers's outburst, William Mason wrote a long poem on *The English Garden*, to be followed in 1774 as a result of the *Dissertation* by his highly amusing *Heroic Epistle*.

All these essays showed an obvious admiration for Brown's work and a sympathetic understanding of his large-scale compositions, but the authors were themselves more involved in the smaller scale and were interested in more eventful scenes. Although they were clearly shocked by Chambers's bitter attack, they shared many of his less extreme ideas. At the beginning of the century young improvers were excited by Prospect. Fifty years later their grand-sons were alive to the new idea of the Picturesque. The publication of Gilpin's *Tours* from 1787, and in 1795 of both Richard Payne Knight's *The Landscape* and Uvedale Price's *The Picturesque*, could have sparked a return to the more complicated and more intimate landscape of William Kent had it not been for the rapidly increasing importance of a fundamentally new influence in gardens, a veritable tidal wave of new plants.

6

Eighteenth-century Plant Introduction

The eighteenth century is often characterized, quite reasonably, as the age of the English landscape garden. However, if this over-simple view is extended to imply 'a time when the English lost their heads and scrapped their gardens', nothing could be further from the truth.

Capability Brown landscapes might have been simple in their materials (although much less simple than surviving remnants would suggest), but no more so than the great formal gardens of London and Wise in the seventeenth century. What is often for-gotten is that Brown's landscapes, like their precursors, incor-porated extensive, usually walled, kitchen gardens in which unusual plants could be collected and cosseted for their intrinsic interest. Furthermore, owners of the great estates laid out by Brompton Park or by Brown also had town houses in and around London with small gardens – sometimes only two or three acres – in which the cultivation of plants was made easier and more interesting by the proximity of professional nurserymen and of like-minded friends.

Plants and Prospect

The improvement of estates, which formed the basis of the English landscape garden, required a combination of practical skills and philosophical inquiry. The creation of a landscape garden was an experimental investigation into the underlying order of the natural world and the aesthetic principles founded on that order. What could be more logical, therefore, than to allow the experimentation to overflow into the collecting and detailed study of the component parts of that natural world, whether fossils, minerals, animals, insects or plants? In the eighteenth century the landscape garden and the botanic garden advanced side by side.

In 1731, when Kent was working at Holkham, Philip Miller produced the first edition of his monumental *Gardeners Dictionary* from the Chelsea Physic Garden. In 1743, while Henry Hoare was shaping Stourhead and Lancelot Brown was finding his feet at Stowe, James Lee and Lewis Kennedy founded one of England's greatest nurseries at the Vineyard, Hammersmith.[1] In 1759, when Lancelot Brown was engaged at Burghley, Moor Park and Longleat, a botanic garden was established at Kew. In 1795, the year in which Richard Payne Knight produced his long poem *The Landscape*, his younger brother Thomas Andrew Knight met Sir Joseph Banks and was inspired to publish his research on fruit trees.[2]

Not only did the two aspects of gardening proceed side by side: they were often combined into a single passion, not least by the dowager Princess Augusta, her son George III and their adviser Lord Bute. Lord Bute was a distinguished amateur botanist, collecting and introducing rare local plants from the downland around his seaside house at Highcliffe, near Christchurch, Hampshire. Lancelot Brown was consulted for the general development of Highcliffe and also at Bute's principal seat of Luton Hoo in Bedfordshire. Frederick, Prince of Wales, leased Kew House in 1730 and engaged William Kent to remodel the grounds. After Frederick's death in 1751 Lord Bute became adviser to his widow, Princess Augusta, bringing in William Aiton from Chelsea to supervise botanical aspects of the garden, and William Chambers, in 1757, to add several more ornamental buildings, including the orangery and pagoda which still adorn the garden.

When George III succeeded to the throne in 1760 he actively encouraged his mother's interest in the garden. In 1761 one of the largest stove-houses then known was built at Kew; in 1762 a major collection of trees was added, and within the nine-acre walled garden a botanic garden proper was established. On Augusta's death in 1772 George III purchased the lease of Kew House and combined it with the royal property of Richmond Park. In the following year Lancelot Brown supervised the formation of the hollow which is now the rhododendron dell, the excavation itself being carried out by the Staffordshire militia. Thus Brown added to the garden which encompassed his arch-enemy Chambers's entire efforts at garden-making.

Kew was typical of the parallel interest in landscape and in plants which continued throughout the eighteenth century. The interest

in plants was aided in no small measure by the rapid expansion of trade and the building of the Empire. The settlement of Virginia in 1607 and Plymouth in 1620 began a long process of English colonization of the eastern seaboard of North America, and by 1700 the French, Dutch and British had all established island colonies in the Caribbean Sea. These sugar-producing possessions in the West Indies were immensely prized in Europe and were serviced regularly by ships plying to and fro across the Atlantic. As shipping increased, so did the opportunity of bringing new seeds and plants into Europe.

Three of Chambers's exotic buildings at Kew: the Alhambra, the Pagoda and the Mosque.

An Atlantic alliance

One of the most fruitful transatlantic associations was between Peter Collinson in London and John Bartram.[3] Collinson, one of the key figures of eighteenth-century gardening, was the son of a draper with trading interests in America. In 1730 he was introduced to a fellow Quaker, John Bartram of Philadelphia. Bartram had started a botanic garden in 1728 (a garden which still survives), and Collinson supported him by finding subscribers for his plants and seeds at the rate of £5 per box, twenty boxes to be sent each year. By 1740 Bartram was firmly established, corresponding regularly with Philip Miller, Hans Sloane, J.J. Dillenius and other leading botanists, sending consignments of plants to Collinson and making long collecting expeditions. He introduced about 2,000 species in all, including lilies, phlox, rhododendrons and magnolias.

Trade routes to the Far East were established even earlier. The English East India Company was formed in 1600 and its more vigorous Dutch counterpart in 1602. By 1619 the latter was the biggest trading company in Europe. In 1652 the Dutch settled the Cape and developed a virtual trading monopoly in the Spice Islands of the Malay Archipelago. In Japan only the port of Nagasaki was open to the West, and even this was restricted to a Dutch monopoly from 1639.

English trade was directed primarily to India, with stations at Bombay, Tellicherry and Madras supplying cotton and pepper, but by 1685 there was a modest trade in tea and porcelain from Canton.

Throughout the Orient trading posts were small specks on the edge of vast land masses, but glimpses of its exotic dress, buildings, customs and art fired Europeans with excitement: *chinoiserie*, the European notion of Chinese design, affected all aspects of Western culture. Plants, too, were exquisite, often highly developed by centuries of cultivation, but were tantalizingly unavailable to the West. Nevertheless, the Dutch East India Company's physicians, confined to the small island of Deshima in Nagasaki harbour, contrived to send a number of plants back to Europe. Andreas Cleyer (1682), Engelbert Kaempfer (1690) and especially Carl Peter Thunberg (1775–6) prepared the way for the nineteenth-century physician/collector Philipp Franz von Siebold.

The physic garden

The great increase in worldwide travel throughout the eighteenth century fostered the establishment of plant collections, private and institutional.

The Oxford Physic Garden, founded in 1621, was not ready to receive plants before 1640, but in the care of the Bobarts, father and son, it then acted as a significant collecting and distributing centre for new plants. Edinburgh Botanic Garden was founded in 1670, but it was not until 1763 that the activities of several small gardens were combined and moved to a much larger site.

The most important garden by far was that of the Society of

Apothecaries on a site in Chelsea, leased in 1673. In 1676 the new physic garden was walled to protect it from thieves and from the winds which swept across the open fields around the village of Chelsea. Sir Hans Sloane, who purchased the Manor of Chelsea in 1712, granted inheritance of the garden to the Apothecaries on condition that it be maintained as a physic garden and, at Sloane's suggestion, Philip Miller was appointed as head gardener. Miller continued in this capacity until 1770 when he was seventy-nine. He died the following year.

Miller's energy was boundless. His correspondence with collectors and fellow botanists throughout the world was vast. In 1724 he published the two-volume *Gardeners and Florists Dictionary, or A Complete System of Horticulture*. In 1728 he presented a paper to the Royal Society on the raising of difficult exotic seeds, and subsequently gave papers on the raising of coconuts and the cultivation of sugar, coffee and cocoa. In 1731 his monumental *Gardeners Dictionary* was published, listing more than 1,000 plants grown at Chelsea and dealing with all aspects of cultivation. The dictionary appeared in eight editions before his death in 1771 and eight more to 1830.

Between the appearance of the first and the eighth editions of the *Gardeners Dictionary* the number of plants cultivated at Chelsea increased from 1,000 to 5,000 as Miller received plants from America, the West Indies, the Cape, Siberia and nearer home in Europe.

In Europe Miller was known as the 'prince of gardening'. In England he might appropriately have been termed the 'father of horticulture': the garden at Chelsea served as a nursery in more ways than one, for his pupils included William Aiton, William Forsyth and Joseph Banks.

William Aiton worked as Miller's assistant from 1754 to 1759 and was then appointed curator of the Princess Augusta's new botanic garden at Kew. Three years later the Cambridge Botanic Garden was established, with advice from Miller and with his son Charles as its first curator. Forsyth replaced Philip Miller at Chelsea in 1770 when, increasingly cantankerous in old age, Miller was dismissed.

Exiguus spatio, variis sed fertilis herbis.

Horticultural riches and clipped green galleries in Philip Miller's Gardeners Dictionary.

Sir Joseph Banks

Joseph Banks was undoubtedly Miller's most distinguished pupil. Elected to the Royal Society at the age of twenty-three, he later replaced Lord Bute as unofficial director of the botanic garden at Kew.

In 1768 Banks spent £10,000 on Captain Cook's voyage in the *Endeavour* in order to indulge his own passion for natural history.[4] The main objective of the voyage was to observe a total eclipse in the South Seas. The government provided an astronomer and an assistant. Banks took two artists, two scientists, a secretary, two white servants and two black.

Three years later, having mapped New Zealand and encountered the conjectural southern continent, the *Endeavour* returned to England. Only three of Banks's nine assistants survived.

Plants, animals and drawings were exhibited in Banks's Soho house: there were 3,000 plants, of which a third were new to science. Most of the plants were, of course, dried herbarium sheets, but some seeds survived the journey. New Zealand spinach was introduced, and the *Sophora microphylla* now in the Chelsea Physic Garden is a direct descendant of Banks's introduction.

Flushed with success, Banks planned a second, more elaborate, voyage. The ship was turned into a floating laboratory, despite Cook's protests. It was so top-heavy that it barely made the journey from Woolwich to the river mouth at Sheerness. Banks went back to London. The ship was refitted and Francis Masson was sent from Kew by William Aiton as the King's Botanist, settling on Banks's advice in Cape Town.

In 1775 Masson returned to Kew to assist with the care of his Cape introductions, but by 1778 he was tired of England. He travelled to Madeira, the Canary Isles, the Azores and the West Indies, to North Africa and the Cape and finally to North America, where he died in Montreal, aged sixty-five, in a freezing winter.[5] His introductions to England were numerous – after one journey in the Cape he sent over 400 new plants back to Kew – and they had a great impact in English gardens. Pelargoniums, heaths, gladioli, cinerarias and other brilliant flowers still play a part in conservatories and greenhouses. The plants which survived the sea voyages would not survive an English winter, but the means for ensuring their survival were becoming increasingly widespread in the eighteenth century.

The glasshouse

The seventeenth-century 'orangeries' and 'greenhouses' were generally makeshift structures, portable sheds erected around tender plants and heated by open fires in the winter, then dismantled in the spring. In 1619 Salomon de Caus suggested building a per-

manent shelter with a roof and low stone walls so that only
windows needed to be added for winter protection. By the mid
seventeenth century most major English gardens had such permanent features. It was not until the very end of the century,
however, that roofs were glazed. The Jardin Royal in Paris had the
first known glass-roofed structure, *c.* 1693, and the first in England
was reputedly the greenhouse at Wollaton Hall in Nottinghamshire, *c.* 1696.[6]

*Early greenhouses in Thomas
Fairchild's* City Gardener.

The heating of greenhouses was achieved by open fires or pans of charcoal, later by enclosed stoves of Dutch design standing within the house, or by subterranean furnaces with flues passing up through the back wall of the greenhouse.

In 1731 when Miller first published his *Gardeners Dictionary* he described in considerable detail the types of greenhouses available and, although favouring flues if they were well managed, he particularly recommended the stovehouse with pits of tanners' bark to provide a constant and less drying heat. By this means he managed to preserve in good condition 'the most tender exotic trees and herbaceous plants, which before the use of bark it was thought impossible to be kept in England'.

Patrons . . .

During the eighteenth century the passion for collecting and cultivating exciting new plants spread to an ever wider spectrum of garden owners. Wealthy landowners and merchants often had their own contacts abroad, but commercial nurseries rapidly multiplied to provide for those who did not. The proprietors were often distinguished botanists, as well known for the advancement of botanical science as for their dissemination of plants, and many of them sent out their own collectors as well as exchanging new introductions with their patrons.

Among private collectors, Robert James, 8th Earl Petre, was outstanding. He began planting his estate at Thorndon Hall, Essex, when he was fifteen, moving two dozen sixty-foot high elms from Ingatestone to extend an avenue. He was among the recipients of plants sent, via Collinson, by John Bartram and, in addition to his renowned collection of hardy trees, claimed to have 'the greatest part of stove plants, whether succulents or others, as are yet known in England'.[7] In the last three years of his short life James planted 40,000 trees, and when he died in 1743, aged thirty, 200,000 plants were sold from Thorndon, many of them going to Goodwood and Woburn for the Dukes of Richmond and Bedford.

Dr Robert Uvedale (1642–1722), a master of Enfield Grammar School, devoted so much attention to his collection of exotics that he was threatened with dismissal from his post. Among his collection, reputedly the largest in England at that time, were the first plants of *Lathyrus odoratus*, progenitor of the modern sweet pea, raised from seed sent to him in 1699 by a Sicilian monk, and one of the earliest cedars of Lebanon.

Sir Hans Sloane (1660–1753), the owner of Chelsea and Philip Miller's patron, had more than a purely medical interest in plants long before his connection with Chelsea. In 1684, when he was twenty-four, he wrote to his friend Charles Hatton at Kirby: '... there is a vast number of East and West India seeds come over this year'.

Dr James Sherard (1666–1737) had his own botanic garden at Eltham, where James Gordon worked before moving to Lord Petre's estate at Thorndon Hall. His older brother William (1659–1728) was consul at Smyrna from 1703 to 1715 and sent many seeds and plants from Greece and Asia Minor to Eltham. Dr John Fothergill's botanic garden at Upton House, East Ham, started on his retirement in 1772, had one of the largest greenhouses in the country, 260 feet long, attached directly to his house. Fothergill amassed a collection of 3,400 species of tender plants in his stoves and 3,000 species of hardier exotics in his garden.

... and nurserymen

From its establishment in 1681, the Brompton Park nursery of London and Wise was pre-eminent, but there were five commercial gardens in London by 1690 and another ten by the end of the century, with a few in the rest of England.[8]

Thomas Fairchild at Hoxton in east London was quite typical of the new breed of nurserymen, dealing predominantly with ornamental plants rather than selling fruit trees as an extension of an orchard or market garden business. Fairchild, a friend of Mark Catesby, one of the earliest plant collectors to visit America, distributed many North American trees, most notably the tulip tree, *Liriodendron tulipifera*. He is also noted as the first person to produce a deliberate hybrid, crossing a carnation and a sweet william to produce 'Fairchild's Mule Pink'.

Robert Furber established a nursery in Kensington Gore, and Christopher Gray another in Fulham. Both nurseries benefited substantially by buying many of Henry Compton's exotics when, on Compton's death in 1713, his successor ordered the plants to be disposed of to make room for more useful vegetables.

On the death of Lord Petre in 1743, his gardener James Gordon left Thorndon Hall to start a nursery at Mile End. He established an unparalleled reputation for raising North American plants from seed, and distributed kalmias, rhododendrons, azaleas and other plants to fellow nurserymen as well as to private buyers. *Ginkgo biloba* was brought to Mile End from the Continent *c.* 1754, and was the sole source of layers for English gardens for many years.

Soon after Gordon's departure from Thorndon Hall, an even more important nursery was established on the site of a former vineyard (now the site of Olympia) by Lewis Kennedy and James Lee. In 1760 Lee published *An Introduction to Botany*, in which he used Linnaeus's new binomial system of naming plants. It went through ten editions and brought widespread acclaim for the nursery. In 1774 there followed a seventy-six-page catalogue, with plants listed by their English and Latin names for ease of reference and accuracy in identification. Also from the Vineyard came a handful of sturdy young gardeners, all Scots, whom Lee sent along to Joseph Banks to be dispatched to all parts of the world. The most distinguished of these, and the most dogged by misfortune, was David Nelson.[9]

Nelson joined Cook's fateful third voyage, in 1776, in search of a north passage to the Atlantic. Cook was hacked to pieces in the Hawaiian islands, but Nelson returned to England after four hazardous years with many new plants from the north-west seaboard of America. After seven years at Kew he began an even more remarkable voyage, again at the instigation of Sir Joseph Banks, to bring breadfruit plants from Tahiti to the West Indies as a cheap source of food for slaves. The journey, with Captain Bligh on the *Bounty*, began well and Nelson secured his plants but, after eighteen months at sea, he was sent overboard by the mutinous crew. Ironically he survived a 3,500-mile journey in an open boat to the Dutch settlement at Campang only to die there of fever.

As the eighteenth century advanced, the network of plant collectors, distributors and cultivators, both amateur and professional, extended and ramified. The expansion of overseas trade and administration which created the opportunity for plant introduction also fostered a rapid expansion of a middle class of people, often immensely wealthy and eager to establish their position in society by acquiring substantial estates. The growth of wealth and of the middle class was even more dramatic at home: with the building of canals from 1760, Hargreaves's spinning jenny in 1769 and Watt's steam engine in 1775, the industrial revolution rapidly gained momentum.

Improvement of great country estates, enrichment of town gardens and the philosophy, science, craft and art of gardening were all inextricably interwoven in a furore of interest which swept the country.

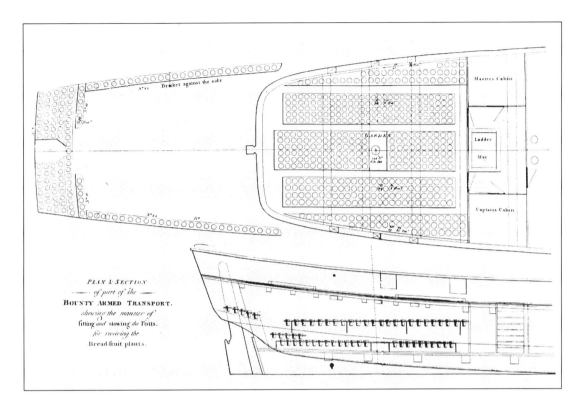

PLAN & SECTION
of part of the
BOUNTY ARMED TRANSPORT.
shewing the manner of
fitting and stowing the Pots,
for receiving the
Bread-fruit plants.

The Bounty, *transformed from naval vessel to floating garden until mutiny struck.*

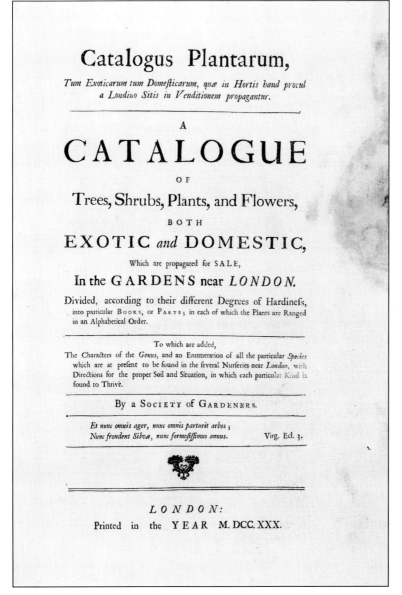

Catalogus Plantarum,

Tum Exoticarum tum Domesticarum, quæ in Hortis haud procul a Londino Sitis in Venditionem propagantur.

A

CATALOGUE

OF

Trees, Shrubs, Plants, and Flowers,

BOTH

EXOTIC *and* DOMESTIC,

Which are propagated for SALE,

In the GARDENS near *LONDON*.

Divided, according to their different Degrees of Hardiness, into particular BOOKS, or PARTS; in each of which the Plants are Ranged in an Alphabetical Order.

To which are added,

The Characters of the *Genus*, and an Enumeration of all the particular *Species* which are at present to be found in the several Nurseries near *London*, with Directions for the proper Soil and Situation, in which each particular Kind is found to Thrive.

By a SOCIETY of GARDENERS.

Et nunc omnis ager, nunc omnis parturit arbos ;
Nunc frondent Silvæ, nunc formosissimus annus.   Virg. Ecl. 3.

LONDON:
Printed in the YEAR M. DCC. XXX.

The Catalogus Plantarum *issued by London nurserymen in 1730, probably compiled by Philip Miller.*

The fifteen London nurseries of 1700 had increased to about twenty-five by 1730, with at least as many springing up in the provincial cities. By 1760 there were about 100 substantial nurseries in the country, and by 1800 the number had doubled.[10] With a network of canals to provide cheap transport, and priced catalogues and newspaper advertisements to publicize the availability of plants, regional nurseries such as William Lucombe of Exeter, William

Falla of Gateshead and Robert Dickson of Hassendeanburn grew to rival those of London.

To a very large degree, the improvement of estates and the enriching of gardens in the eighteenth century proceeded as geographically distinct but intellectually related activities. Plant cultivation was mainly a London-based activity, facilitated by ease of communication with the other major nurseries and with fellow enthusiasts, whereas estate improvement was a rural and extensive activity.

In the nineteenth century this clear dichotomy was shattered and confused. The three forces which combined to create this confusion were the opening of the Orient, the development of the industrial revolution and, not least, the arguments between garden theorists, arguments which began with verbal attacks on Lancelot Brown and have continued to be waged for the succeeding 200 years.

7

Into the Nineteenth Century

The terms 'nineteenth-century garden' and 'Victorian garden' are often considered synonymous, but the length and extraordinary eventfulness of Victoria's reign, from 1837 to 1901, renders the word 'Victorian' a very clumsy adjective. It is more meaningful, in terms of garden history, to divide the nineteenth century into three broad phases, the subjects of the next three chapters.

The assembly of garden ingredients, associated especially with the ageing Humphry Repton and with John Loudon, was already largely complete by the time of Victoria's birth in 1819 rather than of her coronation. The blending of these ingredients to produce the highly decorated 'cake' of the High Victorian garden then took place in the first half of Victoria's reign, while the reaction against the exuberant excesses of such gardens surfaced at the time of Albert's death in 1861 rather than at the end of his beloved queen's reign.

The long reign of George III (1760–1820), nearly matching that of his granddaughter, saw immense changes in Britain and a great expansion of its influence abroad, changes reflected faithfully in its gardens and gardening.

East and West

With Nelson's victory at Trafalgar in 1805, Britain's navy was supreme, and Wellington's defeat of Napoleon at Waterloo in 1815 put an end to French expansionism. Britain controlled the sea routes to the Far East and India was effectively under British rule.

Rosa chinensis, delicate but truly perpetual in flower.

China proved much more difficult, remaining virtually a closed country with trade limited to the ports of Macao and Canton until 1842. Lord Macartney's Embassy in 1792–3, attempting to establish diplomatic links, did increase slowly the number of plants sent directly from China to England, and the few plants introduced in the early years of the nineteenth century had a tremendous impact on English gardens. In 1803, Sir Joseph Banks sent William Kerr from Kew to Canton. The double *Kerria japonica*, named after him, and *Rosa banksiae*, named after his sponsor, were but two of many good plants introduced before Kerr left Canton for Ceylon.

Sir Abraham and Lady Amelia Hume were perhaps the most successful amateurs. Sir Abraham had several relatives in the East India Company, not least a cousin in charge of the English factory at Canton. Through these connections *Magnolia denudata* came to their Worsley Bury garden in Hertfordshire in 1801, a form of *Paeonia suffruticosa* in 1802, *Camellia japonica* 'Lady Hume's Blush' in 1806, seven different chrysanthemums from 1798 to 1808, and 'Hume's Blush Tea-Scented China Rose' in 1809.[1]

In the Western hemisphere, too, British influence expanded. By 1763 Britain controlled North America east of the Mississippi and held most of the Caribbean with its rich sugar plantations. Over-extension of British interests led in 1776 to the American War of Independence, but the new nation which emerged in 1783 was English-speaking; new trade links were rapidly established and, as settlement of the country extended to its Pacific coast, many new plants were introduced to Britain from a region in which the climate was not much different from our own.

Archibald Menzies brought the immensely rich north-western flora to the attention of English botanists in 1795, but it was the spectacularly successful explorations by David Douglas from 1824 that brought living material to English gardens in quantity.

An urban society

The effects of this overseas expansion were, of course, manifold. It not only created great wealth for merchants involved in tea, silk, spice and other imports, but also opened up new markets for English manufactured goods. The replacement of home workshops by factories, the opening of canals and the expansion of British shipping spurred industrial production and stimulated a population boom. The population, which increased from 6 to 10 million between 1750 and 1800, doubled in the following half-century.

People needed houses. In 1800 the Duke of Bedford dismantled his London town house and developed the Bloomsbury estate. It was but one of many lucrative developments in the West End of London and was echoed in all the important centres of population. In country estates too there were coal, iron ore, limestone, building materials to be quarried and mined, providing handsome profits to revitalize traditional estates and to produce a new class of immensely rich industrialists.

Much of this new wealth was expended on improving or acquiring estates, on new houses and new gardens. As in earlier periods of growth, the style of the new houses and gardens reflected the mood of the age, and in the late eighteenth/early nineteenth centuries this was a mood of fundamental change in the order of society and of man's relationship to his surroundings.

Greeks and Goths

The mid eighteenth-century landscapes of Lancelot Brown reflected
the supposed perfection of a classical order, a pervading sense of
good taste measured against infallible rules of right and wrong.
Long before Brown's death, however, this sense of order and
infallibility was being disturbed. Descriptions of the ancient Greek
settlement at Paestum threw doubt on the 'correctness' of Palladian
architecture. James 'Athenian' Stuart's garden temple at Hagley,
Herefordshire, built in 1758, heralded the Greek revival in England and, by the time Stuart and Nicholas Revett had published
their *Antiquities of Athens* in 1762, 1789 and 1795, it was clear that
there was not one 'correct' classical style but many.

The Greek revival was paralleled by a growing admiration for
Gothic architecture. Early Gothic buildings, the temple at Shotover
for example, were intended to shock: to contrast with noble classical
buildings. Later, Gothic assumed a lighter, more frivolous character,
suitable for umbrellas, garden seats and airy temples with the
occasional more awesome ruin. Examples abound in the pattern
books and drawings of Batty Langley[2], Thomas Wright[3] and
Thomas Robins.[4]

As it gained in respectability, Gothic became suitable even for
substantial houses. James Wyatt, the most distinguished Gothic
architect of the eighteenth century, worked with equal ease with
classical and Gothic, merely interchanging colonnades with cloisters
and balustrades with finials. In 1775 he rebuilt Sheffield Park,
Sussex, acquired in 1769 by J. B. Holroyd, Earl of Sheffield, and the
centrepiece of Lancelot Brown's landscape erupted into pointed
arches and pinnacles.

Wyatt's most spectacular building was Fonthill Abbey in Wiltshire, built initially as a garden ornament for the recluse William
Beckford but enlarged from 1796 to 1807 as the principal feature
in the landscape and as a major house.[5] In 1807 the central tower
collapsed, and in 1822 the estate was sold, but not before Beckford
had created a masterpiece of brooding, melancholic landscape
extending for six square miles around the fantastic building.

One of Wyatt's last buildings was at Ashridge, Hertfordshire,
for the Earl and Countess of Bridgewater. Started in 1808, alterations and additions were continued after Wyatt's death in 1813 by
his nephew Jeffrey Wyatville. It dominated a garden which was to
have far-reaching influence in the nineteenth century.

The fine, severe buildings of the Greek Revival and the eventful
silhouettes of Gothic architecture might seem poles apart, but there

was a strong, significant link between them. The striking remains of Greek buildings were appreciated not only as fine architecture but also as romantic ruins. They were portrayed in irregular outline, with plants springing from the bases of columns and creepers veiling fallen masonry, as signs of a great civilization succumbing to the even greater forces of nature; and to the potent romantic stimulus which these illustrations provided was added a new and equally potent word, 'Picturesque'.

Wyatt's Sheffield Park, its pinnacles echoed by nineteenth-century conifers.

The Picturesque

William Gilpin, a master at Cheam School, had been to many parts of the country during his summer holidays observing and analysing the scenery. Horace Walpole and William Mason persuaded him to publish his notebooks, and in 1782 the first of them appeared, *Observations on the River Wye, and several parts of South Wales &c: relative chiefly to picturesque beauty; made in the summer of the year*

A sketch in Gilpin's Observations. *Human figures were welcomed as a vertical accent among picturesquely grouped sheep.*

1770. Similar *Observations* followed on Cumberland and Westmorland, on the Highlands of Scotland and on the New Forest. Gilpin's own interpretation of the Picturesque was quite straightforward. 'By Picturesque I mean precisely nothing more than such ideas as could be formed into a picture.'[6] The effects of light were of paramount importance in making pictures, so it is not surprising that Gilpin favoured rugged scenery, the irregular outlines of ruins and of sparsely branched oaks and shaggy-coated animals, rough textures which catch the light. People in the landscape were also appreciated, in part because they helped to distinguish roads from rivers.

Gilpin's books were immensely popular. He brought the more rugged parts of Britain a new respectability, as cherished scenes to be sketched rather than as unproductive wastes to be abhorred. In his own mind the 'idea as could be formed into a picture' might just as equally be a passage from the classics as a piece of natural scenery, but his avid followers applied the idea almost entirely to the seeking of scenery which might be judged by the same aesthetic principles as would be used for a painting.

Gilpin did not follow his argument to the conclusion that one might make a landscape to look like a picture, but it was not long before the word 'Picturesque' was applied to man-made as well as to natural landscapes, and eventually to buildings.

Horace Walpole's villa at Strawberry Hill, begun in 1747, was probably the first instance of studied asymmetry in the plan of a building. With the addition of the great round tower in 1761 and the Beauclerc tower in 1776, Strawberry Hill became the masterpiece of deliberate asymmetry. In 1794 Richard Payne

Knight began Downton Castle in Herefordshire, a rambling, picturesque building calculated to ornament the Downton estate. In 1798 John Nash built his own house, East Cowes Castle, on the Isle of Wight, deliberately exploiting irregularities of plan and silhouette, and went on to design dozens of castles, houses and cottages in a similar vein throughout England. The enthusiasm for Gothic, for picturesque castles and for melancholy ruins increased as the eighteenth century drew to a close.

There were other styles too. William Kent had built Egyptian temples and pyramids. When George Anson (later Admiral Lord Anson) returned in 1744 from a four-year voyage around the world, he brought back with him a substantial fortune which he spent enlarging his house at Shugborough, Staffordshire, and decorating its gardens with numerous monuments including a Chinese house and pagoda from sketches made in China by an officer on his ship.

In 1752 the French Jesuit priest Jean Denis Attiret's *A particular account of the Emperor of China's gardens near Pekin* was translated into English. Chambers's *Design of Chinese Buildings* (1757) was followed by his pagoda, mosque, house of Confucius and other exotic buildings at Kew, but China was too little known, too distant both culturally and geographically, too heavily mysterious to be taken seriously as a model. Chinese buildings in England were usually lighthearted confections for garden ornament, scarcely distinguishable in their most diluted forms from their Gothic counterparts. Chambers's outrageous *Dissertation* in 1772 did nothing to further the use of Chinese buildings or gardening in England.

A totally different reception met the first works on Indian architecture. Thomas and William Daniell's *Select Views of India* (1788) appeared when correctness of taste and absolute standards had given way before a new generation of romantic idealists. *Select Views* was followed in 1808 by *Picturesque Voyage to India*, a publication as important in the nineteenth century as the Athenian drawings had been in the eighteenth: it caused an unprecedented stir by portraying buildings and landscape together in a way which was both accurate and picturesque.

Romantics abroad

The climate of romanticism which so ecstatically received news of India marked a radical change in outlook. The Romantic move-

The palace at Rhotas, Bihar, by Thomas and William Daniell, c. 1790.

ment is often seen simply as a reaction against eighteenth-century autocracy, as a triumph of sentiment over reason, nature over artifice and simplicity over pompous display, but it contained, too, a deeper current of distaste, even fear, of the future. The shattering of the inevitability and order of eighteenth-century society by the meteoric rise of a wave of self-made men would be welcomed by the Romantics; that the new order, with its populace rigidly ordered by the factory clock and subservient to noisy and filthy machinery, might be worse than the old was deeply disturbing.

Rebelling against the immediate past and the foreseeable future, the romantics suspected man-made order: nonconformity was admired; the medieval sagas of romantic literature fostered a closer study of medieval culture and an admiration, even envy, of the simple moral integrity of the medieval craftsman who could believe without question in the Creation. As man and his doings were despised, so nature and its wonders were increasingly revered. The majesty of a mountain or a storm made man seem puny. The beauty and purposefulness of a flower or an unfolding fern frond made man's art ineffectual. The romantic could abandon himself to nature and escape the unpleasantness of social turmoil. Rousseau's rhetorical question, 'If the Author of nature is great in His great works how much greater is He in His smallest works?' led a generation of young men and women to seek escape from the man-made world in a study of the beauty, intricacy and extraordinary ingenuity of the natural world.

Underlying these aesthetic ideas was a growing social sensitivity. The eighteenth-century Establishment was not only oppressive in art, it also symbolized oppression of the poor.

When Oliver Goldsmith walked through the Home Counties on his arrival in England in 1756 he saw a countryside thickly studded with parks and gardens. In 1760 he estimated that there were 400 parks in the Chilterns alone, often touching adjacent parks: the land was parcelled out among the rich, not merely squeezing out the poor but forcibly displacing them in order to 'improve' the scene. At Normanton, Sir Gilbert Heathcote rebuilt the church as a garden pavilion. At Audley End, Bowood, Harewood, Chatsworth, Shugborough, Warwick and a string of other famous parks, villages were destroyed or removed to new sites along the main road and at a convenient distance from the house. Usually the inhabitants moved on without complaints: the landlord was too strong to be opposed. At Nuneham an old lady's pleading to be left in peace for the few remaining years of her life was successful: the incident was commemorated with a plaque after her death as a romantic garden feature.[7] At Milton Abbas, where villagers protested and dug in their heels, Lord Milton ordered the dam holding Brown's half-filled lake to be released, washing away the opposition.

The publication of Goldsmith's *The Deserted Village* in 1770 was directed specifically against the changes at Nuneham but applied more widely. In 1775 Nathaniel Kent's *Hints to gentlemen of landed property* suggested that cottagers might be regarded as a superior rather than an inferior race, leading as they did a simple, primitive existence free of vice. Kent implied that gentlemen of landed property would gain by gathering their peasants around them in good, plain, honest cottages. One might even add a building or two in which to act out the simple life of a peasant as a release from one's own worldly cares. The model farm and especially the dairy (from which came Mother Nature's own unadulterated food) became necessities of a blameless life.

At Nuneham the second Earl Harcourt encouraged back the villagers displaced by his father and dressed the children in shepherds' costumes to add a note of rustic authenticity. Even before his succession, young Harcourt begged an acre from his father to make a flower garden. The garden, designed by William Mason, had paths winding 'like the steps of an indolent man' and was inspired by Rousseau. Climbers festooned the trees and arched

Mason's flower garden at Nuneham, with the Temple of Flora, Orangery and busts disposed around the meandering circuit walk.

over rustic bowers 'weaving a garland of repose', while urns and weeping trees created a pleasing melancholy which deepened in the gloom of the grotto. Violets, periwinkle and other simple plants peeped with unaffected simplicity from every bank.

Changes in architecture, the proliferation of Gothic and exotic buildings and avid interest in the Maker's smaller works – plants from all parts of the globe – had far-reaching effects on garden design. While a Palladian or even a Greek building might rest nobly on a smooth stretch of grass, a picturesque, Gothic pile looked oddly out of place in such a setting. More enrichment of its surroundings was required, and the new plants provided the enrichment necessary. Chambers had already attacked Brown's bald hills and sun-parched lawns but, in 1794, the criticism was resumed with a new ferocity by two West Country landowners, Uvedale Price of Foxley and Richard Payne Knight of Downton.

Price's *Essay on the Picturesque* applied Gilpin's concept to man-made landscapes. He sought a rougher, more rugged and more interesting landscape than those created by Brown, a landscape in which jagged rocks, tumbling waters and windswept trees in irregular masses would replace the smooth lawns, limpid lakes and rounded clumps.

Knight's essay *The Landscape – A Didactic Poem* appeared in the same year and expounded very similar ideas, preferring even the old formal gardens to Brown's landscapes:

> Though the old system against Nature stood,
> At least in this, 'twas negatively good: –
> Inclosed by walls, and terraces, and mounds,
> Its mischiefs were confined to narrow bounds;
>   .   .   .
> ... Kings of yew, and goddesses of lead,
> Could never far their baneful influence spread;
>   .   .   .
> Curse on the shrubbery's insipid scenes
> Of tawdry fringe encircling vapid greens;
> Where incongruities so well unite,
> That nothing can by accident be right;
>   .   .   .
> ... Prim gravel walks, through which we winding go,
> in endless serpentines that nothing show.
>   O! waft me hence, to some neglected vale;
> Where, sheltered, I may court the Western gale;
> and 'midst the gloom which native thickets shed,
> Hide from the noon tide beams my aching head.[8]

The landscape gardener

In the absence of Lancelot Brown himself (for he had died in 1783), Knight and Price addressed themselves vehemently – and quite mistakenly – to Brown's successor, Humphry Repton; mistakenly because, although it is commonly implied that Repton took up the traces where Brown let them fall, the two were, in fact, very different in their approach to 'landscape gardening' (a term which Repton himself devised).

Repton was born in Norwich in 1752. His parents anticipated a career as a cloth merchant, and to this end Humphry was sent to Holland at the age of twelve to learn the language and the ways of the country. Befriended by Zachary Hope, an international banker and art connoisseur, he developed a taste for, and considerable skill in, painting, poetry, music and the art of polite conversation.

Repton was unsuited to a business career; on the death of his parents in 1778 he bought Old Hall, Sustead, Norfolk, with his inheritance, and there settled happily as a country gentleman, painting, botanizing, planning and overseeing improvements on his estate and in the parish. He wrote to Robert Chamberlayne: 'The wet, hazy meadows which were deemed incorrigible have been drained and transformed into flowery meads.'[9]

Perhaps because the returns on such investments were too small to support a growing family, Repton decided to become a professional landscape gardener. In 1786 he moved to Hare Street, near Romford in Essex, and spent three preparatory years reading all he could of garden design and rural improvement.

Repton's library included Thomas Whately's *Observations on Modern Gardening* (1770), William Mason's *The English Garden* (1771–9), Gilpin's *Observations on the River Wye* (1782) and Girardin's *De la Composition des Paysages*.

In 1788 Repton proceeded to write to his many friends informing them of his intentions. They promised support and gave it. Within two years he was working at thirty houses, including Holkham and Sheffield Park. In 1791 he worked for William Pitt the Younger, who introduced him to Reginald Pole Carew, member of Parliament for Lostwithiel, extending Repton's practice to the South-West and beginning a long association between Repton and Pole Carew over the development of Antony House in Cornwall.

The practice in landscape sketching proved of inestimable benefit. His proposals were illustrated in watercolours with flaps showing the original scene overlaying them. 'Before' and 'after' paintings were interleaved with neatly handwritten reports on the problems, potentials and suggestions for the estate, to make handsome books bound in red leather. These 'red books' were not only working documents and handsome mementoes but excellent advertisements when displayed in the libraries in which they took an honoured place.[10]

By 1816 there were over 400 red books and four more substantial volumes gathering together into a more coherent philosophy of landscape gardening the principles developed during Repton's numerous commissions.

Beauty and utility

Repton saw the skill in his art as the combining of beauty and convenience. Where the two could not coexist, the convenient but unsightly feature must be included but carefully concealed. He saw no point in banishing the kitchen garden or laundry yard to a remote corner of an estate when it could be conveniently at hand behind a dense, attractive shrubbery. His two major contributions to landscape gardening were this insistence on convenience and his tempering of the gloomier aspects of the Picturesque by his fundamentally sunny, cheerful disposition.

For convenience and beauty he reintroduced the terrace, balustraded and often embellished with elegant ironwork to make a covered verandah, as a natural meeting of house and landscape; he reintroduced gravelled forecourts and gravel paths to ensure dry feet when alighting from carriages or inspecting the pleasure grounds, to echo the architectural lines of building groups or to emphasize the undulations of the landform; he introduced the flower garden conveniently near the house but carefully screened from the park where its bright colours and obvious artifice would intrude.

The writings on picturesque landscape which Repton studied before embarking on his career usually portrayed their subject as rough, rugged, foreboding, melancholy and hostile. Repton appreciated and admired picturesque landscape but he had no wish to enforce its gloomier aspects on his patrons. Instead he chose the

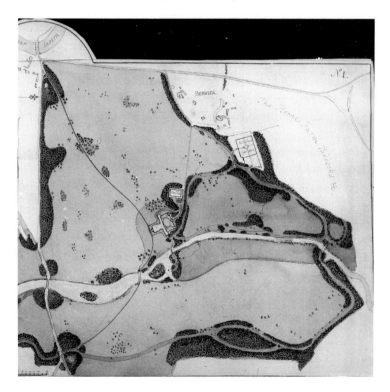

Repton's plan for Attingham; elegant curves and a formal terrace.

*Sheringham, Repton's
'favourite and darling child'.*

cheery shepherd's cottage, the cosy hamlet with smoke rising from tall chimneys, the winding gravel walk, the concealed and colourful flower garden and groups of cattle, sheep or deer to add interest to his landscapes in a more comfortable way.

When Repton began his career many Lancelot Brown landscapes were between thirty and forty years old and in need of revision, not only to bring them 'up to date' but also simply to thin and regroup trees which had grown to obscure views or to crowd each other too closely. Much of Repton's early work involved making, or commonly remaking, extensive landscape gardens.

At Attingham, Shropshire, he reshaped the river and regrouped the trees to draw attention to the ancient bridge. As always, the 'improved' view had an odd number of cattle forming a picturesque group in the foreground. At Endsleigh, Devon, he again thinned and regrouped trees to frame views of the river, added a long flowery terrace walk overlooking the views and designed a charming children's cottage with a circular flower garden. For Abbot Upcher at Sheringham, Repton negotiated the purchase of the estate, designed the house (with his son John) and set it in an elegantly simple park. It was Repton's 'favourite and darling child in Norfolk'.[11]

His career, however, extended over thirty eventful years and, not surprisingly, the emphasis with which he expressed his ideas shifted gradually through those years. The change can be seen clearly by reference to his four major works on landscape gardening, published in 1795, 1803, 1806 and 1816.

A great future change

Repton's *Sketches and Hints on Landscape Gardening* was published in 1795. He had intended to publish the book in 1792 but was delayed by pressure of work, fortunately, as it transpired, as he was able to reply to the criticisms levelled against him by Knight and Price.

In *Sketches and Hints* Repton described the setting of Knight's Downton Castle with admiration:

A narrow, wild, and natural path sometimes creeps under the beetling rock, close by the margin of a mountain stream ... in various places [there are] bridges of the most romantic and contrasted forms; ... caves and cells, hovels and covered seats or other buildings in perfect harmony with the wild but pleasing horrors of the scene. Yet, if the same picturesque objects were introduced in the gardens of a villa near the capital or in the more tame yet interesting pleasure grounds which I am frequently called upon to decorate they would be as absurd, incongruous and out of character as a Chinese temple, from Vauxhall transplanted into the Vale of Downton.[12]

For the enrichment of his 'tame but interesting pleasure grounds' Repton chose especially the flower garden. He knew Lord Harcourt's concealed flower garden well: his sketch of it appeared in Peacock's *Repository* of 1800. In *Observations on the Theory and Practice of Landscape Gardening*, published in 1803, he said:

A flower garden should be an object detached and distinct from the general scenery of the place ... rare plants of every description should be encouraged, and a provision made of soil and aspect for every different class ... bog-earth ... for the American plants ... aquatic plants ... on the surface or near the edges of water ... rock-plants should have beds of rugged stones ... without the affectation of such stones being the natural production of the soil; but, above all, there should be poles or hoops for those kinds of creeping plants which spontaneously form themselves into graceful festoons, when encouraged and supported by art.[13]

When James Wyatt remodelled or rebuilt and the houses erupted into spiky finials, towers, crenellations and pointed arches, they looked oddly out of place in expansive shaven grass: a more picturesque treatment of the grounds was necessary. With the furore of interest in Indian architecture created by the Daniells' illustrations of India, it was time for a more radical change.

In 1806 Repton published his *Inquiry into the Changes of Taste in Landscape Gardening*, in which he concluded:

After tracing the various past changes of taste in gardening and architecture I cannot suppress my opinion that we are on the eve of some great future change in both those arts, in consequence of our having lately become acquainted with scenery and buildings in the interior provinces of India.[14]

Exotic buildings demanded an exotic setting.

At Sezincote, Gloucestershire, Repton put his ideas into practice. In 1795 Colonel Cockerell returned from India and bought the Sezincote estate. Ten years later it passed to Charles Cockerell, also an Indian nabob, who appointed his brother Samuel Pepys Cockerell as architect. Repton was consulted for the landscape. His contribution at Sezincote is difficult to assess, but he would almost certainly have advised on the most suitable of Thomas Daniell's sketches of India for Cockerell to use as the basis for his designs and positioned the resulting features in the landscape. The site planning is superb. The main approach crosses a small valley by a massive Indian bridge decorated with Brahmin bulls. At the head of the

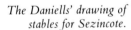

The Daniells' drawing of stables for Sezincote.

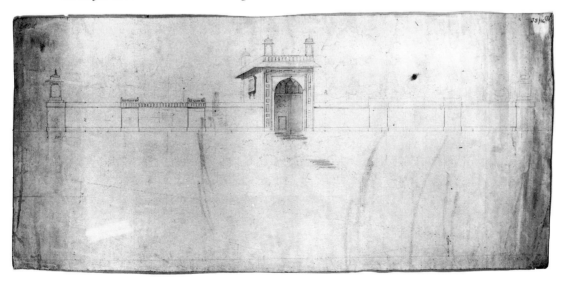

valley are caves for monks, a Hindu temple and a watercourse flowing down under the bridge, around writhing serpents and over rocks. Beyond the valley, the curving hillside gradually reveals the house with long-topped windows beneath a huge copper dome. Attached to the house is a curving, cast-iron conservatory, half enclosing a second U-shaped valley.[15] A second ridge hides the Indian stables, and the whole sits above a typically English scene of lake, woods and trees.

Repton's Thornery at Sezincote, below an Indian bridge guarded by Brahmin bulls.

The Prince Regent saw Sezincote while staying at Ragley and was delighted. Repton was summoned to Brighton, where William Hordern had already built the sensational Indian stables. The red book for Brighton had, as its frontispiece, Flora with the motto 'Gardens are works of art, not nature'. The pavilion was adorned with flowers and shrubs but within the narrow confines of the site 'to accomplish the great object of a perpetual garden, it will be necessary to provide for a regular succession of plants; and the means of removing and transplanting'.[16] The flower garden, the *changeable* flower garden, had arrived.

A dispute at Brighton brought to an end the short-lived partnership between Repton and John Nash, but not before their

'Gardens are works of art, not
of nature', from Designs for
the Pavilion at Brighton.

A perpetual garden in the
flower-filled gallery at
Brighton.

collaboration in the West End of London, where many town houses were being demolished and replaced by terraces of elegant houses around leafy squares, a humane, profitable and far-reaching development.

Equally humane, in a very different setting, was the planning of Blaise Hamlet on the outskirts of Bristol. Humphry Repton was called in by John Harford in 1795 to advise on the planning of his newly acquired estate. Under Repton's guidance the impressive 'castle' atop the hill was framed in hanging woods, to be seen intermittently as the carriage drive wound through a rocky ravine under the hill and across the open ground to Blaise Castle House. By 1806 Nash was involved: a picturesque thatched dairy nestled in a small hollow near the house and a conservatory added to the mansion itself was nearing completion. In 1810 Nash and George Repton (who stayed with Nash after his brother John left acrimoniously) began Blaise Hamlet, nine cottages grouped apparently artlessly and casually but with studied picturesque effect around a green.

The flower garden

In 1811 Repton's carriage overturned when he was escorting his daughter home from a ball. He sustained spinal injuries which resulted in progressive disability and increasing confinement to a wheelchair.

Fragments on the Theory and Practice of Landscape Gardening, published in 1816, was delayed, like *Sketches and Hints,* by the pressure of business but also by Repton's growing infirmity. Poignantly he noted:

Having so long dedicated the active part of my professional career to increasing the enjoyment of rural scenery for others, my own infirmities have lately taught me how the solace of garden scenery and garden delights may be extended a little further, when the power of walking fails ... These remarks are equally applicable to the fruit garden, the flower garden, or the pleasure ground: they should all be accessible to a garden-chair on wheels, and all should be provided with ample grass walks, to avoid the offensive noise of gravel.[17]

He suggested cordons and arches of trained fruit within reach from a wheelchair, and illustrated a raised bed of strawberries being watered by a gardener and sampled by an invalid.

Repton's garden for the disabled, with strawberries and other fruits accessible from a wheelchair.

Repton's increasing involvement with smaller gardens and his skill at combining utility with beauty are very evident in *Fragments*. Criticizing estates where the kitchen garden might be two miles from the house, requiring that 'the choice fruits are removed with as much care and trouble in the package and conveyance, as if they came from Brentford to Covent Garden market',[18] he suggested smaller, concealed gardens nearer the house. A method

... which I have successfully adopted in several villas near London, has been to surround with a border of shrubs and flowers, three or four acres of different dimensions, from an eighth to three-quarters of an acre of garden ground; to raise crops of fruit and vegetables, perfectly hid from the lawn and walks by the surrounding screen of flowering shrubs and evergreens ... By this means, the lawn of the pleasure ground may be varied in its shapes, and the quantity of mowing curtailed: and if we choose to view the interior of the masses which serve to diversify the landscape, we find new objects to amuse the eye or gratify the taste, at the time those fruits are ripe, which are most delicious when gathered by our own hands.[19]

This concept of using concealed gardens as islands to enclose and diversify the lawn was used not only in small London gardens but in one of Repton's last and most significant commissions, at Ashridge. Because of his increasing infirmity, Repton largely ignored the 3,500-acre estate bequeathed by Brown and concentrated his efforts on a mere fifteen acres near the house. To emphasize the site's long history he chose an area between the house itself, the remains of an ancient moat and old lime and elm avenues in which to create a series of separate and concealed gardens. The Holy Well and Monks' Garden commemorated the pre-Dissolution monastery. The Rosarie represented modern elegance, while the fernery, grotto and flint-studded tunnel (suggested by Repton but not constructed until 1850) provided a contrasting rugged mystery. The tunnel led from the melancholy shade of the grotto, with its dark pool, through an artificial hill to emerge into a cheerful flower-filled valley.

As in many of his commissions it is difficult to determine the extent of Repton's influence at Ashridge. He recorded events there from memory in 1816, and many additions were made later by the Countess of Bridgewater, but the surviving garden shows his ingenuity in creating enclosed flower gardens within a larger landscape.

Repton died in 1818, praised by Loudon as 'a man not less eminent for his artistical genius and taste than for his goodness of heart, and amiability of character'.

The science of gardening

While Repton led the nation in artistry and taste, the science of gardening was also making rapid advances. The great wealth of plants introduced during the eighteenth century became more and more widely disseminated as nurseries established, expanded and flourished. The need to preserve unfamiliar plants in cultivation led inevitably to a closer investigation of the plants' requirements: the mainstream of botanical effort shifted imperceptibly from medicine to taxonomy (how plants are classified) in the eighteenth century and to physiology (how a plant functions) in the nineteenth.

Increasing familiarity with glasshouses and their management led to multiplication and specialization: pineries (for pineapples), vineries, peach houses, melon pits, orangeries, conservatories, greenhouses and aquaria became essential adjuncts of the kitchen garden and pleasure ground. Steam heating was developed by Wakefield of Liverpool in 1788 and rapidly improved. In 1818 it was recognized that heated water would circulate, although the reason remained uncertain, and by the mid nineteenth century

circulation of hot water in large-bore pipes from a boiler outside
the glasshouse was almost universally used for heating.

Plant-breeding was a natural extension of physiological investigation. The first deliberate hybrid, Fairchild's Mule Pink, was
made by the nurseryman in 1717. Philip Miller noted in 1731 that
'farina' (pollen) of one tulip placed upon the stigma of another
resulted in fertile seed, but systematic plant breeding was another
century in gestation: eighteenth-century plant-breeding consisted
almost entirely in the selection of chance variations in plants raised
from seed or in perpetuating naturally occurring mutations.

Nevertheless new varieties appeared. *Pelargonium zonale* was
introduced from the Cape in 1710 and had crossed with *P. inquinans*
by 1714 to produce the forerunners of our zonal pelargonium or
'geranium'. By the mid eighteenth century it was a popular garden
flower. *Lobelia erinus* came from the Cape *c.* 1752. The chrysanthemum, an ancient flower in China, was introduced to Kew via
France in 1793 and several varieties were known by 1796. The
dahlia came from Central America to France in 1798 and was
rapidly developed.

The queen of flowers, the rose, also took a tremendous leap
forward as a result of new introductions from China, following
the establishment of Macartney's embassy. Among the first were
'Slater's Crimson China' (1792), 'Parson's Pink China' (1793) and
'Hume's Blush Tea-Scented China' (1809). Rather later came
'Parks's Yellow Tea-Scented China' (1824), the first yellow rose.
These roses brought new colour in the clear, lasting reds and pinks
('Parks's Yellow' was a pale creamy yellow), a new form in the
few-petalled high-pointed buds, a new sharper fragrance and, most
important of all, a recessive character for truly perpetual flowering.
It was half a century before these characteristics were combined
with the vigour of the older European gallicas, damasks and albas
to produce hybrid perpetuals (*c.* 1850) and the hardier hybrid tea
roses (*c.* 1870), but the noisettes, Bourbons, tea roses and other
intermediates were immensely popular.[20]

The temptation to acquire and cultivate the myriads of newly
introduced and newly created plants stretched the resources of
many noblemen and gentlemen but none more spectacularly than
the Marquis of Blandford at White Knights near Reading.

Blandford acquired White Knights in 1798.[21] With an extravagance verging on madness he proceeded to fill the house with
treasures and the garden with rare plants. White Knights soon had
few rivals in the kingdom for the quantity, rarity and variety of its
contents: an American border, a French garden, pavilions, grottoes,

Swan fountain in the Marquis of Blandford's White Knights by Hofland.

urns and fountains, an extensive wilderness full of the rarest and choicest plants. In 1804 Blandford owed Kennedy and Lee £15,000. For the magnolia wall, 145 feet long and 24 feet high, the nursery supplied twenty-two *Magnolia grandiflora* at five guineas each, an outlay which would have paid a top quality gardener for a year.

In 1816 Blandford borrowed £50,000 to stave off disaster. In 1817, when he succeeded to the Dukedom of Marlborough, he owed over £600,000. In 1819 the contents of the house and grounds were sold and the Duke moved to a corner of Blenheim, where he continued to gather rare and expensive plants around him, albeit on a more modest scale.

The only garden which seriously rivalled White Knights was Woburn, but here the collecting was done on a sounder basis: the fifth Duke of Bedford not only collected paintings, sculpture and plants, remodelled the house and added an indoor tennis court and riding school but he also developed the Bloomsbury estate on the site of his London house and poured large sums of money into farm improvements and scientific farming.

Although progress in the world of flowers and trees was most spectacular and best documented, similar advances were occurring in other branches of horticulture. One of the most outstanding plant scientists was Thomas Andrew Knight, the younger brother of Richard Payne Knight of Downton. A member of the Royal Society, he worked with enormous energy on the raising of new, improved fruit trees. From 1795 he published his experiments in *Philosophical Transactions of the Royal Society of London*. His work on transmission of debility of fruit trees by grafting predated by 150 years the discovery of viruses which caused such debility; his experiments on peas recognized characteristics of dominance and recessive behaviour a century before Mendel quantified such observations; his paper 'On the Direction of the Radicle and Germen during the Vegetation of Seeds', read to the Royal Society in 1806, discussed the influence of gravity on seedling growth half a century before Darwin carried out parallel experiments on the effect of light and established the existence of plant auxins.[22]

Botanic gardens

Again it was about half a century before such pioneering work was reflected in a surge of activity in established botanic gardens, but the steady increase in plant introductions accelerated the more or less traditional activity of the botanic gardens in collecting and classifying plants.

A site was given for a new botanic garden at Cambridge in 1761, and two years later a much older but fragmented garden at Edinburgh, founded in 1670, moved to a new five-acre site at Haddington Place. Chelsea Physic Garden lost much of the reputation built up by Miller when William Forsyth replaced him from 1770 until 1784, and little happened at Oxford for many decades, but the focus of activity moved to Kew. With the King's blessing, Banks's enthusiastic direction and the skilful management of the Aitons, father and son, Kew became one of the world's leading gardens as plants from Cook's voyages of 1768–71, 1772–5 and 1776–9 came to it. In 1789 William Aiton published his *Hortus Kewensis*, listing 5,500 species in the garden. From 1810–13 William Townsend Aiton, who managed both Kew and Richmond after his father's death in 1793, revised the *Hortus* and issued it in five volumes.

The Horticultural Society of London

In the nineteenth century, however, the focus shifted again from the botanic gardens to the newly formed and prestigious Horticultural Society of London. The idea of the new Society was put forward by John Wedgwood, a son of Josiah Wedgwood, to William Forsyth in a letter of 29 June 1801.[23] Joseph Banks and William Townsend Aiton were soon involved, but it was not until 7 March 1804 that the group, enlarged to seven by the addition of Charles Greville, R. A. Salisbury and James Dickson, held its inaugural

Chrysanthemum indicum, sent by John Reeves to the Horticultural Society of London.

meeting in Hatchard's bookshop in Piccadilly. By the fourth meeting, on 11 April, there were sixty members.

Apart from occasional exhibits of plants at meetings and the celebrated display (and consumption) of fruits which soon became a tradition at the Anniversary Dinner, the Society's activities consisted almost entirely of regular meetings (eight general meetings, monthly from November to June) and the reading of papers.

In 1818 the Society acquired its own small experimental garden, an acre and a half in extent, in Kensington, and in 1819 it moved to its own house in what is now Lower Regent Street. These were timely acquisitions, as the Society's library was growing rapidly and the Society as a body was beginning to acquire new plants.

One of the most important agents in the collection of both drawings and plants was John Reeves, a tea broker from West Ham who spent twenty years in China from 1813, corresponding regularly with Banks and sending drawings and plants from China to the Horticultural Society. The first consignments of plants were entrusted to James Lee at the Vineyard and to William Anderson at the Chelsea Physic Garden, but the arrival of Reeves's plants doubtless spurred the Society to acquire its own garden. Reeves was more influential still in the long term because of his success in bringing rather than sending plants. In 1816 he returned briefly to

London, bringing with him 100 carefully tended plants, of which
ninety survived. John Livingstone, chief surgeon to the East India
Company in China and like Reeves an overseas Corresponding
Member of the Horticultural Society, heard of Reeves's success on
his return and wrote at once to Sabine, the Secretary, urging him
to send out trained gardener/collectors. The difficulties of sending
plants from China were enormous. Livingstone estimated that only
one plant in 1,000 survived, representing a cost, if purchased at
three plants for £1 in Canton, of over £300 pounds for each
survivor. How much more sensible to send a collector to establish
plants in pots of soil before the voyage, then to accompany them
home. At £100 a year for a good man, it was folly not to do so.[24]

Livingstone's letter to Sabine was sent in February 1819. It was
not acted on immediately, perhaps because of the memory of Kerr's
unfortunate existence as a virtual prisoner in Canton. However,
Banks died in June 1820, Kew ceased to send plant collectors and
by November Sabine was making arrangements to send John Potts
to Bengal and China. The Horticultural Society took over from
Kew the role of patron-in-chief of plant introduction, and a new
wave of systematic introduction of living plants for gardens rather
than dried specimens for botanical cabinets continued throughout
the nineteenth century.

The garden bookshelf

Advances in the art and science of garden-making in the early years
of the nineteenth century were profound, but the most fundamental
effect on the shaping of gardens by succeeding generations lay in a
third field of endeavour: the field of publishing and, in particular,
the publishing of periodicals.

Miller's *Gardeners Dictionary* remained in the forefront of gardening books from its first edition in 1731 to the eighth in 1768,
shortly before Miller's death.

In 1767 John Abercrombie, a gardener at Kew, produced *Every
Man His Own Gardener*. Fearing that he was too little known for
the book to succeed, he offered the Duke of Leeds's head gardener,
Thomas Maw, £20 for the use of his name. He need not have
worried: the book was immensely successful. In 1770 Abercrombie
bought a nursery in Hackney. In 1776 the seventh edition of *Every
Man* was issued by Maw and Abercrombie and in later editions
Abercrombie's portrait was included. There followed a steady
stream of practical works: *The Garden Mushroom* (1779); *The*

Complete Forcing Gardener (1781); *The Complete Wall Tree Pruner* (1783); *The Propagation and Botanical Arrangement of Plants and Trees* (1784); *The Gardener's Pocket Dictionary* and *The Gardener's Daily Assistant* (1786), *The Universal Gardener's Kalendar* and *The Gardener's Vade Mecum* and *The Hothouse Gardener* in 1789, and *The Gardener's Pocket Journal c.* 1790. This last work ran to thirty-five editions by 1857.

It was not unknown for very expensive and time-consuming illustrated works to be published in parts. Catesby's *Natural History of the Carolinas* ... was an outstanding example. Richard Bradley, Professor of Botany at Cambridge, was the first to produce a gardening book in parts, intending publication to continue indefinitely as a periodical. *A General Treatise of Husbandry and Gardening* appeared in fifteen parts from 1721 to 1724.

In 1777 William Curtis, a demonstrator at Chelsea Physic Garden before he acquired his own London Botanic Garden in Lambeth Marsh, produced the first part of *Flora Londinensis* as a periodical, intending to illustrate all the wild flowers growing around London. The enterprise involved Curtis in serious loss and he turned instead, at the suggestion of patrons of his garden, to portraying exotic plants drawn from life and accurately hand-coloured for 'the use of such ladies, gentlemen and gardeners as wish to become scientifically acquainted with the plants they cultivate'.[25] Curtis's *Botanical Magazine* was an instant success from its appearance in February 1787. Three thousand copies of each issue were sold at a shilling each.

In 1797 *The Botanist's Repository* appeared, describing newly introduced plants, but only ten volumes were issued. In 1815 came the *Botanical Register*, followed, before its demise in 1847, by another twenty magazines for botanists, florists and gardeners.

All these early publications dealt solely or mainly with individual plants, their botanical characteristics and, in some cases, their individual culture.

A suburban gardener

By far the most important writer on gardens and general culture of plants in the early nineteenth century was John Claudius Loudon. If Philip Miller represents the cornerstone of gardening and garden publishing in the eighteenth century, his counterpart in the nineteenth is surely this enterprising and enormously energetic Scotsman.

Born in Lanarkshire in 1783, Loudon went to live with an uncle in Edinburgh while attending school there, distinguishing himself in writing and drawing. On leaving school he assisted John Mawer, a nurseryman and landscape gardener, then joined Robert Dickson in Leith Walk near the Botanic Garden. Here he used every opportunity to further himself, attending university classes in agriculture, botany and chemistry and going without sleep on two nights each week to read and write.

In 1803 he moved from Edinburgh to London. Before the year was out he wrote an article in the *Literary Journal* on his 'Observations on the laying out of the Public Squares of London', criticizing the gloomy, soot-laden evergreens and suggesting

Eclecticism in print: the title page of Loudon's Hints on the Formation of Gardens.

HINTS

ON THE FORMATION OF

GARDENS

AND

PLEASURE GROUNDS.

WITH DESIGNS
IN VARIOUS STYLES
OF

Rural Embellishment:

COMPRISING PLANS FOR LAYING OUT

FLOWER, FRUIT, AND KITCHEN GARDENS,

AND THE ARRANGEMENT OF

Glass Houses, Hot Walls, and Stoves;

INTERSPERSED WITH REMARKS ON VARIOUS SUBJECTS OF

HORTICULTURAL IMPROVEMENT.

TO WHICH IS ADDED, A

PRICED CATALOGUE

OF FRUIT AND FOREST TREES, SHRUBS, AND PLANTS,

ADAPTED TO

VILLA GROUNDS,

FROM ONE PERCH TO A HUNDRED ACRES IN EXTENT.

LONDON:

PRINTED FOR JOHN HARDING, No. 36, ST. JAMES'S STREET.

1812.

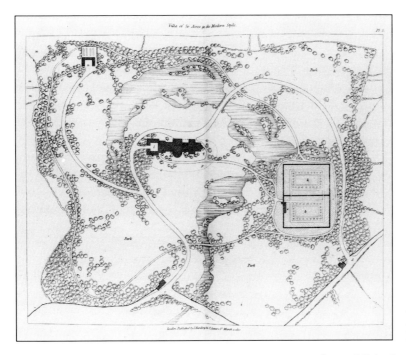

A villa of fifty acres from Loudon's Hints on the Formation of Gardens.

sycamores and planes to lighten the effect. In 1804 he published *Observations on the Formation and Management of Useful and Ornamental Plantations: on the Theory and Practice of Landscape-Gardening, and on gaining and embanking of Land from Rivers or the Sea*. His widespread activities as a landscape gardener continued until 1806 when, drenched with rain during an all-night coach journey from Caernarvon, he contracted a chill and then rheumatic fever.

Loudon's recuperation in a farmhouse at Wood Hall, Pinner, allowed time for reflection and writing, learning German and painting landscapes (some to be exhibited at the Royal Academy)! As a result of his deliberations he persuaded his father to move to Wood Hall, and joined him in farming. In 1808 came the pamphlet *An immediate and effectual Mode of raising the Rental of the Landed Property of England; and rendering Great Britain independent of other Nations for the Supply of Bread Corn. By a Scotch Farmer, now farming in Middlesex.* Loudon moved to Great Tew in Oxfordshire that autumn at the invitation of General Stratton, and stayed to carry out improvements until 1811.

In 1812 he produced *Hints on the Formation of Gardens and Pleasure Grounds*. Its full title, *Hints on the Formation of Gardens and Pleasure Grounds with Designs in various Styles of Rural Embellishment: comprising plans for laying out flower, fruit, and kitchen gardens, and the arrangement of glass houses, hot walls, and stoves; interspersed with remarks on various subjects of horticultural improvement. To which is added, a priced catalogue of fruit and forest trees, shrubs, and plants, adapted to villa grounds, from one perch to a hundred acres in extent,* was printed in a dozen or so different typefaces, as if to emphasize Loudon's liking for variety. His aim was to produce guidelines and model solutions for the design of smaller properties, a subject neglected for the previous century, and thus to raise the standard of design.

From the expence of consulting eminent professors in this line, many are deterred from applying for their aid. Nurserymen and builders, therefore, have been necessitated to supply their places, and it is for their aid, as well as for the information of the amateur who lays out his own grounds, that the author of this work submits it to the candid examination of an impartial public.

By 1812 Loudon's farming and landscape gardening activities had brought him a fortune of £15,000. He decided to broaden his education by travelling abroad, and spent the next eighteen months in Europe. Sadly his investments were not sound: he returned to find himself impoverished and plunged back into writing in order to earn his living.

In 1822 came his all-embracing *Encyclopaedia of Gardening*, over 1,000 pages of solid, fine print and innumerable illustrations. Loudon's solvency was restored. In 1825 he designed his own villa in the fashionable rural suburb of Porchester Road, Bayswater – in fact a pair of semi-detached dwellings built to look like one imposing

Four treatments for front gardens from Loudon's Hints on the Formation of Gardens.

residence. Loudon sensibly chose the half with the quarter-acre garden on the south side, and proceeded to collect and cultivate all the plants that could be squeezed in, about 2,000 species at any one time. There were mosses and alpines, roses and vines, trees and shrubs, bulbs and hothouse plants and even a salt-water tank for seaweeds.

His writing and gardening did not proceed without difficulty. The rheumatic fever of his youth had left him with a rheumatic right arm. Increasing pain drove him to laudanum for relief and he became addicted. In 1825 clumsy bone-setters broke his arm and then decided it must be amputated. It was only with difficulty that the doctors persuaded him to stay in bed for the afternoon after the amputation. He cured himself of laudanum addiction by topping up the pot with water each time he drew off a glassful until, by sheer will power, he was drinking virtually plain water. Eventually rheumatism spread to his left arm: he was just able to hold a pencil between his third and fourth fingers.

Despite his misfortunes the first issue of his *Gardener's Magazine* appeared in 1826, at five shillings quarterly. With typical Loudon zeal the magazine was intended 'to disseminate new and improved information on all topics connected with horticulture, and to raise the intellect and character of those engaged in this art', despite a price which kept it beyond the reach of most practising gardeners. In 1828 the magazine carried a review of a novel called *The Mummy*, set in the twenty-second century and predicting many advances in society. In 1830 Loudon met the writer of *The Mummy* and was surprised to find not an author but an authoress. In the following September John Loudon, then forty-seven, married the twenty-three-year-old Jane Webb.

With Jane as an able and willing right hand always at his side, Loudon's output continued unabated. In addition to the *Gardener's Magazine* and the newer *Magazine of Natural History* (begun in 1829), *The Encyclopaedia of Cottage, Farm and Villa Architecture* appeared in 1833 and his *Architectural Magazine* commenced in 1834. *The Suburban Gardener and Villa Companion* was published in 1838, and in the same year came the eight weighty volumes of *Arboretum et fruticetum Britannicum, or the Trees and Shrubs of Britain*. The effort which Loudon poured into this immense work, travelling to visit rare or fine trees, long hours every day supervising artists in the field without rest or food, and the worry occasioned by the financial failure of the work, hastened his death, but it is incredible that he survived as long as he did. In 1839 he worked on Derby's arboretum; in 1840 he was in Paris, in 1841 in Scotland

(Above) The excitement caused by Indian architecture is clearly evident in Cockerell's elegant conservatory at Sezincote, skilfully set into the hillside.

(Right) 'China', one of the many compartments of James Bateman's garden at Biddulph Grange, before its rescue by the National Trust.

(Above) Easton Neston, Northants, typifies the Victorian gardening tradition but its scale and dramatic central vista reflect the garden's early eighteenth-century origins.

(Left) One of the most opulent late-Victorian gardens, Waddesdon combined lavish bedding displays with a richly planted parkland setting.

Ludwig Messel's Nymans before it was devastated in the storm of October 1987.
Restoration is progressing steadily.

(Above) The eighteenth-century landscape at Stourhead was richly embellished with conifers, hardy hybrid rhododendrons and other new exotics which now dwarf the Pantheon and other buildings.

(Left) Steep slopes, lofty trees and rushing streams at Bodnant recreated the Himalayan hills from which so many of the plants in the garden were derived.

(Opposite above) Benthall Hall: many a quiet country house, aside from the maelstrom of Victorian extravagance, provided inspiration for a new way of life.

(Opposite below) Nurserymen and artists combined to make the Edwardian garden as gay as a party dress.

(Above) The Madonna lily (one of Gertrude Jekyll's favourite flowers), adds a monastic calm to this simple garden scene by Lilian Stannard.

(Left) On the Great Plat at Hestercombe, Lutyens's geometry is matched by the boldness of Gertrude Jekyll's planting.

(Opposite above) The white garden at Hidcote Manor, with arching roses and free-growing herbaceous plants contained within trim hedges.

(Opposite below) Hidcote's red borders, gazebos and stilt garden extend the garden vista from the old walled garden to the brow of the hill.

(Above) Achille Duchêne's water parterre at Blenheim: one of the most splendid pieces of historical reconstruction in England.

(Below) Harold Peto's water garden at Buscot (1905–10) typifies the Italian influence evident in much professional garden design early in this century.

and the North of England, resting in a friend's house in Paisley for six weeks after contracting a fever. In 1843 he became involved in the then popular aspect of landscaping cemeteries. Knowing that he was dying, he completed the cemetery in Southampton and went on to complete one in Bath before returning to Bayswater to finish his *Self Instruction for Young Gardeners*. He died in December, while standing dictating to his wife.

The Gardenesque

The forty years of Loudon's career in London, overlapping with that of Repton, marked the end of one era in garden planning and the beginning of another. In appearance, social background and manner the two men were very different: Repton was elegant, cultured and eternally cheerful, Loudon was thick-set, solidly down-to-earth and very serious. Despite these outward differences, however, they had much in common. Both were widely interested in rural improvement, adornment and architecture, in employing the latest aids to convenient and civilized life. Both were talented artists and knowledgeable botanists, practically acquainted with farming and estate improvement. Both were prolific writers. The generation which separated them, however, determined that they addressed themselves to very different audiences. Repton wrestled with ideas of the Beautiful and the Picturesque to create often substantial landscape parks for wealthy individuals. Loudon's larger commissions were usually of a public nature – public parks, aboreta and cemeteries. His most notable contribution lay in advising, through his books and periodicals, the thousands of smaller estate and garden owners who could never have afforded, or would never have thought to employ, a distinguished professional landscape gardener to lay out their grounds. His *Hints on the Formation of Gardens* of 1812 began with 'Parterres of Turf and Earth for small Ground Plots'. Plate 3, for a plot of 2–10 perches, included 'A design in the French style, intermingled with what may be called the picturesque manner'. Many of Loudon's layouts showed ingenious combinations of formal (ancient or French style) and informal (picturesque or modern) features, but Plate 16, a 'modern English parterre', showed the inherent dangers of combining ancient and modern. Its limpid, weak shapes warned of the fate of changeable parterres of tender plants almost before this system of gardening was devised.

In his *Suburban Gardener* Loudon dealt systematically and in fine
detail with first, second, third and fourth rate gardens. Plans, plants,
costs and hints on cultivation were offered for substantial villas and
walled backyards. When dealing with a small estate of a few acres
or even, as in Loudon's own Bayswater villa, a mere quarter of an
acre, niceties of distinction between the Beautiful and the Picturesque had very little relevance. For such circumstances he devised
a third system of design, the 'Gardenesque'.

Loudon described the Gardenesque as 'the production of that
kind of scenery which is best calculated to display the individual
beauty of trees, shrubs and plants in a state of culture; the smoothness
and greenness of lawns; and the smooth surface, curved directions,
dryness, and firmness of gravel walks'.[26] Furthermore, he suggested
that 'as a garden is a work of art and a scene of cultivation, every
plant or tree placed in it should be so placed as never to be
placed there by nature or accident or as to prevent the practices of
cultivation being applied to it'.

This encapsulation of the Gardenesque style had several major
implications. Firstly, a garden is a work of art, not of nature.
Loudon overturned convention by inferring that nature and art
were distinct, even opposites, implying that one might emphasize
artistry by unnaturalness; avenues, quincunx, formal groves and
individual specimen trees were more artistic than were spinneys
and copses where trees grew deformed and spindly in mutual
competition.

A further, more subtle inference was that a garden might be
made more artistic by growing plants which were clearly not
'natural', lending support to the crazes for collecting crested, frilled
and other aberrant ferns, conifers (especially the monkey puzzle),
purple beech, blue spruce or cedar, golden yew, weeping ash and
elm, fastigiate oak and other vegetable freaks of later nineteenth-
century gardens. Our recent eagerness for fastigiate cherry and
dwarf, multi-coloured conifers perhaps reflects this same ancestry.

A third point was that the garden is a work of art *and a scene of
cultivation*, a place for working in. Plants should be spaced out to
reveal their individual forms, the grass kept away from stems and
each plant set in a circle of earth meticulously hoed and mounded.
The garden was no longer a reminder of classical Rome, an ideal-
ization of Nature's beauty, a scene of awe or repose, of poetical
inspiration. It was a plot in which to grow as many, and as many
different plants as possible to the highest standards of individual
cultivation.

Such inferences were far from what Loudon intended. He saw the Gardenesque as the production of *that kind of scenery* calculated to display plants – a landscape, not a collection, but such subtleties were largely lost on his readers.

A rapidly growing and increasingly wealthy population was making England an urban rather than a rural nation, with countless new suburban gardens to be made. New styles of building, new materials for construction, new plants both tender and hardy, and a rapidly developing nursery industry for their distribution offered unlimited scope for the makers of gardens. A new means of communication, the gardening periodical, ensured rapid distribution of the best, the latest, the most outrageous ideas: it was the most potent force in shaping the later nineteenth-century garden and largely instrumental in ensuring the establishment of Loudon's answer to the Beautiful and the Picturesque – the Gardenesque.

The need to consider Loudon as a single key figure in the early nineteenth century rather than in pre- and post-1820 fragments has stretched the chronology of this chapter a little, even straying into Victoria's reign, but, by 1820, the ingredients of the High Victorian garden were assembled.

8

The High Victorian Garden

In most respects the changes which occurred in gardens from 1820 to 1870 can be seen simply as the maturation and combination of ideas already apparent in the reign of George III. With the end of the Napoleonic Wars and the succession of George IV, Britain returned to a period of buoyant prosperity and garden-making.

The plant collectors

The introduction of exotic plants, which had flourished under the patronage of Sir Joseph Banks, increased rather than declined after his death in 1820. Kew curtailed its activities but Joseph Sabine, secretary of the young Horticultural Society of London, was quick to step into the breach by persuading the Society to engage plant hunters.[1]

John Potts left England in 1821 for China to meet John Reeves and returned in 1822 with a large collection of plants – chrysanthemums, camellias and a quantity of *Primula sinensis* among them.

In November 1821 Sabine took advantage of an offer from his brother, a captain in the Royal Artillery, to send George Don to West Africa, South America and the West Indies. He returned in February 1823 with a rich collection of stove plants and especially tropical fruits.

In January 1822 John Forbes was sent, at the invitation of the Admiralty, on a survey of the East African coast via Spain, Brazil and the Cape of Good Hope. Small but healthy and adaptable plants, including several orchids, arrived from Brazil during the year and more came from East Africa in 1823, but news arrived at the end of the year that Forbes, aged twenty-three, had died while making his way up the Zambesi river.

In April 1823 John Parks was sent to China. Again John Reeves helped with the growing, packing and dispatch of plants, among which were chrysanthemums, camellias, the yellow Banksian rose, 'Parks's Yellow Tea-Scented China Rose' (for eighty years the only yellow repeat-flowering rose) and a plant which came almost to symbolize the Victorian era, *Aspidistra lurida*.

Increasing unrest in China dissuaded Sabine from sending a second collector to China to assist Parks. Bitterly disappointed, David Douglas was sent instead to New England. Douglas arrived in New York in August 1823 and left in December, but in four months he made innumerable contacts, visited fruit-growing areas in New York, Pennsylvania and Canada and saw apples, pears, plums, peaches and grapes growing in abundance. The Council of the Horticultural Society hailed the expedition as a success beyond all expectation, and in July 1824 Douglas set out on a second mission, under the protection of the Hudson Bay Company, to explore the largely unknown north-west coast. Douglas wrote to a friend: 'By degrees the goddess of night threw her veil over the rocky shores of Cornwall and my delightful view of happy England closed – probably for ever!'[2]

Douglas's energies were prodigious. Arriving at the Columbia River in 1825 he walked 2,000 miles in the remaining eight months of that year, 4,000 miles in 1826, then walked from coast to coast in 1827 back to Hudson Bay, arriving in Portsmouth in October 1827. Douglas returned a national hero. For a cost to the Society of less than £400 he introduced over 200 species of plants: lofty pines, spruces, firs and the handsome Douglas fir, shrubs such as *Garrya elliptica*, berberis and the now ubiquitous *Ribes sanguineum*, oenotheras, penstemons, *Lupinus polyphyllus* and many annuals including clarkia, *Mentzelia lindleyi* and the charming *Limnanthes douglasii*.

Douglas could not settle in London. In October 1829 he went to California for the Horticultural Society, sending back many more exciting plants, but on his second excursion to Honolulu in 1834 he fell into an animal trap and was gored and trampled to death by a trapped bullock. Douglas was not only extraordinarily successful in his innumerable introductions, his influence was exceptionally durable. Nearly all the plants introduced from the Pacific North West proved very much at home in Britain, and his memory lives on especially in the towering conifers which break the skyline around every substantial nineteenth-century house in the country.

In September 1824, only two months after Douglas first sailed for New York, James Macrae also left England for Brazil, Hawaii, Chile and Peru, sending back seeds and plants and returning to England in 1826 with another large collection, including fresh seed of another characteristically Victorian plant, the monkey puzzle (or monkey puzzler), *Araucaria araucana*, first introduced by Menzies in 1795.

Theodore Hartweg was sent in October 1836 to the mountains of Mexico. In February 1837 two boxes arrived in London with sixty species of orchids and eighty other plants including cacti, trees and shrubs, one of which, *Fuchsia fulgens*, is one of the main parents of the modern fuchsia. In 1845 Hartweg left England again, for California. Most of his introductions were not hardy in Britain, although *Ceanothus dentatus* grows well in the south and the Monterey cypress, *Cupressus macrocarpa,* transforms itself from the gnarled, windswept specimens of the Californian coast to stately bright green columns on our south coast, where it provides excellent protection from salt-laden gales.

The Orient unveiled

In 1842 the troubles which prevented Douglas going to China subsided to an uneasy peace with the defeat of China in the Opium Wars. The Horticultural Society lost no time in sending a collector, and selected Robert Fortune, who had worked in the Edinburgh Botanic Garden and at Chiswick. He sailed in February 1843 via Hong Kong to Chusan and Shanghai.

Fortune travelled and collected for two years. Plants, including some sent from Japan to Shanghai, were taken back to Hong Kong. Half were sent to London and half were taken to Canton for Fortune to accompany back to England.

Fortune was told that 'hardy plants are of the first importance to the Society'; the warning was well heeded. Among his introductions were *Jasminum nudiflorum* and *Lonicera fragrantissima* to dispel the winter gloom, *Weigela florida, Viburnum macrocephalum* and *V. tomentosum* 'Plicatum', *Cryptomeria japonica, Rhododendron obtusum, Dicentra spectabilis* and *Platycodon grandiflorum*. In October 1846 he was able to see quantities of Japanese anemones (now *Anemone hupehensis* var. *japonica*) in flower in the Chiswick greenhouses but this, too, was soon recognized as being quite hardy and an excellent border plant.

Much of Fortune's success was due to his careful briefing and his thoroughness in collecting and packing, but he was also assisted by a new development, the Wardian case, invented by Dr Nathaniel Bagshaw Ward.[3] Ward, a physician practising in the East End of London, was a keen naturalist. In 1829 he sealed a chrysalis in a glass jar in order to study its emergence but his interest was taken, instead, by the seedlings which appeared and flourished in the humid atmosphere safely away from gas fumes and desiccating draughts. He experimented with larger glass cases and eventually published his results in the *Companion to the Botanical Magazine* (1836), *The Gardener's Magazine* (1839) and a small book, *On the Growth of Plants in Closely Glazed Cases* (1842). The Wardian case, usually engulfed in heavy ornamentation, became an indispensable part of Victorian furnishing, saving its delicate contents from gas fumes and draughts, but in its simpler and robust form it enabled Fortune to transfer to Britain the most delicate of plants safe from salt spray and desiccation. With the success of the Wardian case proved beyond doubt, Fortune undertook further journeys for the East India Company, smuggling tea plants out of China to establish the plantations in India. He later worked with Kew and, with Fortune as collector and Kew as propagator/distributor, plantation economies of rubber, cocoa, banana and coffee were established in various parts of the ever-expanding Empire.[4]

From 1860–62 Fortune undertook a last expedition, financed this time as a private venture, to the newly opened territory of Japan, before retiring quietly to Kensington where he lived comfortably for nearly twenty years – one of the few collectors to die of old age, at sixty-eight.

Fifteen years elapsed between the return of Robert Fortune from China in 1846 and the departure of the Society's next collector, John Weir, for Brazil and New Grenada. Weir sent back many fine orchids but, tragically, became paralysed in 1864 and never recovered from his disability.

In the forty years from Potts to Weir the Horticultural Society of London, later the Royal Horticultural Society (the Royal Charter was sealed on 8 May 1861), was instrumental in enriching English gardens with an immense number of plants. In 1821 the one-and-a-half-acre garden in Kensington was abandoned in favour of a new site, thirty-three acres of market garden land at Chiswick leased from the Duke of Devonshire. Two years later the garden housed a collection of 1,200 roses, trials of 435 lettuce varieties, 260 peas and 240 potatoes, and in 1826 when a *Catalogue of Fruits cultivated in the Garden of the Horticultural Society of London at*

Chiswick was published it contained 3,825 varieties. The Society took care not to compete with commercial growers but plants of proven merit were distributed to Fellows and thus to nurseries: the stimulus to horticulture was incalculable.

Nineteenth-century nurseries

James Lee's nursery at the Vineyard, Hammersmith (from which John Kennedy relinquished his interest in 1817) continued to flourish as the nineteenth century progressed. Lee had four sons destined for the four departments of the nursery – counting house, seeds, greenhouse and hardy plants – but he died in 1824 when the eldest son, John, was only eighteen. John Lee ran the nursery, outliving his own son, but the business yielded to the inevitable bricks and mortar of a spreading city when he died in 1899, aged ninety-three.

Conrad Loddiges's nursery in Hackney, founded in 1771, grew to rival the older Vineyard. It was known expecially for its American plants, sent by John Bartram's son William. By 1818 Loddiges and his son George grew over 1,200 trees and shrubs arranged alphabetically in a seven-acre collection along a spiralling walk. There were in addition 1,500 roses. In 1821 the firm became one of the first in Britain to grow orchids on a commercial scale. In 1839 their *Orchidae in the Collection of C. Loddiges and Sons* listed 1,600 orchids. George Loddiges died in 1846; the nursery lost its unrivalled position and closed in 1856.

Joseph Knight founded the Exotic Nursery in King's Road, Chelsea, in 1809, having worked previously as gardener to George Hibbert, a man wealthy enough to send his own collectors to the Cape and to Jamaica. Conifers soon occupied a prominent place in the nursery and in 1840 Knight published his *Catalogue of Coniferae*. The nursery was short-lived, however. In 1853 the King's Road site was acquired by the up and coming firm of Veitch.

Farther afield, Lucombe and Pince of St Thomas's, Exeter, was famed for its fuchsias, cinerarias, calceolarias and other greenhouse plants, but it also grew a wide range of other plants including the upright semi-evergreen Lucombe oak.[5] Lucombe and Pince continued to the end of the nineteenth century.

Even further from London was the nursery of Peter Lawson and Son of Edinburgh, founded in 1770. In 1820 Charles Lawson succeeded his father and secured immortality for the family's name when, in 1854, he obtained seed of Lawson's cypress from the Secretary of the Oregon Association, William Murray.

The nineteenth century also spawned many new nurseries. A. Paul and Son was founded in 1806 in Cheshunt, later the centre of the glasshouse industry as inner London sites became increasingly polluted. In 1810 William Jackman established a nursery at Woking, to the west of London. The nursery was continued by his sons George and Henry from 1832 and then by George alone. It specialized in clematis (*Clematis* x *jackmanii* was shown at a Royal Horticultural Society exhibition in 1863 and received a First Class Certificate) but also produced a wide range of other plants. Backhouse of York (founded in 1816 by James and Thomas Backhouse) was another general nursery which developed a specialist interest:

The new periodicals and penny post rapidly spread new varieties of plants throughout the country: Gardener's Chronicle, 1862.

it became renowned for the construction of large, naturalistic rock gardens.

Introductions alone in the nineteenth century would have filled even the largest garden to overflowing, but the wealth of new plants was further supplemented by the establishment of specialist nurseries with prodigious output of new hybrid varieties.

Home-grown hybrids

The chrysanthemum was introduced in the late eighteenth century already in an advanced state of development. Colvill had a display of Chinese chrysanthemums in his King's Road, Chelsea, nursery in 1796, but seventy more varieties were introduced between 1820 and 1830. The introduction of Japanese varieties by Robert Fortune in 1861 led to the development of large recurving mops of rich colours.

Colvill was also interested in the development of the gladiolus, an interest shared by James Kelway. In 1850 Kelway left his gardening post to start his own business in Langport, Somerset, and in 1861 he produced the first large-flowered hybrids.

Kelway also took an interest in delphiniums. *Delphinium elatum*, the first truly perennial delphinium, was introduced early in the seventeenth century and other species followed, but Kelway began to specialize in them in 1859. By 1881 there were sixteen varieties, and eight years later 137.[6]

Another flower automatically associated with Kelway was the herbaceous paeony. *Paeonia lactiflora* was first introduced in 1784 and again by Banks in 1805. Several hybrids were produced, but from 1865 Kelway adopted the species and produced a wide range of spectacularly beautiful flowers, many of which continue to grace Kelway exhibits at the Chelsea Flower Show in the 1980s.

Surprisingly the narcissus was very late in attracting interest as a garden plant. It is a Mediterranean genus extending as far north as Britain. Gerard knew twelve varieties in 1597 and Parkinson seventy-eight in 1629, but it was Dean Herbert of Manchester, in the course of his research on the Amaryllidaceae, published in 1837, who sparked off a serious interest in the breeding of narcissus. Edward Leeds, also of Manchester, began to produce large-flowered hybrids. William Backhouse, a Yorkshire banker, was also a keen cultivator and hybridizer, and when ill-health forced him to give up his plants they were acquired by Peter Barr. Barr's interest led to a Daffodil Conference sponsored by the Royal Horticultural Society in 1884 and to continued development of this now popular garden flower.

Nowhere was the interest in plant breeding more apparent nor the results more impressive than in the rose and the rhododendron. The hybrid China roses were mainly sterile triploids, but repeated crossing gave a range of variation and, in 1830, a fertile seedling arose, making possible a further blending of repeat flowering and vigour.

The major nurseries – Lee, Loddiges, Rivers and Paul among them – included long lists of roses in their stock. In 1836 Thomas Rivers published one of the finest rose catalogues in the country, offering 50 perpetuals, 89 hybrid Chinas, 136 dwarf and tea-scented Chinas and over 300 old roses: moss, albas, damasks, etc.

The hybrid perpetual became the dominant type of rose by 1850 and featured heavily in the first Grand National Rose Show, organized in 1858 by Dean Reynolds Hole (who became first President of the National Rose Society on its formation in 1876). East and West became ever more closely united in the rose until, in 1867, Guillot produced 'La France', the rose now generally regarded as the first hybrid tea.[7]

That the rose became virtually England's national flower might well be due to the strategic importance of London, hence the establishment of estates in the Home Counties on clay loams suitable for farming, and also to the unlimited availability of stable manure, for the modern rose is a greedy plant. Increasingly, however, the heaths and woods on the barren sandy soils of Surrey, Sussex and Hampshire were being occupied and cultivated by a new race of commuters, taking advantage of enormously improved transport to work in the city and to live in the country. For these the rhododendron provided a much more suitable flowering shrub.

The European rhododendrons *R. maximum*, *R. ponticum* and *R. caucasicum* and the very hardy American *R. catawbiense*, introduced in the eighteenth century, were cherished as garden plants and resulted in a range of hybrids of pale pink and mauve colouring. In 1817 the tender *R. arboreum* was introduced from India. It flowered simultaneously at Alresford and at Highclere, Hampshire, in 1825. The brilliant red flowers could not fail to create a sensation. By 1832 Michael Waterer, founder of the Knap Hill nursery at Bagshot in 1790, had crossed *R. arboreum* with *R. caucasicum* to produce hardy hybrids of stronger colouring. John Standish was another outstanding breeder of rhododendrons. He was joined in his Bagshot nursery by Charles Noble (after whom the very early-flowering *Rhododendron nobleanum* was named) from 1848 to 1857, and the nursery became famous for its hardy plants. Standish was one of the first to offer Fortune's plants from China and Japan, and when Joseph Hooker, son of the Director of Kew and a near neighbour of Standish, introduced a whole range of beautiful and hardy rhododendrons from Sikkim, Standish was among the first to be given seed. By grafting seedlings on to old rhododendrons he induced them to flower at an early age and produced many hardy hybrids including 'Ascot Brilliant' in 1862.[8]

Deciduous azaleas, too, appeared in great numbers. *Rhododendron molle* from Japan was grown by Loddiges in 1824. Its crossing with *R. japonicum*, introduced from Japan by Siebold in 1830, produced the Mollis hybrid azaleas and these were later crossed with *R. occidentale*, introduced by William Lobb for Veitch in 1851, bringing fragrance and good autumn colour as added attractions. Michael Waterer was once again a leading figure in the development of deciduous azaleas, creating a precedent for Anthony Waterer's Knap Hill hybrids which appeared from 1870.

All these hardy plants had a considerable effect on garden design, but it was a group of tender plants which most symbolized the achievements of the High Victorian garden: bedding plants.[9]

The bedding system

Surprisingly, perhaps, neither the range of plants nor the concept of bedding was particularly new. Parkinson grew double larkspurs of several colours and six varieties of wallflower. The calves' snout or snapdragon, *Antirrhinum majus*, was already so familiar that Parkinson classed it as an English rather than an outlandish flower,[10] while *Tagetes erecta*, introduced from Mexico to Spain, naturalized so successfully along the Tunisian coast that it was introduced to Britain as the 'African' rather than the American marigold.[11] Parkinson grew this and the smaller (and equally American) 'French' marigold, *Tagetes patula*, in quilled and double forms. Both were among the plants listed under August in Henry Wise's notebook of flowers for each month of the year, together with 'Belvidore' (*Kochia tricophylla*) and scarlet beans,[12] and it was London and Wise at Brompton Park who developed the strain of 'Brompton stocks' used by them in vast numbers for the parterres at Blenheim. *Lobelia erinus* and several pelargoniums were introduced from the Cape early in the eighteenth century. By 1750 'Geranium Africanum', the zonal pelargonium, was a popular plant.

(*Above*) *Lobelias, rediscovered for bedding schemes after a century in cultivation (from Mrs Loudon's* Ladies' Companion to the Flower Garden*)*.

(*Above right*) *Brilliant salvias from Central America.*

(*Right*) *Verbenas, vivid but elegant flowers 'to be seen in every London window box'.*

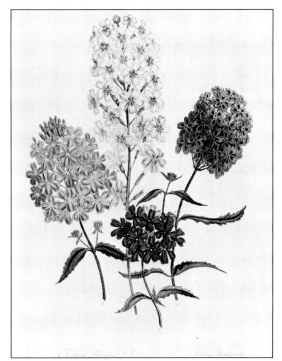

In the nineteenth century, however, the tempo of introductions changed. When, in the tumult caused by the Napoleonic Wars, South American countries established their independence from Spain and Portugal between 1810 and 1826, other European countries quickly stepped in to trade with the newly independent states.

A botanic garden was established in Rio de Janeiro c. 1809; another in Buenos Aires in 1826 through the influence of John Hallet, Consul-General of South American States in London, and with a German superintendent. Another was started in Caracas in 1828 by Mr Fanning, and there were several others around the Caribbean at about the same time.

Some plants had already crossed the ocean to Europe: the two *Tagetes*, the beautifully scented *Heliotropum peruvianum* in 1757, *Zinnia elegans* in 1796 and the dahlia from Mexico to Spain c. 1800, but renewed exploration led to a spate of new introductions. In 1822 the Horticultural Society received the brilliant yellow *Calceolaria rugosa* from Chile. In the same year came the scarlet *Salvia splendens* from Mexico. *Petunia nyctaginiflora*, with sweetly-scented white flowers, was introduced from Brazil to France in 1823, and *P. violacea* came to Scotland in 1831. Their meeting in Europe produced a race of hybrid petunias. Also from Brazil came *Begonia semperflorens* in 1829. In 1826 *Verbena chamaedrifolia* (*V. peruviana*) was sent from Buenos Aires to England. In the next decade came *V. incisa* and *V. tweedyi*, parents of the modern hybrid verbenas. Such bright, almost fierce, colours found great popularity, and by 1844 Mrs Loudon reported seeing *V. chamaedrifolia* on every balcony in London.[13]

The idea of plunging tender exotics in the open ground during the summer to recuperate from the rigours imposed by dark, fume-filled greenhouses dates back at least to Philip Miller. Repton suggested regular changes of planting for the vases and baskets in the exotic garden of the Royal Pavilion at Brighton, to maintain perpetual flowering. In 1824 Loudon referred briefly to 'the changeable flower garden',[14] and by 1830 gardeners were rapidly appreciating the dazzling effect of planting exotics in bold masses of one or two colours. Bedding had arrived.

Hortus Veitchii

Plant introduction, plant breeding, plant distribution were major facets of the development of gardens in the nineteenth century and nowhere were these three more successfully combined than in the dynasty founded by John Veitch in 1808, of all nurseries in the nineteenth century the most worthy successor to London and Wise in the seventeenth and Kennedy and Lee in the eighteenth. Born in Scotland, Veitch moved down to Devon and, after working as a landscape gardener, worked for Sir Thomas Acland at Killerton as land agent. In 1832 he moved, with his son James, to Mount Radford, much nearer to Exeter. In 1853 James and his son (also James) acquired Knight and Perry's nursery in King's Road, Chelsea, thus establishing themselves firmly in the capital, and further land was soon acquired at Coombe Wood in Surrey for tree and shrub production, at Langley and at Feltham, Middlesex for fruit. In 1869 Harry James became the main driving force, maintaining and extending the Veitch reputation in all directions, and being knighted for his services, but there was no younger member of the family to continue the family name and in 1914 the stock and land were sold.[15]

In all aspects Veitch shone. Cultivation was of the highest standard. The collections of shrubs, orchids, fruit, seeds, etc. were second to none. Staff trained in the Veitch nurseries were placed in the most prestigious positions in the country. Veitch breeders worked to improve or develop apples, raspberries, begonias, fuchsias, gloxinias, escallonias, hemerocallis and roses. The first man-made orchid hybrid, *Calanthe × dominii*, flowered in 1856 from a cross made by John Dominy, Veitch's leading hybridizer in Exeter.

In plant collecting, too, the nursery was of enormous significance. William Lobb and his younger brother Thomas, born in Cornwall, were their first collectors. In 1840 William Lobb went to Brazil and Chile, sending back large amounts of seed of the monkey puzzler, *Araucaria araucana*, until then a rare plant, and by 1843 Veitch were able to offer it in quantity at £10 per hundred. In 1843 Thomas went to Java and hence to India, Burma, Malaya and Borneo, bringing back a wonderful collection of orchids, tender rhododendrons and other stove plants. In 1845 William returned to Chile, from where he introduced many good garden plants – *Berberis darwinii*, *Cortaderia selloana* (the pampas grass to decorate innumerable Victorian lawns), *Escallonia macrantha* and *Tropaeolum speciosum*, for example – as well as tender plants such as *Sinningia speciosa*, the 'gloxinia' from which Veitch breeders produced an extensive range of hybrids. In 1849 he went to California and reintroduced in quantity several of Douglas's plants. In 1853 he brought back a large amount of seed of the wellingtonia, *Sequoiadendron giganteum*, which made even more impact in English gardens than the already popular monkey puzzle.

In 1859 Richard Pearce was sent to Chile, Peru and Bolivia and introduced the tuberous begonia, the hippeastrum and other fine plants.

The meteoric rise of the Veitch nursery, one of many great establishments of the nineteenth century, symbolizes the scale and excitement of plant cultivation as wave upon wave of new introductions reached our shores and hundreds upon hundreds of new hybrids poured from the trial grounds. The phenomenal range of plants led to a garden revolution as remarkable in its way as the industrial revolution which it paralleled. Indeed, progress in the garden was inextricably linked with progress in the factory.

The industrial revolution and the gardener

In 1830 the Liverpool–Manchester Railway provided the world's first scheduled rail service, using the immortal 'Rocket'. A web of railway lines soon spread across Britain, both creating an enormous demand for more steel and providing a means whereby steel and many other commodities could be carried quickly to any part of the country. Ready availability of steel and its associated technology led not only to bridges, rails and locomotives but to buildings including glasshouses, to reliable boilers and heating pipes, to decorative ironware – arches, seats, flower-baskets – and tools. Budding's mower, patented in 1832, was the most significant of many items of equipment. The small cylinder mower, infinitely more manoeuvrable than a scythe, made it possible to cut around complex-shaped beds or other obstructions in a lawn, thus preparing the way for Victorian elaboration. Smaller machines provided a healthy recreation for gentlemen owners of small gardens, while for larger estates the choice lay between the ultra-modern, steam-driven lawn-mower weighing half a ton and the more traditional horse-drawn version which included in its equipment a set of leather boots to prevent the horse's hooves from damaging the turf.[16]

Another material which developed rapidly in the nineteenth century was glass. In 1832 Lucas Chance's cylinder glass replaced bubble glass. In 1845 glass tax was repealed, and over the next twenty years the price of glass fell to a fifth of its pre-1845 level. In 1851, 300,000 sheets of Chance's cylinder glass were used to clad Joseph Paxton's Great Exhibition building in Hyde Park.

With the twin stimuli of rapid advances in engineering and a torrent of new tender orchids and other spectacular plants to be housed, advances in glasshouse design came rapidly.

Budding's mower, 1832,
simplifying grass cutting
around complex flower beds.

John Loudon made many significant advances in glasshouse design. He extended Sir George Mackenzie's spherical house upwards as an elegant bell for large trees or outwards as a curvilinear lean-to for forcing. Loudon also devised slender glazing bars of iron and suggested, but did not develop, a ridge and furrow glazing system to improve morning and evening light penetration while also strengthening the structure. His inventiveness extended to suggesting a glass promenade encircling London, for winter exercise of its inhabitants, and less detailed plans to encase a whole city within a glass dome with an artificial climate.

W. & D. Bailey, who collaborated with Loudon, built many beautiful glasshouses. Perhaps the most adventurous and exciting house was the conservatory at Bretton Hall, Yorkshire, for Mrs Beaumont. Built in 1827, it spanned 100 feet and was 60 feet high with a roof top ventilator opening discreetly within a gilt coronet.[17] Of similar age but more traditional appearance was Fowler's conservatory erected at Syon Park, London, in 1824.

As the century progressed, many manufacturers produced standard structures for glasshouses designed for a range of purposes, from lofty palm houses to sunken cucumber pits. In many gardens the focal point of the kitchen garden became a substantial glass complex, with ranks of frames subordinate to the main range of glass rising to a stately vinery or palm house in the centre. None could rival the range built for Queen Victoria herself at Windsor. In an attempt to rationalize production for the royal household,

The Glasshouses, Waddesdon Manor, Bucks.

The magnificent range of glass at Waddesdon, from an early postcard.

old-fashioned gardens were closed and, in 1844, a thirty-one-acre walled garden was laid out at Windsor with stoves, pineapple houses, apricot houses, vineries, cherry houses and a variety of structures for asparagus, mushrooms, cucumbers and melons, flowers and decorative pot plants. At the centre of the main range was the head gardener's house, from which he could supervise the 150 gardeners.

For heating, the open fire and flue which created a dry heat suitable for introductions from the Cape in the eighteenth century gradually gave way to steam and hot water. From the 1820s hot water heating became more and more widespread and, with the realization that heated water would rise to create a current, four-inch iron pipes sloping gently up from the boiler and back to the boiler carrying hot water through the glasshouse became the standard method of heating from the mid nineteenth century. Pipes usually ran in conduits below the floor, topped by elegant cast-iron gratings so that they could be damped frequently, creating ideal hot humid conditions for the tropical orchids and other tender exotics around which the nineteenth-century gardener's life revolved.

The scientific garden

The general climate of research and investigation in sciences and industry prevailed, too, in the world of plants. The Horticultural Society served as a focus for exchange of ideas on plant physiology, glasshouse design, breeding, variety trials, rootstocks and other aspects of scientific horticulture. Interest was apparent, too, in the new lease of life given to the botanic gardens.

Edinburgh Botanic Garden, which had moved from Holyrood to a five-acre site in Haddington Place in 1763, moved again in 1823 to occupy fourteen acres of the Inverleith estate at Broom Park. James McNab, a principal gardener at Edinburgh, devised a machine for transplanting large trees, and for many months the garden's mature trees moved through the Edinburgh streets drawn by teams of horses.

Cambridge Botanic Garden, founded in 1761, moved in 1831 from a five-acre site in the centre of the city to its present forty-acre site and, after a slow start, planting began in earnest in 1846.

Oxford, too, took on a new lease of life with the appointment, in 1834, of Charles Daubeny as Professor of Botany. He raised money to build a laboratory and rebuild the glasshouses, and established at Oxford the basis of experimental botany. To signify the new role of the garden its name was changed from the Oxford Physic Garden to Oxford Botanic Garden in 1840, in which year Daubeny also laid out plots to study the mineral requirements of plants. This inspired one of his pupils, John Bennet Lawes, to found his own agricultural experimental station at Rothamsted, Hertfordshire, in 1843.[18]

Kew was neglected as a botanic garden after the death of Joseph Banks and for a time the Government contemplated its abolition, but in 1841 the garden was transferred from the Crown to the State, with Sir William Hooker as its first Director. The garden expanded rapidly from fifteen acres in 1841 to 250 in 1846. In 1844 the great Palm House was begun, with Decimus Burton as architect and Richard Turner, proprietor of a major ironworks, as engineer. In 1845 the four-and-a-half-acre lake was dug, providing material for paths and mounds as well as a body of water, and in 1848 the Museum of Economic Botany was opened. In that same year Joseph Hooker, Sir William's son and eventual successor as Director, left England for China. His introductions in the years 1848–51 included forty-three rhododendrons, many of them scarcely hardy but of brilliant colouring. Seed was distributed from Kew to gardens and nurseries throughout the kingdom.

Art or Nature?

The influx of plants and their rapid improvement by breeders, the products of manufacture, the ability to transport plants, manu-factures and building materials by rail, scientific and technical advances in the cultivation of plants – all these changes expanded enormously the palette of the landscape gardener and the craft of the gardener, but what of the garden's design?

Repton and Loudon bequeathed their successors an increasingly burdensome dilemma by making a distinction between Art and Nature. Repton himself had no difficulty accepting the eighteenth-century view of Nature as an imperfect specimen to be corrected by man in the park, and he drew freely on the natural world to adorn his Art in the flower garden. Loudon, too, saw Nature as a raw material. He could hardly wait to see the impressive but un-tidy hills of the Lake District covered in elegant villas.[19] Their successors, though, were increasingly troubled by the notion that a garden, as a work of Art, should not be an imitation of Nature.

One escape from the dilemma was to use plants which in them-selves looked unnatural in Britain: the spectacular exotics pouring in from the Empire and the fastigiate, weeping, contorted, crested, variegated or grafted standard plants readily available from the burgeoning nursery trade. Bedding plants, especially, with their brilliant colours arranged in geometrical arrays, could never be accused of imitating nature and, as the nineteenth century advanced and the thirst for exotic novelty increased, more and more elaborate forms of bedding were devised.

Hardy annuals from North America, many introduced by Douglas, were used first in the 'changeable flower garden' but, with the introduction of the more durable and more spectacular half-hardy plants from South America, hardy annuals soon lost favour. With the emphasis on contrast in Art, as distinct from harmony in Nature, bright colours were eagerly sought after and the less adventurous gardeners soon settled into a routine with concentric circles of purple heliotrope, yellow calceolaria and scarlet salvias or geraniums.

By the late 1860s the idea of carpet-bedding evolved, using dwarf subtropical and succulent plants with purple, yellow, green, grey and crimson foliage massed and clipped into elaborate patterns. In 1868 John Fleming used such plants at Cliveden to creat a mono-gram of the initials HS for his employer, Harriet, Duchess of Sutherland, and his technique was rapidly adopted for making abstract patterns.[20] In 1875 George Thomson, superintendent of the

*Carpet bed at Kew (*Gardener's Chronicle, *1870).*

Crystal Palace Park, planted a series of six huge beds each shaped and realistically coloured to represent a different species of butterfly.[21]

The more extreme examples of carpet-bedding were denounced in the gardening press in much the same tone as Bacon had dismissed knots of coloured earths 250 years earlier, but the gardeners and their urban audience took great delight in these 'childish toys'.

Another method of tackling the dilemma between Art and Nature was to retreat into history and to seek inspiration from what had long been recognized as gardens and must therefore be counted as Art. Loudon's *Encyclopaedia of Gardening*, in 1826, was the first authoritative account of garden history. His descriptions of a succession of historical styles of gardening, each suited to its period, was plagiarized by landscape gardeners to yield a rich catalogue of stylistic options.

John Hughes[22] was typical in recognizing two major styles: the 'Ancient or Geometric' including Italian, Dutch and French, and the 'Modern or Natural' including Rural, Gardenesque and Picturesque. However, as the Natural could not really be natural, and the Rural/Picturesque gardens were known to have included elements which were themselves classical (Palladian temples and bridges), exotic (Indian, Chinese and Turkish tents and seats) or primitive (Gothic and rustic features), practitioners were soon enmeshed in a maelstrom of styles. French, Italian, Dutch, Egyptian, Greek, Hindu, Chinese, Turkish, Tudor, Jacobean, Swiss, Gothic,

Bedding at Blickling.

Rustic and Prehistoric were discovered, rediscovered and revived in a whirlwind of fantasy.

The potential hazard of unlimited opportunity was highlighted early in the nineteenth century in the controversial garden of Alton Towers in Staffordshire.[23] In 1814 Charles Talbot, 15th Earl of Shrewsbury, began to embellish his ancestral home. The house was encased in a huge shell of mock fortifications. A lake was added, the waters held by a mock bridge designed by J. B. Papworth, and the valley below the house was studded with features ancient and modern: Stonehenge, a Chinese temple, a pagoda spouting water from its peak, arbours and statues, bridges, temples classical and Indian, flower-baskets, rockwork, moss-houses, cottages and seats. The Earl died in 1826. His son tried to unify parts of the garden by removing many of the smaller features but he, too, made his own additions: the monument to his father, conservatories and a box and gravel knot designed by Nesfield in the form of a giant S. He also commissioned A. W. Pugin to alter the house in the new Gothic taste. Loudon was appalled by the 15th Earl's handiwork – a work of morbid imagination joined to the command of vast resources. He also disapproved of the 16th Earl's alterations 'because no trifling alteration can ever improve what is so far out of the reach of reason', but by the 1840s the Earl's gardener provided his own solution. The landscape was filled with trees, rhododendrons and other shrubs, heathers and rockwork absorbing the architectural features into an increasingly picturesque jungle.

The only redeeming features of Alton Towers were its scale and the dramatic impact of the individual features, many designed by the leading practitioners of the day. It carried a portent, however, of what could happen when every small garden could be embellished by every feature of Alton Towers, mass-produced, miniaturized and scattered across the suburban lawn.

For the architect, the choice of style and the decision to be 'pure' or 'derivative' were serious matters. Thomas Hopper considered 'it is the architect's business to understand all the styles and to be prejudiced in favour of none'.[24] Hopper's Penrhyn Castle in Gwynedd (1827) was solidly Norman, while in Buckinghamshire Cliveden (1850) was an Italian villa, Waddesdon (1874) a weighty French château and Ascott (also 1874) a rambling Tudor house with French terraces and a Dutch flower garden.

Landscape with flowers

For the landscape gardener the choice was less momentous. There was scope for more than one style. Documentary evidence for the form of older gardens was at best fragmentary, so interpretation could be fairly liberal. As for the contents, there was a common belief that the ancients would have used modern plants if they had had the opportunity, so there was an entirely free hand. The dilemma for the landscape gardener was often eased, too, by the existence of an eighteenth-century landscape park. In such instances he could sensibly appropriate a portion of the all-too-abundant foreground to practise his art, leaving the background of lakes, hills and woods to display the beauties of Nature – as Repton had done on many occasions.

At Clumber Park, Nottinghamshire, William Sawrey Gilpin (nephew of the 'Picturesque' William Gilpin and an eminent landscape gardener), lamenting the lack of separation between house and park, designed an expansive double terrace ornamented with vases, fountains and parterres.[25] Gilpin also created the terraces at Sudbury Hall, Derbyshire,[26] and planted pines in picturesque groups to frame views from the new terrace at Nuneham, Oxfordshire.

Whether the excuse for this new formality was French, Italian, Dutch or Old English (modelled on Haddon Hall, Montacute and other survivors from Elizabethan England), it provided great scope for bedding in all its forms, and great flower-filled parterres of elaborately patterned beds became an essential feature of every garden. Ernest Field, gardener to Alfred de Rothschild at Halton, Buckinghamshire, 'once heard it said that rich people used to show their wealth by the size of their bedding plant list: ten thousand for a squire, twenty for a baronet, thirty for an earl and forty for a duke'.[27] Rothschild had 41,000.

As the interest in historical styles extended from the relatively modern French and Italian to the older, and native, Jacobean, Elizabethan, early Tudor and medieval, so other garden features were revived. Mazes were made in several gardens: Glendurgan, Cornwall, in 1839, Hatfield (the most notable survivor) in 1841, and Somerleyton, Norfolk, c. 1850 for example. Topiary also increased gradually in popularity, mainly in the form of shaped hedges, balls and finials. Topiary specimens in the truly Old English garden of Levens Hall were restored and added to from 1810 to 1862. The Moorish and other exotic gardens at Elvaston Castle in Derbyshire relied heavily on hedges and architecturally shaped greens in the 1840s, and in the West Midlands Packwood's 'Sermon on the Mount' was planted in the following decade. It was towards the end of the century, though, that more elaborate topiary became very popular, both in the High Victorian garden (where it was considered essentially Dutch) and in the Old English garden which developed as a reaction against Victorian excesses. In High Victorian gardens the topiary was often elaborate but purely geometrical, with variegated hollies and golden yew literally outshining the duller greens. In the Old English gardens topiary was often representative – peacocks, other animals, orbs and other objects – and in dull green yew or box.

The rock garden

A feature which became immensely popular in the nineteenth century, and which was considered, rather remarkably, to straddle the divide between Art and Nature, was the rock garden.

Early rock gardens evolved from classical grottoes such as Pope's grotto at Twickenham, and the complex of caves and arches at Painshill, Stourhead and Stowe. Later an interest in mineralogy led to the collection of rock specimens and sometimes to their arrangement, literally, as a rock garden. In the 1780s William Forsyth used minerals (many brought back by Banks from Iceland) for their geological interest in the Chelsea Physic Garden.[28] The development of the Picturesque led to a third phase of rockwork, using rocks to roughen the surface of the landscape and to simulate

Rockwork at Hoole House, from the centre of the Flower-garden.

Lady Broughton's rock garden at Hoole House.

rocky pinnacles and bluffs. Repton's rock-strewn valley at Sezin-cote is an early example of such rockwork, and Sir Matthew Digby Wyatt's gloomy valley and tunnel at Ashridge in 1851 (suggested originally by Repton) is an extreme one. At Elvaston William Barron moved large rocks just as he moved large trees, and piled many thousands of tons of rock up into a spectacular picturesque feature.

Loudon considered that because rocks were usually imported to make a rock garden it was exotic and therefore Art. Many rock gardens were made on lawns and in view of the house, but as the attempts at realism became more successful or native rock was exposed by excavation, the rock garden was seen more and more as a work of Nature and removed from the house. Sometimes the naturalism verged on mimicry. Lady Broughton's rockery at Hoole House in Cheshire, constructed at the end of the main lawn in 1838 and greatly admired by Loudon, was a scale model of the Savoie and the valley of Chamonix.[29]

Rock-garden construction advanced rapidly after 1849, the year in which Edward Cooke first visited Biddulph Grange in Stafford-shire to advise James Bateman on the design of his garden.[30]

Bateman was an authority on tropical fruits and orchids. His immense *Orchidaceae of Mexico and Guatemala*, issued in parts from 1837–43, is one of the rarest books (and is the heaviest) in the RHS Lindley Library.[31] Edward Cooke started his career at the age of nine, in 1810, drawing exotic plants in the Hackney nursery of Loddiges, and later married Jane Loddiges. Cooke was a typical Victorian, passionately interested in all aspects of natural history and scientific advance; his two abiding interests were plants and ships. In addition to his painstaking delineation of ship's gear, he made detailed studies of coastal rock formations, wielding both his brush and his geologist's hammer. He was made an RA for his paintings and an FRS for his geological studies, as well as being a Fellow of the Linnaean and Zoological Societies. At Redleaf, near Groombridge, Cooke first applied his diverse talents to gardening for William Wells, exposing the remarkable rock formations of Sussex sandstone, and this accumulated experience was employed for nearly twenty years at Biddulph Grange. The rockwork, planned with the aid of clay models, combined geological accuracy, picturesque effect and dramatic inventiveness with concealed flights of steps, rocky arches to frame views and high cliffs to separate the various areas of the garden.

Another major advance at Biddulph Grange, marking the fourth stage of rock gardening, was the planning of the garden to provide a range of habitats for plants. Hitherto there had been an interest in rock gardens for scenic effect and in alpine plants, usually grown in pots, but the Biddulph rockwork was realistically clothed in bilberry, gaultheria, junipers, dwarf bulbs, ferns and other plants which flourished on the rocky ledges or shaded crevices.

In the late 1850s the York nursery of James Backhouse began to specialize in alpine plants and in the construction of picturesque rockwork, so it became possible to buy a rock garden and its plants in much the same way as one might buy a conservatory or garden seat, without engaging a geological artist.

Where supplies of local stone or the resources to move stone over long distances were lacking, a cheaper alternative became available from 1848 when James Pulham started his business in Broxbourne making Pulhamite stone. Pulham's father, also James, was a pioneer in the manufacture of Portland cement and developed a method of simulating stonework by heaping up brick rubble, pouring over cement and moulding the material, as it was hardening, into astonishingly realistic stratified masses.

As the rock garden took on a more studied geological accuracy it moved from the realm of Art to the realm of Nature, and increasingly the rock garden was built at a distance from the house, ideally in a secluded dell.

Chatsworth ne plus ultra

During the nineteenth century the majority of older parks were embellished by terraces and other formal features around the house. New estates were also designed on a similar pattern: geometry within the balustrade, serpentine curves beyond. Thus Art and Nature coexisted. Where the gardener inherited not only a Capability Brown park but also the substantial remains of earlier formal gardens, the ageing rhetoric of Art *versus* Nature evaporated in the face of unlimited opportunity. Such was the case with the most influential of all Victorian gardens, Chatsworth.

The story of Joseph Paxton's career at Chatsworth is well known[32] but bears retelling. Born in 1803, he was admitted to the Horticultural Society's new garden at Chiswick as a trainee and was soon promoted to under-gardener in the arboretum. Here he came to the notice of the Duke of Devonshire, from whom the garden was leased and who had a private door into the garden from Chiswick House. When, in 1826, the Duke needed a gardener at Chatsworth he offered the post to Paxton, who readily accepted.

The Great Conservatory at Chatsworth. The figure right of centre gives some idea of the huge scale of Paxton's glasshouse.

I left London by the Comet coach for Chesterfield, and arrived at Chatsworth at half past 4 o'clock in the morning of the 9th of May, 1826. As no person was to be seen at that early hour I got over the greenhouse gates by the old covered way, explored the pleasure ground, and looked around the outside of the house. I then went down to the kitchen garden, scaled the outside wall, and saw the whole of the place, set the men to work there at 6 o'clock, then returned to Chatsworth, and got Thomas Weldon to play me the water works, and afterwards went to breakfast with poor dear Mrs Gregory [the housekeeper] and her niece; the latter fell in love with me, and I with her, and thus completed my first morning's work at Chatsworth before 9 o'clock.[33]

Paxton married the niece, Sarah Brown, the following year. Sarah Paxton played an increasing role in managing her husband's affairs at Chatsworth while he travelled with the Duke, to Russia, to Europe and frequently to London, and later to meetings connected with his own involvement in railways and public parks as well as in the design of houses and gardens.

Chatsworth was already noted for the substantial remains of a splendid seventeenth-century garden set in a Capability Brown park, and much of Paxton's early work was directed at bringing the existing gardens up to an acceptable standard. Aucubas and laurels, cedars and monkey-puzzlers were planted in quantity. Portugal laurels in tubs were clipped into formal shapes to simulate the bay trees and oranges of more southern climes, in order to give a suitably classical air to the long terrace. In 1829 newly introduced 'Douglas pines' (Douglas firs) travelled from London as seedlings in Paxton's hat. By 1845 they were 35 feet high. The great cascade was restored and partly rebuilt to correct the alignment.

Then the expansion began. In 1835 an arboretum was created, its cost more than recouped in timber sold from the wooded site. In 1836 work began on the Great Conservatory, in which Paxton adapted Loudon's ridge-and-furrow principle to a curvilinear glass-house. Four years later it was complete: an acre of tropical paradise through which a coach and horses could be driven. In 1842 Paxton began the stupendous rockwork at Chatsworth. Partly imitating local scenery, partly artificial, the rockwork encompassed an immense 'ruined' aqueduct from which water fell 80 feet to supply the restored cascade. The Wellington Rock, 40 feet high, also featured a waterfall. On a smaller scale, Paxton also rebuilt the weeping willow fountain, replacing the seventeenth-century original. From a reservoir high in the hillside Paxton created the Emperor Fountain, planned for the abortive visit of the Tsar in

1843 and the highest fountain in Europe. Perhaps his greatest triumph was the flowering of *Victoria regia* in 1849. The giant waterlily was first discovered in the Amazon in 1836. Seed was sent to Kew and plants were raised in 1849. Paxton obtained one of the seedlings and built a special glasshouse for it with an uninterrupted span of 62 feet by 47 feet. In the centre was a tank 33 feet in diameter, heated to 85°F and stirred by a little wooden paddle wheel to create just the sluggish movement which Paxton calculated would be experienced in the Amazon River itself. It was the giant waterlily and its Chatsworth home which stimulated Paxton's scheme for the Great Exhibition Building of 1851, for which he was awarded a knighthood.

During Paxton's life thousands of visitors flocked to Chatsworth each year. Even more visited the 1851 Exhibition and its successor at Sydenham. His books and magazines spread his ideas to gardeners too poor or too distant to visit either. Paxton, more than any other single person, characterizes the Victorian gardener, and Chatsworth, more than any other garden, demonstrated what could be achieved when botany, science, technology, art and wealthy patronage were combined.

The Italianate garden

Many of the other notable gardens of the age were designed not by gardeners but by architects, the most successful of whom was Sir Charles Barry. Barry represented the classical school of architecture, although when the design competition for the new Houses of Parliament stipulated that it should be Gothic he was not averse to dressing up his classical building in Gothic pinnacles, with the able assistance of Pugin. When the Duke of Sutherland summoned Barry to Trentham, just outside Stoke, to enlarge and modernize his seat, Barry resorted to an elaborate 'adaptation' of Palladian architecture. The garden presented a problem. It was virtually flat and very cold. Barry transformed the almost imperceptible slope into two vast terraces, separated by only a few shallow steps. With much gravel, balustrading, statuary, a central circular fountain and, as at Chatsworth, clipped laurels replacing Italian orange trees, he created a magnificent 'Italian' garden extending from the mansion to adjoin the formalized edge of the lake.

Trentham's glory was short-lived. The industrial wealth of the Potteries which enriched the Duke of Sutherland so fouled the air and polluted the river that the house was eventually abandoned.

Barry went on to redesign Dunrobin, on the Sutherlands' shooting estate in Scotland, and in 1849 Cliveden, their residence conveniently situated for London and on a site more propitious for Italian garden-making. At Harewood, Yorkshire, Barry also designed elaborate terraces overlooking the eighteenth-century lake, but his most admired work, after Trentham, and Barry's own favourite, was Shrubland Park, Suffolk, for Sir William Middleton. The house stood on a 70-foot-high escarpment which Barry carved into a series of terraces. The main terrace, a string of elaborate gardens nearly a mile long, was connected to the upper level by an immense staircase bordered by pots of scarlet pelargoniums and edged in clipped box, which sloped up to emphasize the pinnacles of new conifers substituting for Italian cypress. The focal point of the main terrace was a semicircular parterre of yew, turf, silver sand and flowers in elaborate scrollwork.

Barry's immediate success at Trentham established 'Italian' as the most characteristic style in Victorian gardens. It was a style which found favour equally with the patron, who could ostentatiously display his wealth and good taste, the architect, who could display his classical learning and geometrical inventiveness, and the gardener, who found, in the large, level terraces, the ideal site for

Barry's immense Italianate terrace at Trentham.

exuberant displays of plants, the bedding schemes described earlier in the chapter.

Philip Frost, head gardener at Dropmore, near Cliveden in Buckinghamshire, is often accredited as the 'inventor' of bedding[34] and Joseph Paxton with being its Henry Ford, perfecting and systematizing the mass production of bedding plants. But John Fleming also played a major role. Fleming was head gardener at Trentham when Barry wrought its transformation, and soon became famed for the quality and originality of his bedding schemes. He assisted Barry, too, with the planting of the terrace at Harewood. When the Sutherlands left Trentham for the sweeter air of the Thames Valley in 1849, Fleming went with them to Cliveden, thus becoming a near neighbour of Philip Frost at Dropmore.

At Cliveden, Barry superimposed his Italian villa on the ancient terrace and designed the great parterre below the house, which Fleming filled with a succession of carefully recorded schemes. Each bed was edged with privet or spruce clipped 8 inches high and 9 inches wide. Each bed was over 80 yards round the outer edge and was planted with rhododendrons in the centre. It required 2,000 plants 'to fill the beds moderately'.[35]

The problem with bedding . . .

Fleming, though, identified a major weakness in even the best devised bedding schemes.

No one can deny that a well-filled flower garden, with a bright season, is very beautiful. It is, however, soon over; and then comes a much longer space, with nothing to look upon but the bare soil of the beds, in bad contrast often times, with the beautiful green sward with which they are surrounded.

If no provision is made for the garden in spring, which is generally the case, we frequently find at the end of the dull winter months fine midday weather, which is a strong inducement to extend and prolong to the fields and wood the casual walks of the past dull months. Many little flowers are then beginning to peep from every sheltered corner; and long before the garden is attractive, many rustic spots are studded with beautiful little flowers and bright colours. The garden is, in most instances, the point from which the walk begins and ends, and it generally fares but indifferently by comparison. Why then should we not in this matter take a lesson from nature? and if flowers at that season bloom in the fields and woods, they can also be made to bloom in the garden.[36]

VIEW OF THE GREAT FLOWER GARDEN AT CLIVEDEN FROM THE MANSION.

THE GREAT GARDEN.—PLAN NO. 2.

Plan No. 2, that accompanies this, is a part of the flower garden in front of the mansion, and contains 3 acres, 2 roods, and 10 poles. It was figured in a highly-coloured plate given in "The Journal of Horticulture and Cottage Gardener" for July, 1862.

That season some of the beds were planted in chains of colour formed by the plant; others in a strip of colour taken down the bed in a separate form, dividing it into ovals, each of which was filled alternately with a different colour. The following is the planting for the season of 1862 :—

No. 1 bed, mixed Anemone and yellow Jonquil; centre chain, Silene pendula and yellow Tulip.

2, blue Myosotis; chain, white Myosotis.

3, white Silene; chain, pink Silene, with Tournesol Tulip.

4, blue Myosotis and La Candeur Tulip.

5, all pink Silene and Rex Rubrorum Tulip.

6, Limnanthes Douglassii; chain, blue and white Myosotis and mixed Tulips.

7, mixed Anemone; chain, pink Silene.

8, blue Myosotis and yellow Rose Tulip; chain, white Myosotis.

This arrangement, although very pretty and neat, was found to diminish the grand effect pro-

The Great Flower Garden at Cliveden with notes on its planting scheme by John Fleming.

Fleming filled his Great Garden with anemones and wallflowers, arabis, alyssum and daisies, forget-me-nots and pansies, tulips, hyacinths and narcissus, with permanent edgings of crocus. The Duke's garden had forty beds similarly planted among spring-flowering shrubs, and

> In another part of the ground is a ribbon made to wind round a group of Evergreen Oaks, with at open places bows and ties, having the appearance of binding them together. It is 2 feet wide and upwards of 300 yards long. There is difficulty at all times in getting this perfect, from a portion being under the drip of the trees . . .[37]

In 1863 it was filled with white forget-me-nots and 'Cliveden Blue' pansy.

Fleming also referred to the established practice of winter bedding (using evergreens plunged in their pots), and to the difficulties of preventing such schemes looking like nursery-yards.

Another method of introducing colour in the winter garden, noted but not commended by Fleming, was the use of coloured minerals, a technique known in Francis Bacon's time but revived especially by William Andrews Nesfield. Nesfield retired from the army to become a successful watercolourist but became interested in gardens. In 1826 his sister married Anthony Salvin, the architect of many picturesque country houses, and Nesfield launched on a career as a landscape gardener of the Italian school. His garden at Grimston, Yorkshire, included an Emperor's Walk flanked by busts of the Caesars, but he was more noted for his elaborate 'Italian' parterres, some copied directly from French pattern-books. In the plainer examples the gardeners were able to fill the box-edged beds with flowers. More often they were of green only, and in the most elaborate scrollwork, plants were too fickle to be admitted. The pattern was drawn with coloured minerals or painted on the gravel. Eaton Hall, in Cheshire, was Nesfield's most notable example. Here 'the scrolls run out to great length, and are, in many places, not six inches wide!! nay, even less than that. This struck us as rather bordering upon the ridiculous.'[38] At Kew his parterres around the new Palm House were not implemented, although the terrace, the formalized edge of the basin and the *patte d'oie* of radiating vistas survive.

Nesfield's designs, published in 1860, for the new gardens of the Horticultural Society at Kensington, one of the last enthusiasms of the Prince Consort, were so heavily architectural that there was very little room for plants and the cost of the garden seriously impaired the Society's finances.[39] The Society terminated its lease at Kensington in 1882 and removed entirely from Kensington to Westminster in 1888.

History at large

Throughout the country, houses and gardens were being enlarged and modernized. At Montacute, Somerset, the Tudor mount was removed to make way for a new 'Elizabethan' garden! At Lyme Park, Cheshire, Lord Newton created the impressive 'Dutch' garden below Wyatt's orangery. At Wrest Park, Bedfordshire, the Earl de Grey designed his own house, a perfect and restrained French château, and added a magnificent parterre to supplement the seventeenth-century canal which Lancelot Brown had earlier been ordered to leave untouched. With family fortunes restored by the 7th Earl, later 1st Marquess of Salisbury, the great house at Hatfield was 'restored' in the Jacobean style, the terraced gardens extended into the landscaped park and, in 1841, the famous maze was planted. At nearby Knebworth the remaining wing of the original Tudor brick quadrangle erupted in stuccoed turrets and battlements overlooking a sunken parterre.

Later in the century a localized flurry of activity broke out in Buckinghamshire as a new aristocracy, the Rothschilds, established themselves in spectacular country seats. On the death of her husband, Mrs Nathan Rothschild moved from Gunnersbury Park, which was inherited by her son Lionel, to the Vale of Aylesbury. Her youngest son Mayer followed, and commissioned Joseph Paxton to build Mentmore Towers. Baron Anthony de Rothschild moved to Aston Clinton, and Lionel then acquired Tring Manor (a Wren house in a 3,500-acre park), Halton and finally Ascott.

Halton has been described as 'an exaggerated nightmare of gorgeousness and senseless and ill-applied magnificence'.[40] Ascott was much more modest – a hunting lodge on the Mentmore estate. The original farmhouse was encased in a long, discreet, half-timbered house set on grassy terraces. The gardens were designed and made by the Veitch nurseries (and almost certainly designed by Sir Harry Veitch personally). As the house was used mainly during the winter it had many evergreens, including a large sundial clipped in box, but a sheltered Madeira Walk and the enclosed Dutch Garden provided flowers to relieve the solemnity.

In 1874, the year in which work on Ascott began, Lionel's son-in-law Ferdinand bought 2,700 acres in Buckinghamshire from the Duke of Marlborough and began an entirely new house, Waddes-

Carving the hill top at Waddesdon into a garden.

don, on the windy summit of Lodge Hill. The top of the hill was sliced off (an average of nearly ten feet over ten acres), a steam tramway was built for fourteen miles to bring building materials from the nearest railway, and Waddesdon Manor arose. Mature oaks were moved to make the avenues, drawn from the surrounding countryside on Barron transplanting machines by teams of ten Percheron horses imported from France (as was the landscape gardener, Lavine). The formal gardens were relatively limited in extent, giving way to rolling greensward and winding paths, but the whole estate was richly planted and embellished. The rockwork marking the approach to the house initially housed a group of deer or mountain sheep, but the smell of the animals in a hot summer was too much for polite society and the animals were removed to the park.

Despite the enormous changes during the Victorian era, the spectacularly splendid gardens described thus far differed only in degree – and not in kind – from the gardens of Humphry Repton. Nowhere is this more clearly seen than at Tatton Park, where Repton was consulted in 1791 and Paxton in 1856. The lightness of Repton's arbours and flower-beds was replaced by the massive

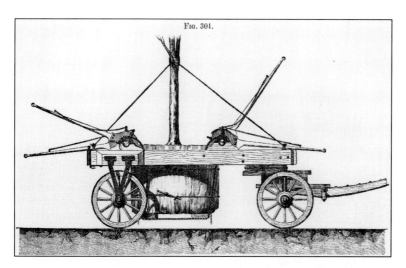

Fig. 301.

Tree-moving equipment for an instant landscape.

splendour of Paxton's balustraded parterre, but the basic organization of the garden was unaltered: artistic geometry and flowers near the house, natural beauty beyond the balustrade.

The inner garden

Few gardens broke with the convention of the house and its terraces commanding views over parkland to distant prospects. Of these few the most influential by far were Elvaston Castle, Derbyshire, and Biddulph Grange, Staffordshire. Both gardens were compartmentalized, like many others, but they looked inwards on themselves rather than outwards to distant prospects.

At Elvaston the introspection was symbolic. The Earl of Harrington scandalized society by living openly with his mistress, an actress. The two married, retired to Elvaston and lived in total isolation from the outside world. The garden became famous as a shrine of romantic love but was virtually unvisited until the Earl's death in 1851. Its fame rested partly on the reputation of its head gardener, William Barron. When called upon to create a new garden on inhospitable soil, Barron spent four years trenching and draining the ground then devised techniques for moving mature trees over long distances.[41] Multi-ranked avenues of coniferous trees were another Barron trademark. Monkey puzzle, noble fir and cryptomeria lined one avenue, with an inner row of cedars (Lebanon and deodar) and finally pines, spruces, firs and hemlock within. The pinetum was immense but the remarkable features which set Elvaston aside from other gardens were the four hedged enclosures drawing on all the imagery of chivalry and chaste love. Moorish patterns, lovers' knots, rose-bowers and statuary, including the Earl kneeling before his love, were interspersed with new exotics.

At Biddulph the separation from the outside world was not for social but for climatic reasons. James Bateman moved from his father's home at Knypersley Hall to Biddulph Grange in 1842. His reputation as a collector and cultivator of plants, especially orchids, was already considerable. Biddulph was on a high and windswept site, but Bateman and Edward Cooke combined to create a garden in which hedges and the outer defences of a pinetum and arboretum

Biddulph Grange, with numerous compartments connected by tunnels, galleries and rockwork.

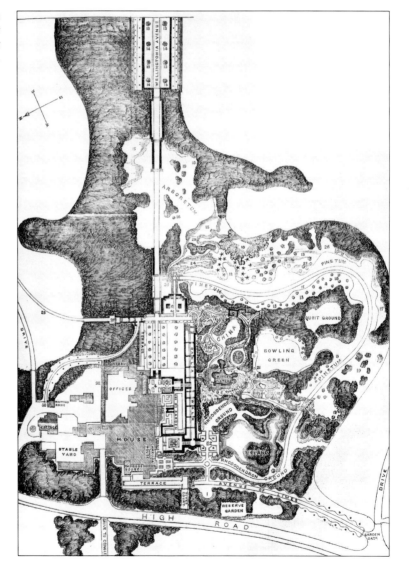

*'Egypt' at Biddulph Grange,
connecting the Pinetum and the
Dahlia Walk.*

provided shelter for a series of garden compartments. Each com-
partment was complete in itself, and the links between one garden
and the next were brilliantly contrived to ensure the separation. A
gap in the rockwork, a stone tunnel, led to China. Another tunnel,
a cunning flight of steps and the visitor was in the quiet green of
the pinetum. The Cheshire Cottage at the end of the pinetum
became, on entry, a dark tomb from which one emerged into
Egypt. It was fantastic, it was historic and exotic, and for Bateman
it provided the sheltered niches for the cultivation of a huge range
of plants.

Elvaston Castle and Biddulph Grange, both brought to public
notice by long descriptions in the *Gardener's Chronicle* in the 1850s,
were compelling examples of what could be achieved in gardens
without recourse to distant vistas. Both were extraordinary gardens,
successful only because they were made by people of considerable
discernment. The stone frogs, bulls and dragons at Biddulph were
the work of outstanding sculptors. (Cooke was working simultaneously at Sydenham, where prehistoric monsters and other

Wimbledon House, a Chatsworth in miniature.

animals were being carved for Paxton's gardens. He commissioned the carvings for Biddulph and was himself a distinguished artist.) In less skilled hands both gardens could have been ludicrous – and into less skilled hands the examples fell.

What changed fundamentally during the nineteenth century was not the style of the large, professionally designed gardens but the evolution of an entirely new type of garden, Loudon's 'Suburban Garden'. In 1800 there were 10 million people in England and Wales. By 1850 there were 20 million and by 1900, 40 million. The majority lived in or clustered around towns. Far too many were crowded in back-to-back houses in hideous conditions, but the more fortunate had substantial villas and ample gardens, the gardens classified by Loudon as First Rate (10 acres plus), Second Rate (2–10 acres), Third Rate (1–2 acres) or Fourth Rate (1 perch to 1 acre).[42]

Amateurs unlimited

For the owners of such gardens there was no recourse to a Capability Brown, Humphry Repton or Sir Charles Barry. Instead they turned for inspiration to the nurseries, to books and to the new periodicals.

For the technical aspects of gardening there was no shortage of information. Vegetables, dahlias, roses, pineapples, orchids, grapes, trees and flowers each had detailed and informative manuals. There was no shortage, either, of advice on artistic aspects, but this was not always so helpful to the beginner. Edward Kemp (Paxton's assistant at Birkenhead Park and subsequently superintendent there), for example, divided his *How to Lay Out a Garden* into four parts; the two central parts being 'What to Avoid' and 'What to Attain'. To be avoided were, essentially, bad taste, undue plainness and excess. Included in the last were: 8. Too great a Mixture of Styles; 9. Unsuitable Decorations; 10. Tricks for Surprising People; 11. All kinds of Eccentricity: every sort of Sham. To be attained were simplicity, intricacy, convenience, unity and congruity, richness and polish, originality and freshness.

Of course, to steer a path between avoidance of eccentricity and attainment of originality was a delicate matter, on which Kemp offered helpful advice:

> The scenes of nature are continually sought, because, while they are 'ever charming', they are likewise 'ever *new*'. And a garden should be made to combine some little freshness, – something that will distinguish it from other gardens. Departure from rule is not, it will be readily believed, the kind of originality to be desired.
>
> Originality is antagonistic to all sorts of tameness. Even a slight deviation from established laws will often be preferable to their dull and expressionless embodiment, though such a course cannot at all be allowed to be necessary.[43]

Amid the generalities, Kemp advised attempting originality by seizing on the peculiarities of the site (consulting the genius of the place), by growing what others do not and by perhaps specializing in particular groups of plants.

J. A. Hughes, in *Garden Architecture and Landscape Gardening*, reduced his advice to one golden rule, 'If a thing looks wrong, it is wrong.'[44] He then proceeded, amid many diagrams of steps, balustrades, finials, and other details, to explain what he considered to be 'wrong'.

Not surprisingly the majority of garden owners adapted what they saw around them in the larger gardens and public parks, and seized upon the more tangible offerings of the books and magazines: the seats, statues, remarkable trees and conspicuous flower beds. Every garden became a miniature Alton Towers, Chatsworth and Biddulph Grange combined: a parterre or two decorated with statuary and urns surrounded by a landscape of tortuous paths through pineta, ferneries, rockeries and shrubberies, richly embellished with every product of rustic work and cast iron from innumerable catalogues. Many skeletons of such gardens remain, much overshadowed by the more tenacious evergreens. It is evident from such remains and from innumerable contemporary illustrations that many suburban gardens were ingeniously planned and attractively planted, if a little rich for modern taste.

However, the temptation to collect was considerable, and the misinterpretation of Loudon's 'Gardenesque' encouraged a uniform scatter of plants and objects. The *structure* of the garden, the distinction between open space and the masses of hills, trees, evergreen shrubbery or walls, and the overlay of decorative planting which had been the characteristic of all designed landscapes ancient and modern, atrophied. The typical suburban garden became an amorphous collection of excessively decorative objects. In this respect little has changed in a hundred years.

As the century passed its zenith, those who cared about design fought a rearguard action against the tidal wave of garden-making by accretion and then, in frustration, turned angrily on each other.

9
The Battle of Styles

The most renowned protagonist in the battle of garden styles, which finally came to a head in 1892, was William Robinson. In 1861 Robinson left the garden of Ballykilkavan, some twenty-five miles outside Dublin, and sailed for England. There he obtained a post in the Royal Botanic Society's garden in Regent's Park, under the designer and curator of the garden, Robert Marnock. As he was responsible for the maintenance of the native plant collection, Robinson travelled widely through Britain and took obvious delight not only in wild flowers but in the endemic cottage gardens, charming and unaffected mixtures of fruit trees, vegetables and simple, hardy flowers.

A wild gardener

In 1867 Robinson went to Paris as agent for the Veitch nurseries and horticultural correspondent for *The Times*, to report on the Paris Exhibition. His *Gleanings from French Gardens* appeared in 1868, and the weightier *Parks, Promenades and Gardens of Paris* in 1869. From Paris he travelled through the Alps to Italy, and a slim volume on *Alpine Flowers for English Gardens*, announced in a foreword to *Parks, Promenades . . .*, was published in 1870, followed almost at once by *The Wild Garden*.

In these early works Robinson's likes and dislikes were already apparent. He was clearly impressed by the re-planning of Paris: its numerous wide, tree-lined boulevards, leafy squares and the new parks planned by Barilett Deschamps with horticultural assistance from Alphand. He was even more impressed by the bold planting in the parks, of which he distinguished two types.

First was 'subtropical gardening', using plants with especially striking foliage to create an exotic effect, a system which had already made some impact in England thanks to the experiments by Gibson, the Superintendent of Battersea Park.[1] Although many of the plants thus employed were truly subtropical (canna, castor oil, wigandia, palms, banana, etc.), Robinson drew particular attention to the possibility of using hardy plants for the same purpose, citing especially the pampas grass, giant reeds, yuccas and such herbaceous plants as *Crambe cordifolia, Rheum emodi*, acanthus and giant fennel.

His second type of planting was

the system of naturally grouping hardy plants ... In the rich alluvial soil in level spots, near water or in some open break in a wood, we might have numbers of the fine herbaceous families of Northern Asia, America and Europe. These, if well selected, would furnish a type of vegetation now very rarely seen in this country, and flourish without the slightest attention after once being planted.[2]

Conservatory in the Jardin d'Acclimatation, from William Robinson's Parks, Promenades and Gardens of Paris.

Robinson's ideas of plant grouping had much in common with Loudon's idea of the Gardenesque and, as with the Gardenesque,

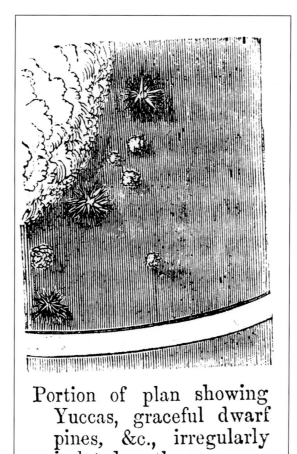

Portion of plan showing Yuccas, graceful dwarf pines, &c., irregularly isolated on the grass.

Softening the edges of the shrubbery, from Parks, Promenades and Gardens of Paris.

the ideas were open to misinterpretation. In an attempt to soften the hard line between expanses of mechanically mown lawn and overstuffed shrubberies, Robinson suggested using isolated specimens of fine-leaved plants as outliers of the border, blurring its margin in much the same way as seedling trees blur the edges of a natural wood. In the small illustrations which exemplify the idea[3] the grouping is quite naturalistic *if one bears in mind the large areas of adjacent grass which do not form part of the figure.* However, the illustrations taken in isolation could be seen as a suggestion to scatter yuccas, pampas, reeds and retinosporas freely over the whole lawn, a suggestion entirely contradictory to Robinson's vehemently expressed views; but readers are apt to see what they wish in the printed word, and many a Victorian lawn was peppered with pampas, monkey puzzle and yucca in the belief that this was the word of the prophet.

In his writing Robinson struggled perpetually to combine the botanical opportunities of the Gardenesque with the scenic qualities of the Picturesque, and he is most notable for something he did only unconsciously: to extend the idea of the Picturesque from the large canvases of Salvator Rosa to the vignettes of natural plant compositions portrayed for *The Wild Garden* by Alfred Parsons. For Robinson, columbines and geraniums in meadow grass,[4] the large-leaved Cretan borage[5] or the stately spike of *Mulgedium* (now *Lactuca*) *plumieri*[6] were just as suitable subjects for a picture as were the rocky streams of the Wye Valley or the classical ruins of an Italian hillside.

Broken-brick gardening

While Robinson heaped praises on the plantsmanship evident in Parisian parks, gardens and nurseries, his dislikes were numerous, extending to all things mechanical and artificial. In particular he

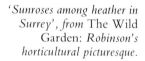

'Sunroses among heather in Surrey', from The Wild Garden: *Robinson's horticultural picturesque.*

disliked extensive and unnecessary terracing (railway embankment gardening), the cutting of innumerable geometrical flower beds in the lawn (pastrycook gardening), the use of coloured minerals to replace flowers in a parterre (broken-brick gardening) and excessive use of statues, fountains and closely shaved lawns.

Two gardens above all symbolized for Robinson all that was evil: Versailles and Crystal Palace. Of Versailles his descriptions were detailed, his prose appropriately leaden.

This being one of the most celebrated gardens in the world it behoves us to examine it somewhat in detail – were we, however, to treat of it in proportion to its real merits as a garden, a very small amount of space would suffice. Let us pass through the vast stone courtyard ... the eye first rests on a vast spread of gravel, some marble margins of great water basins, sundry protuberances from the level of the water, and away in the distance an effect like that afforded by a suburban canal in a highly practical and unlovely country.[7]

Versailles was vast, bold, hideous, depressing, but at least it was old. It had almost earned redemption by inciting the Revolution which freed the country from further monstrosities, and it had its compensations in the School of Horticulture and the wonderful fruit and vegetable gardens. No such clemency could be bestowed on the Crystal Palace, built in an age when men should know better and in a country which claimed freedom and democracy as its birthright. At the Crystal Palace 'in the region of the great fountain basins ... a more horrid impression is received than in any part of Versailles'.[8] Robinson wept, verbally at least, for lost opportunities, vast expenditure and ruined shareholders.

In the autumn of 1870 Robinson travelled to America with his brother, to trace his father who had left Ireland with his employer's wife. Robinson obtained a substantial sum of money from his father, but was also permanently enriched by the impressions of endless forests and meadows glowing with autumn colour.

The Wild Garden, first published in 1870, borrowed freely from the ideas and phrases already rehearsed in his earlier publications to illustrate a system of gardening in which 'beautiful hardy plants ... might be naturalized ... in our plantations, fields and woods'.[9] Initially many of the examples were of native plants, but in later editions the impressions left by autumn meadows of asters and golden rods, as by his travels to the alpine meadows of southern Europe, made their mark. The section on native plants gradually dwindled and eventually disappeared.

Robinson's recognition of the charms of wild flowers was by no means new. Even high priests of the formal garden such as John Fleming, head gardener to the Duke of Sutherland at Trentham and Cliveden, were not blind to Nature's charms. It was the flowers peeping from hedgerow and copse which inspired Fleming's ideas for spring bedding in the great parterre at Cliveden. Neither was his idea of substituting hardy exotics for native plants original. His descriptions of the parks of Paris show that such planting was already established in professional practice, and Shirley Hibberd's prolific literary output, predating Robinson's by a decade, was often occupied with similar ideas.

In 1855, at the age of thirty, Hibberd edited *Brambles and Bay Leaves: essays on rural life*. On the proceeds of this he moved from Pentonville to suburban Stoke Newington, where for thirty years he ran his own experimental garden in addition to his publishing activities, and finally to Muswell Hill. A stream of books followed, among them *Rustic Adornments for Homes of Taste, The Amateur's Rose Book, The Fern Garden, Beautiful Leaved Plants* (predating Robinson's *Subtropical Gardening*), *The Ivy* and *Field Flowers: a handy book for the rambling botanist*. Hibberd also edited four magazines, including, for its first two years, *Amateur Gardening*.

Garden style

However, what Robinson lacked as an originator he more than made up for in evangelical zeal. With a single-mindedness which often disturbed his more catholic and tolerant contemporaries, he preached the cause of hardy flowers and naturalistic planting as the only true path of gardening. Whereas Loudon and Hughes had catalogued many styles of gardening, Robinson distinguished only two:

. . . one straitlaced, mechanical, fond of walls or bricks, or it may be gravel; fond also of such geometry as the designer of wall papers excels in, often indeed of a much poorer and less graceful kind than that; fond too of squirting water in an immoderate degree, with trees in tubs as an accompaniment, and perhaps griffins and endless plaster and stone work. The other, with true humility and right desire, though often awkwardly and blunderingly, accepting nature as a guide, and endeavouring to multiply, so far as convenience and poor man-power will permit, her most charming features.[10]

Gardening, for Robinson, was not a matter of mere styles but a battle between good and evil. Ruskin was invoked to demonstrate that formal gardening was but a strand of the evil which emanated from the industrialized world.[11]

As Robinson wrote, voluminously and vehemently, other developments at home and abroad ensured that his words would fall upon fertile ground. The steady influx of plants from all parts of the world took a dramatic new turn, and the opening up of the Orient sparked a chain of developments in English gardens. Much was already known about the spectacular flora of Japan from reports of the Dutch East India Company's physicians Engelbert Kaempfer, Carl Thunberg and especially Philipp von Siebold. In 1858 Japanese ports were opened to the West under pressure from America. Siebold returned to Japan briefly and, on this last voyage, introduced variegated hostas to Europe.

The Orient unleashed

The Veitch family were quick to realize the opportunity presented by the opening of Japan. In the wave of diplomatic activity which ensued, John Gould Veitch became attached to the staff of the British Envoy and collected many first-rate plants – Japanese larch, cypresses, pines, *Primula japonica*, *Parthenocissus tricuspidata* (still sometimes referred to as *Ampelopsis veitchii*) and the spectacular *Lilium auratum*. Veitch travelled on to China, the Philippines and Australia, introducing maples, bamboos and many other plants. In 1875 Peter Veitch also collected in Fiji, Australia, New Zealand and Borneo.

The Veitches were not slow, either, in recognizing the importance of reports by French Jesuit missionaries of the rich flora in the hitherto unexplored regions of China away from the coast, near the source of the great rivers. Armand David (1860), Jean Marie Delavay and Paul Farges (1867), and later Jean Soulie (1886) sent many botanical specimens and seeds back to Europe. Most of the seeds failed but the herbarium sheets caused great excitement. In 1877 Veitch sent Charles Maries to Japan and China, particularly to the Yangtze valley. His introductions, including the Chinese witch-hazel, *Primula obconica* and many others, amply justified the journey but in 1879 he turned back.

In 1881 Dr Augustine Henry entered the Chinese Maritime Customs and in the following year went to Hupeh as Assistant Medical Officer. To relieve his boredom he began collecting plants and, in 1886, sent his first collection to Kew. These and later consignments (158,000 specimens in total) caused enormous excitement, and in 1899 Veitch asked Kew to recommend a collector to seek out especially the handkerchief tree, *Davidia involucrata*. Ernest Henry Wilson was engaged and travelled to meet Henry near the Burmese border. Wilson found the davidia, together with a host of other plants: *Acer davidii* and *A. griseum*, *Viburnum davidii*, *Stranvaesia davidiana*, *Magnolia delavayi*, *Abies fargesi* and many others. In the first trip alone he introduced nearly 1,000 species from seed, plus many cases of bulbs and roots. In 1903 he went again to China, also for Veitch, then for the Arnold Arboretum in 1907 and 1910 to China and in 1914 and 1918 to Japan, from where he introduced his selection of the best Kurume azaleas, 'Wilson's 50', flowering cherries and the beautiful *Lilium regale*.

Wilson's introductions were noted by Arthur Bulley, a Liverpool businessman, keen naturalist and gardener. As his garden at Mickwell Brow, Ness, on the Wirral, expanded, he engaged George Forrest to work for him in Western China. In 1913 Francis Kingdon-Ward followed, then R. E. Cooper. William Purdom and Reginald Farrer continued to collect after the First World War, with Ewan Cox and others.

The most obvious yield of these explorations was an incredible array of beautiful plants: maples, rhododendrons, roses, bamboos, camellias, magnolias, mahonias, viburnums, buddleias, hydrangeas, lilies, meconopsis, primulas, gentians, iris, paeonies – the list is endless. Another result, however, was to stir a new wave of romanticism in gardening.

Many of the collectors worked in great peril, partly because of the hazardous terrain but more particularly because the areas in which they searched were torn by warfare and foreigners were not welcomed. Wilson narrowly escaped many disasters. He was caught in a landslide and smashed his leg. (Ironically, he finally met his death, with his wife, in a car accident in Boston.) George Forrest lost sixteen of his team of seventeen collectors during attacks by Tibetans. He escaped after being pursued by man-hunting dogs, despite having his foot pierced through on a bamboo spike. Reginald Farrer disguised himself as a native to facilitate his explorations, eventually became a Buddhist and died in the hills, exhausted by his efforts. All these adventures were recorded in a series of books. Francis Kingdon-Ward's *The Land of the Blue Poppy* (1913), *Mystery Rivers of Tibet* (1923), *Riddle of the Tsangpo Gorges* (1926), etc., and Farrer's *Garden of Asia* (1904), *On the Eaves of the World* (1917) and *Rainbow Bridge* (1921) were more exciting than any fiction. These

Cotehele: plants of the Chinese foothills flourishing in the mild Cornish climate.

and earlier descriptions in journals and letters fuelled an era of scenic gardening, capturing the excitement of Himalayan exploration in much the same way as the eighteenth-century garden-makers had sought to remind themselves of the classical landscapes of Italy.

The mild garden

Many of the early Chinese introductions were not reliably hardy, but it was soon realized that they could be grown to perfection in the moist, mild climate of Cornwall. Trengwainton was started in 1814 by the son of a Jamaican sugar planter. In 1867 it was acquired by the banker T. S. Bolitho, and for three generations the family extended and enriched the garden. Glendurgan was established by Alfred Fox in the 1820s and 1830s with terraces, a walled garden and the remarkable laurel maze (1833). The garden was enormously enriched by G. H. Fox from 1891 until his death in 1931. Trelissick, Trengwainton, Carclew, Caerhays, Cotehele, Lanhydrock, and a dozen or more other gardens spread out of sheltering walls and into wooded glens to create a landscape of rhododendrons, camellias, magnolias and other early flowering plants, growing into tree-like proportions reminiscent of their Himalayan homes.

One of the most remarkable gardens lay beyond Cornwall. When Augustus Smith became Lord Proprietor of the Scilly Isles in 1834, he planted shelter belts around the ruins of Tresco Abbey and soon amassed a vast collection of rare and tender plants, especially from Australasia and South America. Tresco's example spread along the western seaboard as far north as Inverewe, where, in 1862, Osgood Hanbury Mackenzie used Scots and Corsican pines to convert a rocky, windswept site into a paradise of eucalyptus, tree-ferns and other tender plants. In 1875 Henry Pochin bought the estate of Bodnant, overlooking Conway Bay in North Wales, and with the help of Ernest Milner (a protégé of Joseph Paxton) he began his magnificent hillside garden in the steep valley below the house.

Arboreta were important features of many of the largest gardens, but these, too, took on a new significance as new plants poured into the country. Westonbirt was begun by Robert Stayner Holford in 1829 on a freak remnant of acid greensand in the otherwise lime-stone area of Gloucestershire. Three years later the arboretum at Killerton in Devon was established for Sir Thomas Acland by John Veitch, and in 1835 Paxton began his arboretum at Chatsworth. Initially arboreta were seen primarily as plant collections, carefully labelled, botanically grouped and seriously educational. The picturesque potential of towering conifers and billowing broadleaves was soon appreciated, however. Between 1830 and 1844 Edward Harcourt, Archbishop of York, identified another remarkable island of greensand over the heavy clay of his estate at Nuneham, and engaged William Sawrey Gilpin (already at work on the gardens near the house) to lay out a pinetum. By 1863, Holford began reshaping his estate of Westonbirt. The house was rebuilt, the village moved, and the estate planted with vast numbers of carefully massed and grouped trees and shrubs. Sir George Holford, his son, took over in 1892 and began to select and plant the finest of the new introductions from Western China, creating in particular the brilliant displays of autumn colour which are now the most notable feature of Westonbirt. From 1884 the 3rd Earl of Morley, a close relative of Lord Holford, began planting at Sharpitor in Devon, taking advantage of the steep slopes and mild climate.

Plants and the Picturesque

With the introduction of Wilson's hardy plants, opportunities for picturesque gardening in other parts of the country became unlimited. The High Weald of Kent and Sussex, with its dramatic sandstone outcrops, acid soils and deep, wooded valleys, with streams and ancient hammer-ponds – relics of sixteenth- and seventeenth-century iron-workings – provided ideal terrain.[12] As the Southern Railway spread its tentacles from London, the great wastes of pine, oak, birch and chestnut forest of the lower greensand and Bagshot sand areas in Surrey were rapidly settled by commuters to the City.

One of the most influential gardens of the High Weald was Scotney Castle in Kent. The castle dates back to 1378 and was partly rebuilt in 1580 and in 1630, when some parts were plundered for building materials. In 1778 it was sold to Edward Hussey, a

Scotney Castle: Salvin's new house above the picturesque ruins of the old castle.

barrister of the Middle Temple. Hussey died in 1816. His son (also Edward) died in 1817 and the house was abandoned. In 1835 the third Edward Hussey, keenly interested in architecture, gardening and forestry, decided to build a new house. William Sawrey Gilpin advised on the site for the building, and on the treatment of its surroundings, and Anthony Salvin was engaged as architect. Salvin's brother-in-law, W. A. Nesfield, supplied elaborate formal designs for the garden of the new 'castle' but these were rejected. Instead Gilpin's picturesque advice was followed. Stone was quarried from the hill immediately below the new house, so the building literally grew from the site. The quarry and the old castle, partly dismantled to emphasize its medieval origins, became chief features in a romantic, picturesque landscape viewed from the house and its terrace.

In 1836, while the new Scotney Castle was taking shape, Edward Cooke was sketching rocks in William Wells's garden at Redleaf, barely five miles away. Cooke went on to assist with the making of several gardens on the sandstone outcrop of the Sussex Weald, in addition to his more famous work at Biddulph Grange, and retired to the locality in a house designed by Norman Shaw and called Glen Andred.[13]

At Leonardslee, Sussex, thirty miles from Scotney Castle, a new house was built in 1855, perched above a chain of hammer-ponds with distant views of the South Downs beyond. In 1887 Sir Edmund Loder began planting the steep wooded slopes, and for thirty years he continued to collect, plan and plant with an eye equally for fine plants and landscape effect. Viburnums, cherries, magnolias, camellias, sorbus, malus, conifers of all sorts and – especially – rhododendrons were woven into the natural woodland character of the setting with native ferns.

In 1890 Ludwig Messel acquired Nymans, near Haywards Heath, Sussex, and immediately enlarged the house with the help of Ernest George. Here, too, a great garden began to develop: a pinetum, a lime-walk heading out to fine views over the Weald, an early heather garden and other features planned by Messel and his head gardener, James Comber. James's son Harold Comber undertook several expeditions to Australasia and South America, to enrich the garden still further with eucryphias, escallonias, nothofagus and embothriums.

On the opposite slope of the Ouse valley lies Borde Hill, where Colonel Stephenson Clarke began his garden in 1893. Clarke was a sponsor of E. H. Wilson and later of Farrer, Forrest, Kingdon-Ward, Joseph Rock and Harold Comber from Nymans. Plants

Flower borders and topiary in the walled garden at Nymans.

spilled out from the garden proper to infiltrate every copse on the estate, making Borde Hill one of the finest plant collections in the country. One of its most unusual features was the Round Dell, a steep-sided hollow in which Chusan palms, *Trachycarpus fortunei*, found such a congenial home that they still survive among self-sown seedlings of various ages.

In 1903 Sir Edmund Loder's brother Gerald bought Wakehurst Place from Sir William Boord and, in the family tradition, spent the rest of his life embellishing his estate with a magnificent collection of trees and shrubs from all parts of the world.

Less than ten miles from Wakehurst is Sheffield Park, with its James Wyatt house in a landscape by Lancelot Brown. In 1909 Sheffield Park was acquired by Arthur Soames, who extended the lakes, embellished the upper ones with Pulham rockwork and assembled a huge collection of exotic trees and shrubs, with an emphasis on autumn colour reflecting in the waters.

The Japanese garden

In addition to beautiful plants and noble scenery, the Orient provided a third inspiration to gardeners, the example of its own exquisite gardens and houses.

A. B. Freeman Mitford, later Baron Redesdale, spent some time in Japan with the Foreign Service and in 1871 published *Tales of*

Borde Hill: the gardens near the house.

Old Japan. During the 1890s he laid out his own garden at Batsford Park, Gloucestershire, as an arboretum of Japanese plants, especially conifers and maples, with a separate area for bamboos (on which he published a monograph in 1896). Oriental statues also decorated the garden, but in a purely English manner.[14]

The International Exhibition of 1862 and the Vienna Exhibition of 1873 both featured Japanese buildings and sparked an interest in Japanese design. A pagoda from the former now decorates the water garden at Cliveden. In 1891 Josiah Conder, an English architect who became the first president of the Institute of Japanese Architects, published *The Flowers of Japan and the Art of Floral Arrangement*, followed in 1893 by *Landscape Gardening in Japan*. Conder hoped to stimulate, in the West, a more correct and intelligent approach to the creation of 'Japanese' gardens than had been demonstrated in early examples. In 1928 the spring volume of *The Studio* was devoted to a treatise on *The Gardens of Japan* by Jiro Harada. Between these dates many gardens in the Japanese style were created in Britain. At Shipley Glen, Yorkshire, Thomas Hartley laid out his garden in the 1880s with a miniature lake and two islands, one with twin pagodas and the other with a miniature castle.[15]

In 1901 Fanhams Hall, near Ware, was built on the site of a smaller Queen Anne house. Below the formal terraces a wisteria-clad pergola led to a three-acre Japanese garden with a 'fox' lake (shaped like a fox to symbolize wisdom and good fortune), a tea house, bridges, lanterns, dry 'waterfalls', maples and pines. Other ponds yielded spoil which was used to re-create Mount Fuji, and a team of Japanese gardeners came each summer to tend the garden.[16] In 1910 more gardeners came to make the Japanese garden at Tatton Park, which again boasted lakes, lanterns, stepping-stone bridges and a Mount Fuji.[17]

Surpassing all these was the garden at Cottered in north Hertfordshire. Herbert Goode visited Japan on business in 1905 and

The Japanese garden at Cottered.

'The Japanese Nurseries' of V.N. Gauntlett and Co. in Surrey.

acquired several lanterns and other works of art. On his return to Hertfordshire he began to carve the flat pasture adjacent to his house into a miniature landscape of mountains and a sinuous 'fox' lake. More buildings and plants were imported and, from 1923 to 1926, Seyemon Kusumoto completed the design. Fourteen gardeners pinched buds on the conifers to keep them in scale with the landscape, swept leaves, raked gravel and, one assumes, drank tea.[18]

For people of lesser means or lesser ambition it was not necessary to go to Japan for expertise or artifacts. Harada's *Gardens of Japan* included advertisements. William Cutbush and Son Ltd of Barnet (garden artifacts, nurserymen, seedsmen and florists), who were noted importers and distributors of Dutch topiary, also offered a complete service in Japanese gardens. 'The cost is by no means prohibitive.' Pulham and Sons (of rock garden fame) also offered Japanese gardens. Liberty's of Regent Street had miniature gardens from 27s 6d (£1.37) to 15 guineas (£15.75), and J. Suzoki, Professor of Soami School, designed Japanese gardens from New Oxford Street.

Paradoxically, the Japanese garden was so well suited to the English temperament that its immediate influence was less than might have been expected. Devoid of its symbolic rationale, the picturesque rock groupings, lakes and carefully pruned plants were so closely akin to the contemporary taste for alpine gardens that the two ideas merged. Only an occasional bronze crane or stone lantern differentiated a Japanese garden from an alpine garden.

This sympathetic annihilation is well illustrated in the catalogues of V. N. Gauntlett and Co. Ltd, Japanese Nurseries, Chiddingfold in Surrey, a nursery which flourished from *c*. 1890 until the Second World War. Their 400-page catalogue, boasting eight columns of noble patrons, offered a huge range of plants and Japanese garden ornaments. In addition to its enthusiasm for Japanese gardens (the front cover showed two kimono-clad ladies by a wisteria-draped bower), there were special sections in the catalogue for subtropical plants, reeds and grasses, the wild and woodland garden, and other aspects dear to the heart of William Robinson.

A gardening fraternity

Robinson was well aware of the changes which were taking place. Through his position in Regent's Park, his extensive travels and his writing, he observed with great delight the wealth of new hardy plants taking root in the English soil. He advised on several gardens: Viscount Harcourt's new wild garden of Nuneham, for example (where one of Robinson's enthusiasms, the Japanese knot-weed, is only now being conquered by modern herbicides), at Crowsley Park in Oxfordshire, at Killerton, Nymans, and most notably at Shrubland Park, where he smothered the much-detested patterned brickwork of Sir Charles Barry with climbing plants and replaced the 'painted gravel' parterre of Nesfield by borders of hardy flowers. At least as often, though, he benefited from other people's ideas. In each edition of *The Wild Garden* he asked to be informed of any good examples of wild gardening. Sometimes the reports obtained this way were acknowledged. More often Robinson omitted any acknowledgement and claimed the ideas as his own.

Through *The garden; an illustrated weekly journal of horticulture*, which he launched in 1871, and his even more successful *Gardening Illustrated*, begun in 1879, he came into contact with an ever-widening fraternity of distinguished gardeners. In 1884, with the wealth accumulated from his publishing, he acquired Gravetye Manor, an Elizabethan house in Sussex surrounded by 1,000 acres of rolling countryside, thus becoming a neighbour of some of the most influential and successful gardeners of the day. Robert Marnock advised him on the garden, although Robinson often 'forgot' to mention this in later years.

The majority of Robinson's gardening friends were talented amateurs. Many of these were men of the Church, for whom botany and classics, gardening and theology were interwoven into a gentle, restrained and timeless way of life. The Rev. Charles

Wolley-Dod, formerly an Eton master, became a distinguished amateur botanist and gardener at Edge Hall in Cheshire. Canon Ellacombe, who followed his father as vicar of Bitton in Gloucestershire, spent all but five years of his ninety-four-year life in the rectory. He was a valued correspondent of Kew and was welcomed at botanic gardens throughout Europe. The Rev. Henry Honeywood d'Ombrian was first secretary of the National Rose Society, founded in 1876. The Society's first president, Canon Samuel Reynolds Hole, later Dean of Rochester, wrote the immensely popular *Book about Roses* (1869). *Memories of Dean Hole* (1892) went through four editions in a year. In it he recalled his friendship with many professional horticulturists. *Our Gardens* (1899), in which he wrote on the civilizing and harmonizing influence of the garden and its components, was equally successful. Dean Hole considered Robert Marnock 'the champion of the English or natural system, and ... the most accomplished artist we have had in the design of the development of a garden'.[19] He had reason to be personally grateful to him:

He was indeed the brother born of adversity, for I was at that time [when Marnock came to advise Dean Hole on his garden in Nottinghamshire], as a gardener, in a state of extreme prostration and debility from a simultaneous attack of scarlet and yellow fever. In the first delirium of the disease, which went by the name of 'Bedding-out' ... I commited enormities ... for my grand display of half hardy plants. For six summers the symptoms annually returned: then gradually my temperature went down to normal. My reason was restored, and my aching eyes turned away from their kaleidoscope.[20]

It was perhaps the success of Dean Hole's *Memories* which encouraged Canon Ellacombe to write of his reminiscences *In a Gloucestershire Garden* (1895) and *In my Vicarage Garden and Elsewhere* (1902). A very similar autobiographical/advisory tone was prominent in *Pot-Pourri from a Surrey Garden* (1896) by Mrs C. W. Earle, born Maria Teresa Villiers. Art and education, the raising of sons and daughters, advice on household management and a calendar of gardening activities were blended into a delightful narrative.

Such authors exemplified an unbroken tradition of gentility and restrained plantsmanship, but even as they wrote the tradition was rapidly disappearing: suburban railways, omnibuses and a sprinkling of motor-cars transported a new race of commuters into rural England and especially into the sandy wastes of Surrey, Sussex and Kent.

Art and Craft in the garden

The campaign to revive traditional values was fought on a wide front – intellectual, social and artistic. The powerful appeal of the medieval era, of life directed by faith rather than reason, led to the formation, in 1848, of the Pre-Raphaelite Brotherhood of seven, in which the poet/painter Dante Gabriel Rossetti played a leading role. John Ruskin, the immensely influential socialist/ philosopher/critic, supported the revolutionaries in their stand against conventional art.

In 1861 William Morris, an ardent admirer of Rossetti and Ruskin, founded the firm of Morris, Marshall, Faulkner and Co. to design and make decorative work, murals, fabrics, furniture and stained glass for houses and churches. From these beginning evolved the Arts and Crafts Movement. Morris declared that 'Art is the expression of man's pleasure in labour', and he worked to create an environment in which every workman would have a creative and satisfying life. From 1871 Morris spent his summers at Kelmscott Manor in the Cotswolds, and from here he continued to lecture, to write and to exemplify in his own life the importance of simplicity, directness and honesty in all aspects of life, including gardens. He criticized suburban gardens where the sinuous paths and shrubberies of a Victorian park were worried into a few square yards, and pleaded for common sense in gardens: straight paths, ordered rows of vegetables and a profusion of flowers spilling out of straight borders.

The rural survival of Canon Ellacombe, Dean Hole and Mrs Earle, allied to the Arts and Crafts revival led by William Morris, conjured an idealized picture of the Old English garden.

By the turn of the century the Old English garden had as strong an appeal for the new suburban dweller as the 'simple peasant' connotation of the dairy had had for the eighteenth-century nobility. *Some English Gardens* (1904), with text by Gertrude Jekyll and with numerous paintings by George Elgood, captures the blend of old yew hedges, the cottager's instinctive topiary, herbs and sundials, apple trees festooned with roses and flower borders filled to overflowing with simple, old-fashioned flowers. It was just this type of garden which Alfred Parsons not only painted but created at Wightwick Manor, West Midlands, around the Arts and Crafts house of Samuel Mander, a style aptly defined in the simple phrase 'Peacocks and Roses'.

The English Flower Garden

Logically one might suppose that the triumphant advance of cottage gardening and the spectacular examples of hardy planting on a larger scale would persuade William Robinson that the battle had been won. The nation as a whole had cured itself of Dean Hole's 'scarlet and yellow fever'. However, even as the popularity of hardy plants advanced, Robinson embarked on a more and more embittered campaign against bedding and against architects' gardens. Unlike all his close friends, he also developed an intense dislike of topiary. In 1883 came his most important work, *The English Flower Garden*, a book which went through fifteen editions and many reprints in the half century which followed. Half of *The English Flower Garden* was devoted to an alphabetical list of hardy plants (alphabetical by botanical name, although Robinson used English names when he could and often invented English names when none existed), but it began with chapters on garden design in which he berated architects for ruining the English garden.

Of all the things made by man for his pleasure a flower garden has the least business to be ugly, barren or stereotyped, because in it we may have the fairest of the earth's children in a living, ever-changeful state, and not, as in other arts, mere representations of them. And yet we find in nearly every country place, pattern plans, conventional design, and the garden robbed of all life and grace by setting out flowers in geometrical ways ...[21]

... Even when there is no money to waste in walls and gigantic water-squirts the idea of the terrace is still carried out often in plains and other wrong positions in the shape of green banks often one above the other, as if they were an artistic treat.[22]

In 1890, a year after the second edition of *The English Flower Garden*, a very different book appeared: H. E. Milner's *The Art and Practice of Landscape Gardening*. Milner's style was unexceptional and utterly characteristic of his time: curving drives leading to a courtyard and stables, formal terraces and parterres around the house, yielding to nature away from the house. Prospects and practicalities, nature and art were all encompassed in a highly detailed treatise, but Milner's preference was clearly for nature rather than art, and for nature he reserved his most effusive prose. 'The garden proper ... though fine in calculated detail of its plan should express by the breadth of treatment ... that nature has triumphed over art because art has subtly tutored the development of nature's overwhelming beauty.'[23]

The architects' reply

All this was too much for the architects. In 1891 J. D. Sedding's *Garden Craft Old and New* was published. John Sedding was far removed from Robinson's stereotype of 'the architect'. An amiable character, a devoted member of the Art Workers' Guild and a truly vernacular architect, he had always been inspired by natural forms, using flowers and leaves as the only form of decoration in his buildings, but on his move from London to Kent he also became an enthusiastic gardener.[24] *Garden Craft Old and New* was an attempt to establish principles of design for modern gardens by reference to the past.

At first Sedding's history, in language as flowery as the gardens themselves, was dispassionate, then glowing with praise for Elizabethan gardens, then critical of the English landscape garden. Repton was praised for his common sense and for his separation of garden and park, but the criticism began again, rising to a crescendo as 'modern landscape gardening' came within his sights.

Landscape-gardening is, in a sense, still in its fumbling stage: it has not increased its resources, or done anything heroic, even on wrong lines; it has not advanced towards any permanent, definable system of ornamentation since it began its gyrations in the last century. Its rival champions still beat the air ... Their intentions are admirable beyond telling, but their work exhibits in the grossest forms the very vices they condemn in the contrary school ...

... Mr Robinson ... humbly skirts his ground with a path which as nearly represents a tortured horse-shoe as Nature would permit; and his trees he puts in a happy-go-lucky way, and allows them to nearly obliterate his path at their own sweet will! No wonder he does not fear Nature's revenge, where is so little Art to destroy![25]

Sedding's main criticism was not of the opinions of landscape gardeners but of their claims to have a monopoly of right principles. For him the joy of gardens was that each was unique. There could be no recipe or formula for the 'right' garden but it should be avowedly a work of Art. 'I have no more scruple in using the scissors upon tree or shrub, where trimness is desirable, than I have in mowing the turf of the lawn that once represented a virgin world.'[26]

Sedding died just before *Garden Craft* was published and was unable to observe the impact of his ideas, but in January of the following year a second architect joined the fray. Reginald Blomfield had already written *A History of Renaissance Architecture in England* and his own designs showed a strong allegiance to France. His houses, with their deep mansard roofs, overlooked parterres, *pattes d'oie* and other French devices in a restrained but severely geometrical manner. His new book, *The Formal Garden in England*, was equally direct. It was 'an attempt … to clear away mis-conceptions by giving so much of its history as will show the general character of the formal garden in England, its absolute separation from landscape gardening, and the extent and variety of design which it involves'.[27]

Chapter 1 considered 'The Formal Method and the Landscape Gardener'.

It will be well to clear the ground by a statement of the principles and standpoint of the Formal School as compared with Landscape Gardening. The question at issue is a very simple one. Is the garden to be considered in relation to the house … or is the house to be ignored in dealing with the garden? The latter is the position of the landscape gardener in real fact … The object of formal gardening is to bring the two into harmony … Thus the formal garden will produce with the house a homogeneous result, which cannot be reached by either singly. Now let us see how the landscape gardener deals with the problem of house and grounds…

… It is not easy to state his principles, for his system consists in the absence of any; and most modern writers on the subject lead off with hearty and indiscriminate abuse of formal gardening, after which they incontinently drop the question of garden design, and go off at a tangent on horticulture and hot-houses.[28]

Battle positions

There could hardly have been a more barbed taunt: Robinson was apoplectic. *The Formal Garden* was published in January 1892. By July Robinson produced *Garden Design and Architects' Gardens: two reviews illustrated to show, by actual examples from British Gardens, that clipping and aligning trees to make them 'harmonize' with architecture is barbarous, needless and inartistic.*

Sedding, who could not defend himself, was briefly dismissed. 'This gentleman, unfortunately without any knowledge of plants, trees, or landscape beauty, launches out into the dreary sea of quotations from old books about gardens, and knows so little of where he is going, that he is put out of his course by every little

drift of wind.'[29] Most of *Garden Design* was directed at the living enemy with a paragraph-by-paragraph refutation of Blomfield's book.

In October 1892 Blomfield replied in a lengthy preface to the second edition of *The Formal Garden*.

Drummond Castle, a situation in which terracing is appropriate, from Robinson's Garden Design and Architects' Gardens.

Since the publication of the first edition of this book Mr W. Robinson has issued what is no doubt intended for a counterblast to the views advanced in *The Formal Garden* and the late J. D. Sedding's *Garden Craft*. Mr Robinson is annoyed that any one else, and architects of all men, should presume to meddle with garden design; and after an aggressive preface ... he launches into a series of detached paragraphs to prove that landscape gardening is a very beautiful art, that he himself is an eminent professor of it, and that architects cannot possibly know anything about it at all ... Mr Robinson seems to conceive of a garden as a Botanical Museum, a place for the exhibition of specimens from every part of the world, in which no doubt the monkey puzzler would occupy the proud position due to its conspicuous ugliness ... not being an artist Mr Robinson does not understand the artistic importance of mass on the one hand and scale on the other.[30]

Ironically, the two authors had much in common. Both admired Elizabethan gardens with their combination of straight walks,

Haddon Hall, used by both Blomfield and Robinson to exemplify the ideal garden.

(Overleaf above) Robinson's own house and garden, Gravetye Manor.

(Overleaf below) Tea roses and pinks on the terrace at Gravetye.

necessary architectural steps and flower-filled borders. Both detested the absurd extremes of tortuous informality and stiff, over-elaborate parterres. Both chose, as the epitome of all that was wrong in gardens, the ornate Italianate muddle of the Crystal Palace. Ironically, too, William Robinson lived in the symmetrical splendour of an Elizabethan manor house overlooking rectangular gardens, while Blomfield lived in a rambling, picturesque house on the edge of a cliff with not a straight line in sight. However, having taken their respective professional positions neither could compromise. The nineteenth century closed with a bitter wrangle which left the impression that gardens could be *either* designed *or* filled with interesting plants, with no possibility of a middle ground.

In 1901 a third edition of *The Formal Garden* appeared. In its preface Reginald Blomfield declared: 'At the date at which the first two editions of this book were issued, a somewhat acrid controversy raged between landscape gardeners and architects ... In the attempt ... to dislodge a tradition of bad taste, a somewhat polemical treatment was necessary. The occasion for this no longer exists, and

I have therefore omitted the preface to the second edition.'

In the nine years between the second and third editions of *The Formal Garden in England* it had been convincingly demonstrated that gardens were not the subject for gardeners *or* architects but for gardeners *and* architects. Nowhere were the advantages of collaboration more clearly displayed than in the gardens of Gertrude Jekyll and Edwin Lutyens.

I0

The Edwardian and Neo-Georgian Garden

Gertrude Jekyll was born in London in 1843 and moved five years later to Bramley House in Surrey.[1] She showed a keen interest in plants and at the age of nine began her own garden. At eighteen she enrolled at the School of Art in South Kensington, spending day after day in the National Gallery copying Turner's paintings, reading the latest books on colour theory and developing a wide circle of gifted and intellectual friends including Hercules Brabazon.[2]

For much of her early life she travelled widely, to Greece and Turkey with Mary and Charles Newton[3], to Switzerland, Italy and France. Her notebooks showed her acute powers of observation and her love of the aromatic Mediterranean flora.

In 1869 she met William Morris and, through his influence, soon became accomplished at textile design. In 1875 she visited William Robinson at the offices of *The Garden* and became a regular contributor to the magazine.[4]

A garden in West Surrey . . .

In 1876, after eight years in Berkshire, Miss Jekyll moved, with her mother, back to Surrey, to a new house on Munstead Heath. By 1880 the garden was sufficiently advanced to merit a visit from Dean Hole and William Robinson. She continued to travel frequently to London and abroad, fulfilling commissions for embroidery, tapestry, silverwork, woodcarving and interior design, while, from Munstead House, she wrote for *The Garden,* worked in her own garden and occasionally advised her friends on theirs.

In 1882 Miss Jekyll acquired fifteen acres of heath and woodland across the road from Munstead House with the intention of building her own house, but the garden came first. The old trees had been felled some fifteen years earlier, but she carefully thinned the scrubby remnants of birch, pine, chestnut and holly into picturesque groups, carved grassy rides through them and, with infinite care, merged her flower garden imperceptibly with the woodland and its outlying spurs of rhododendrons, foxgloves, ferns and hellebores.

By the age of forty-five, she was an accomplished member of the Arts and Crafts movement and had created a notable garden in addition to planning borders and making other suggestions for her friends' gardens. Within the next five years her life was to take a dramatic turn.

Kindred spirits

Lutyens's shady north court at Munstead Wood, carefully embroidered with Gertrude Jekyll's planting.

In 1889 Miss Jekyll went to tea with her neighbour Henry Mangles, a leading rhododendron grower, and there met the young architect

Edwin Lutyens. Lutyens was invited to tea at Munstead the following Saturday, and the two found in each other kindred spirits.
Lutyens became a frequent visitor to Munstead. He had several
small commissions in the district and together he and Miss Jekyll
explored the Surrey lanes, stopping frequently to examine and
discuss the native ingenuity displayed in the building traditions of
each village.

Miss Jekyll had always been painfully short-sighted and, in 1891,
she was told by a leading oculist to give up her painting, embroidery
and other demanding pursuits. For compensation she turned even
more to her garden. She offered advice to Lutyens on the garden
of his first major commission, Crooksbury near Farnham, and he
was asked, in return, to advise on a small dwelling for Miss Jekyll
at Munstead Wood. The Hut was conceived as a large summerhouse, a workshop–cum–picnic shelter, but when Mrs Jekyll died
in the following year a more substantial dwelling was required.

The new house at Munstead Wood, embodying all the finest
principles of the Arts and Crafts movement and of traditional
building techniques, was completed in 1897, and Miss Jekyll moved
in in October on the day after she had been awarded the Royal

The Deanery, Sonning ... settled the controversy between architects and gardeners.

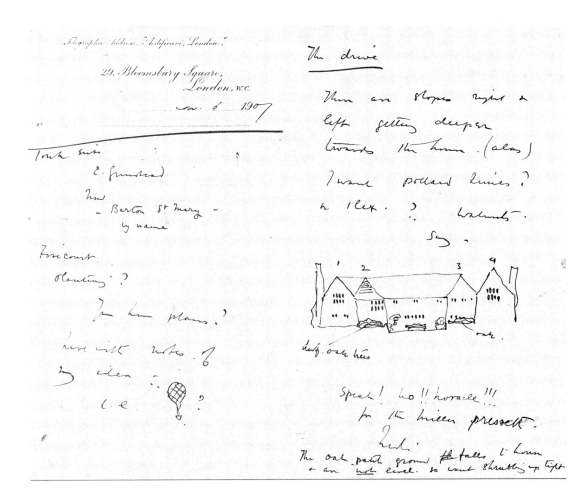

Horticultural Society's highest accolade, the Victoria Medal of Honour.[5]

In the same year, Edward Hudson founded a new magazine called *Country Life* and asked Miss Jekyll to become its editor. She declined, but wrote many articles for the paper which so closely reflected her own interests. She also introduced Edward Hudson to Edwin Lutyens. Lutyens's work (including the Deanery at Sonning, Berkshire, and Lindisfarne, Holy Island, for Hudson himself) was published in *Country Life* and thus disseminated to the most discerning audience imaginable. His career took off, and he became the architect of innumerable country houses. Many of them were planned in the workroom at Munstead Wood, and for many of them Miss Jekyll collaborated on the garden.

The simplistic view of their collaboration is that Lutyens designed the 'hard landscape' – the pools, paths, steps, terraces and buildings – while Miss Jekyll filled in the plant names. In reality they were of one mind. They exchanged a continuous flow of letters discussing the siting of proposed houses, the character of their gardens and the details of planting.[6] The success of their partnership in the creation of Edward Hudson's first house in 1901 was aptly described by Christopher Hussey.

Deanery Garden, at once formal and irregular, virtually settled that controversy, of which Sir Reginald Blomfield and William Robinson were for long the protagonists, between formal and naturalistic garden design. Miss Jekyll's naturalistic planting wedded Lutyens' geometry in a balanced union of both principles.[7]

As Munstead Wood was taking shape, the editor of the *Guardian*, a near neighbour, asked her to write a series of articles for his paper. In 1899 they appeared in book form as *Wood and Garden; notes and thoughts, practical and critical, of a working amateur*. The book was illustrated 'with seventy-one illustrations from Photographs by the Author'. From 1885, Miss Jekyll had added photography to her many other accomplishments. *Home and Garden* was published a year later.

Although she began *Wood and Garden* with a disclaimer – 'I lay no claim either to literary ability, or to botanical knowledge, or even to knowing the best practical methods of cultivation ...'[8] – she clearly chose and assembled her words with just as much care as she did her plants. Her books overflowed with brilliant word pictures, and her many descriptions of flowers, plants and their cultivation showed the complete unity in her life of art, craft, philosophy and religion.[9]

A dozen more books followed the first two, *Lilies for English Gardens, Wall and Water Gardens* (both 1901), *Roses for English Gardens* (1902) and *Annuals and Biennials* (1916) explored the use off particular plants in making garden pictures. *Some English Gardens*, with paintings by George S. Elgood (1904), *Gardens for Small Country Houses*, with Lawrence Weaver (1912), and *Garden Ornament* (1918) dealt with broader issues of design, while *Old West Surrey* (1904) and *Children and Gardens* showed her interest in people and their activities, and revealed many details of her own early life.

Gardens for Small Country Houses was written to demonstrate the importance of 'the right relation of the garden to the house', and drew heavily on the work of Edwin Lutyens. It included the Deanery ('A garden in Berkshire'), her own garden at Munstead Wood ('A garden in West Surrey; poor soil, no definite plan'), and that of Millmead at Bramley, close to her childhood home, a house and garden designed with Lutyens to refute accusations that their designs were only appropriate to large commissions. Millmead was a mere half-acre.

The main hardy flower border at Munstead Wood.

The artist's palette

Gertrude Jekyll's most remembered book is undoubtedly *Colour in the Flower Garden* (1908), first rehearsed as a chapter of that title in William Robinson's *English Flower Garden*. On the basis of this one work Miss Jekyll is often dismissed (sometimes jointly with William Robinson) as the inventor of the herbaceous border, in which colour was the only consideration. In fact, of course, the herbaceous border was never 'invented' and it was certainly known at about the time Miss Jekyll was born.[10] She consistently used the term 'flower-border' in preference to 'herbaceous border' because her own borders contained many plants other than hardy herbaceous perennials. It is worth remembering, too, that *Colour Schemes* was illustrated by over 100 of her photographs, all but one of them in black and white! Form and texture played an equal part in her compositions, as her photographs ably demonstrate.

Miss Jekyll's influence on English gardens was profound. Her knowledge of plants was immense and her interest in them catholic. When visitors expressed surprise at seeing bedding plants in her garden, she was quick to point out that it was not the plants' fault that they had so often been used in crude and inartistic ways.

In her own garden she worked with quiet, meditative purpose in search of perfection, knowing she would never attain it. For others she provided plans, plants and advice appropriate to any situation. For clients, especially clients gardening through the intermediary of contractors and nurserymen, she was obliged to play safe, hence the stereotyped image of a Jekyll garden as a sequence of rectangular flower borders with long drifts[11] of colour-graded herbaceous plants. A closer look at her work, however, reveals a much more versatile artist. At Barrington Court in Somerset her plans were indeed a series of colour-graded borders with strong reds fading to pastel pinks, yellows and blues in one garden, an iris garden of pale pink and lavender and a cool, shaded border of deep green foliage and greenish-white flowers. At Castle Drogo in Devon she planned irregular groups of thorns, furze and heathers to blend the approach to the spectacular castle into its moorland setting.[12] At Hatchlands, Surrey, she planned a sunken parterre filled with marigolds, coreopsis and calceolarias in vibrant oranges and yellows. On the plan she recorded: 'This proposed arrangement too late as they are away in August.' A second scheme was prepared with China roses, pillar roses and a border filled with columbines, lupins, iris and valerian.[13] At Stilemans in Godalming, Surrey, The Old Manor House at Upton Grey, Hampshire, and many other gardens, her contribution was a wild garden with paths flowing in the same easy curves as in her embroidery patterns, or the honeysuckle trails of a Morris tapestry.[14] The walks and small pools were fringed with aruncus, ferns and other favourite plants. She filled Lutyens's huge parterre at Hestercombe in Devon with bold groups of dahlias, cannas and bergenias, while in response to a plaintive newspaper advertisement from a factory boy in Rochdale, she designed a window box three feet long and ten inches wide.[15]

Gertrude Jekyll provided inspiration for a new generation of gardeners. Together with Edwin Lutyens she created a new English garden: inventively geometrical, using local materials in local ways, and filled with planting which was simultaneously disciplined and profuse. Sometimes it was inward-looking and sheltered; sometimes it commanded fine views; sometimes it was largely geometrical (as at Millmead), sometimes the geometry gave way to woodland rides or flower-strewn orchards (as at Munstead Wood itself, Orchards and the Deanery). Always it consulted the genius of the place and the characters of its owners.

Not everyone, though, could draw on the experience of Gertrude Jekyll or the brilliance of Edwin Lutyens. For many garden owners plans came, along with plants, from the larger nurseries, and the

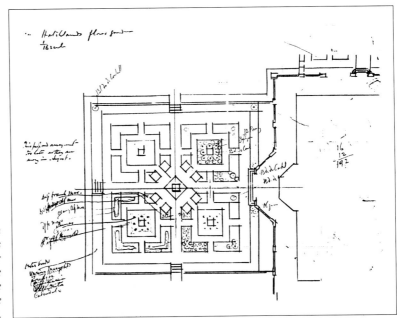

Miss Jekyll's design for an orange garden at Hatchlands (above) was altered to a softer scheme of roses and cottage garden plants (below) when she discovered that the family were away in August.

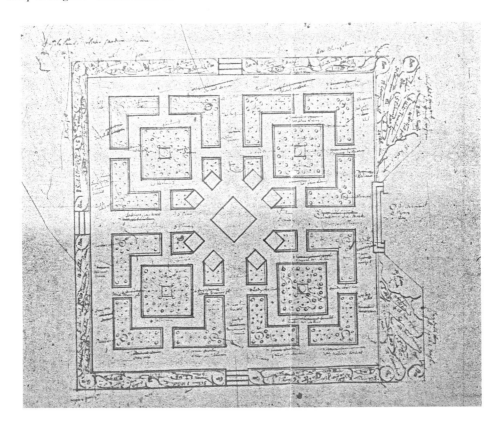

garden became a scattered array of lily pools, rock gardens, pergolas and summer houses, rose gardens, sunken gardens and other features of the nurseryman's stock-in-trade.[16] With no training in design and an understandable enthusiasm for plants, the nurseryman's approach to garden design was, predictably, a rather feeble Gardenesque.

The new formal garden

In other circumstances the design of the garden fell to the architects, who relied on the safety of their T-squares and set squares, often with a minimum of planting. Among the architects the formal – and particularly the Italianate – garden predominated, but it was a style altogether more correct and more restrained than that ponderous corruption practised by Paxton and Barry.

The 'Old English' gardens praised by Sedding, with their flower-bordered lawns, ample topiary, pergolas and simple terraces, steadily became grander and more coherently related as a series of axially connected compartments. C. E. Mallows, for example, an architect much admired by Gertrude Jekyll, designed many large houses –

Mawson's terrace and balustrade at Wightwick.

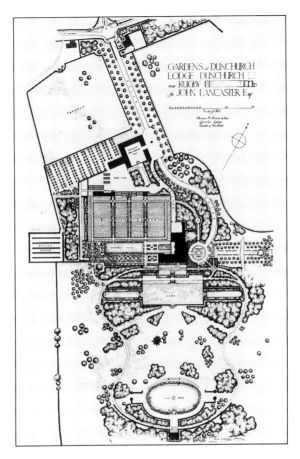

Dunchurch Lodge, Rugby:
characteristic of Mawson's
grander schemes.

strange hybrids between Elizabethan manor houses and vernacular
cottages – surrounded by spacious courtyards, terraces, tennis lawns,
parterres and pergola-shaded walks.[17]

As this interest in the Old English garden expanded, so too did
the enthusiasm for Italian art and architecture. Details of the garden
became increasingly classical in their inspiration until 'Old English'
and 'Italian' fused, a process most clearly seen in the work of
Thomas Mawson and Harold Peto.

Thomas Mawson was a leading exponent of the Old English
garden. From his Lakeland Nurseries at Windermere, run with his
brothers, Mawson studied drawing at the Lancaster Mechanics'
Institute and graduated from making to designing gardens in the
late 1880s.[18] In many respects his work closely resembled that of
the Milners, father and son, but Mawson's work was bolder, richer
in architectural detail and increasingly axial. Furthermore, whereas
the Milners had worked on a large scale, often on public parks,
in which Nature dominated over Art, many of Mawson's

commissions were smaller and related to private houses.[19] Formality predominated, as at Elmcourt in Harrogate. The Hill, designed for Viscount Leverhulme at Hampstead, was strongly classical, with a pergola, colonnade and belvedere overlooking the Heath. At Dyffryn, near Cardiff, Mawson included a sunken Pompeian Garden in addition to the usual rose garden, croquet lawn, lily pool, Japanese garden and other features. Although his work was often grand and heavily architectural, he never quite lost his nurseryman's origins and his interest in colourful plants and elaborate topiary. The garden at Wightwick, designed originally with the help of Alfred Parsons, was redesigned by Mawson in 1910 to include an elaborate parterre, an avenue of alternate yews and golden holly and other geometrical features.

Almost exactly contemporary with Mawson was Harold Ainsworth Peto, who trained as an architect and was a partner of Ernest George from 1876. In the 1890s Peto decided to concentrate on garden design. His elaborate pergola in the garden of West Dean, near Chichester, and the long water-garden at Buscot Park, Oxfordshire, are characteristic of his work, but his main legacy was his own garden at Iford Manor in Wiltshire, a small Palladian house which he bought in 1899. Here Peto wove terraces, steps, his extensive collection of Italian sculpture and many small buildings into the steeply wooded valley of the unmistakably English countryside.

Like Peto, many other artists and architects made their pilgrimage to the source of the Renaissance and were enchanted, not only by what they saw – exquisite architecture in idyllic settings – but by the idea of the Italian Renaissance villa as a setting for a cultured life and a masterpiece of traditional craftsmanship.

In the first decade of the twentieth century the interest in Italian architecture, and more particularly Italian gardens, was manifested in a flurry of publishing. Edith Wharton's *Italian Villas and Their Gardens* (1904) was the first, and one of the most intelligently analytical essays. This was followed by Charles Latham's weighty *The Gardens of Italy* (1905) and W. Inigo Trigg's *The Art of Garden Design in Italy* (1906), with carefully measured plans and sections. Three years later a very different book appeared: George Sitwell's *On the Making of Gardens*. This slight essay, written while the author was recovering from a nervous breakdown, sought to penetrate the soul of the garden, the genius of the place, rather than to dissect it in an academic post-mortem.

★   ★   ★   ★

The dawn of the twentieth century heralded a golden age in gardening. Wealth, inherited and industrial, was increasingly widely spread. Renewed attention to social legislation during Edward VII's reign promised an end to the poverty which had besmirched Victorian achievement, but democracy had not advanced to the point that a garden staff of ten, twenty, fifty perhaps, could no longer be contemplated.

Party dress

The country houses of Lutyens and his contemporaries opened wide doors on to gardens for which Miss Jekyll had provided the recipe. Plants from the Orient were freely available from a growing number of nurseries, many of whom seized upon particular plants and developed them until they were as colourful and gay as the dresses of an Edwardian garden party.

Kelway's gladioli, delphiniums and paeonies were already well established, as were the daffodils of Backhouse, Leeds and Barr, but, with growing demand, the numbers of varieties mushroomed.

In 1900 three new species of iris were introduced: *Iris mesopotanica, I. amas,* and *I. trojana* were used to produce a new race of large, chiffon flowers on branching stems and in a vast range of colours.[20] The simple day lily, known in England since the sixteenth century, suddenly blossomed into unimagined beauty. The oriental poppy, the almost dowdy 'starworts' or Michaelmas daisies rescued by William Robinson for use in the wild garden, polyanthus, phlox and delphiniums bred by Amos Perry, Ernest Ballard, Kelway, Blackmore and Langdon rapidly increased in size, colour range and beauty.

Not all these advances were the products of established professional nurseries. In 1911 a sixty-year-old Yorkshire gardener, George Russell, began experimenting with lupins on his allotment. By constant and rigorous reselection he achieved astonishing results, and Russell's lupins created a sensation when they were shown at Chelsea in 1937.[21]

In 1910, when A. K. Bulley's fortunes were temporarily at a low ebb, he converted part of his famous garden at Ness into a nursery. The venture was so successful that the nursery, named 'Bees' after Bulley's initial, moved to larger premises in nearby Sealand. Bees Seeds was instrumental in distributing widely many of the plants which poured into the country through the garden in Ness. Annuals, too, were rapidly developed. In 1901 the National Sweet

Pea Society was formed and, as if to celebrate the dawning of a new century and a new reign, the sweet pea mutated. In Earl Spencer's garden at Althorp, Northamptonshire, the hood of the pea-flower reflexed and divided to create a larger, frilled flower, the Spencer sweet pea.

The famous seed firms of the country – Suttons, Carters, Thompsons and others – who launched their highly portable wares to the nation at large with the advent of the penny post, also flourished in the golden age. Thick catalogues were produced, handbooks for particular plants were published, and mountains of bedding and conservatory plants – antirrhinums, stocks, schizanthus and primula, gloxinias, nemesias and cinerarias – decorated the great marquee of the Royal Horticultural Society's Great Spring Show (better known, since its move in 1913 from Temple Gardens to the more spacious grounds of the Royal Hospital, as the Chelsea Flower Show).

As always, the new gardening mood was reflected in the development of rhododendrons and roses. Among azaleas especially, the Ghent, Mollis and Occidentale hybrids loved by Gertrude Jekyll contined to develop through the early decades of the twentieth century. Anthony Waterer combined all three groups to produce his own Knap Hill hybrids in an even wider range of more intense colours, and Lionel de Rothschild carried the development further with his Exbury hybrids.[22]

In roses the advances were even more striking. The inherent instability of the cultivated roses, deriving their parentage from vigorous European shrubs, diminutive but repeat-flowering China roses and the newer rampant Japanese *Rosa multiflora* and *R. wichuraiana*, resulted in a flood of hybrid tea roses, including varieties with clear yellow flowers (derived from *Rosa foetida*), vigorous rambling roses with huge trusses of small very double flowers, and low dwarf polyantha roses in which those same huge trusses were borne almost at ground level. The hybrid perpetuals retained much of their popularity, and the Reverend Pemberton crossed these with the sweetly scented *Rosa moschata* to produce his hybrid musks.[23]

Rambler roses on pergolas and pillars lined countless garden paths. The brilliant dwarf polyanthas steadily replaced scarlet geraniums in the flower beds as the need for economy gradually dawned. Hybrid tea roses dominated the cutting garden and the show bench, but the large, opulent hybrid musk roses laden with petal-filled masses of fragrant, softly-coloured flowers and bearing charming names – Penelope, Thisbe, Charity, Pax – really captured the spirit of the new century.[24]

The alpine garden

Great strides were made, too, in the design of rock gardens. Robinson's *Alpine Flowers for English Gardens* (1871) fostered the cultivation of alpine plants in the rock garden. The nurseries of James Backhouse in York and Robert Veitch and Sons in Exeter, combining the resources of skilled craftsmen in rockwork and extensive catalogues of alpine plants, were responsible for many magnificent alpine gardens from the 1870s onwards. James Pulham of Broxbourne also constructed many rock gardens in his artificial Pulhamite stone, including fine examples at Lockinge (Berkshire), Sandringham (Norfolk) and Battersea Park in London, but by the end of James's life the use of concrete was increasingly scorned by the realists. It was quite acceptable to transport stone from the limestone pavements of Westmorland or from Yorkshire to make mountains in the stoneless regions of the Home Counties, but artificial stone was taboo. When James Pulham died, his son J. R. Pulham relinquished the manufacture of Pulhamite stone but continued to make many fine rock gardens in real stone, including, from 1911, the Wisley rock gardens designed by Edward White.

The real champion of the modern rock garden, however, was Reginald Farrer, a Yorkshireman with a prickly personality and a gift for words excelling even that of William Robinson. Born in the limestone country of Ingleborough in 1880 and deeply influenced by the Backhouse nursery at York, Farrer developed an early interest in alpine scenery and alpine plants. As a young man he spent some time in Japan and, in 1904, published his experiences in *The Garden of Asia*. In 1907 he published *My Rock Garden*, in which he ferociously attacked feeble attempts at the making of rock gardens, classifying aberrant styles as devil's lapfuls, dog's graves and almond puddings. Farrer's ideal was a rock garden which was simple and unaffected, which was modelled on nature without stooping to mimicry, and which gave maximum scope for the cultivation of rare and precious alpines. From his slim volume on the construction of rock gardens Farrer went on, with prodigious effort, to produce *The English Rock Garden*, an immense encyclopaedia of alpine plants, meticulous in its botanical accuracy and uninhibited in its praise or damnation of the plants he described.

The English Rock Garden, in two thick volumes, was completed in 1913. In 1914 Farrer travelled to Kansu, a province of north-west China, with William Purdom, taking the proofs of the book with him to correct, but they returned to England in 1915 to find the country at war and publication was delayed until 1919.

In 1919, with peace restored, Farrer travelled again, this time to Burma with E. W. M. Cox, but he died of exhaustion in the rain-soaked mountains in 1920. *The Rainbow Bridge*, his last work, was published posthumously in 1921.

A colourful sunset

The Great War which delayed the publication of Farrer's *English Rock Garden* rudely interrupted the golden age of gardens, but the interruption seemed, at the time, transient. Gardens continued to flourish almost to the eve of the Second World War.

Since 1896 the 9th Duke of Marlborough had been reinstating the formal surrounds of Blenheim, swept away by Lancelot Brown. With a French architect, Achille Duchêne, he made the Italian Garden (the Duchess's Garden) early in the 1900s, replanted the Great Avenue with elms, and repaved the Great Court. During 1925–30 he went on to create the water terraces descending from the palace to Brown's lake. In complete contrast to this formality, the notable rock garden created by the 5th Duke early in the nineteenth century was rescued and greatly extended. More than half a million trees were planted by the 9th Duke, including the clumps of copper beech and blue cedars intended to 'enliven' Brown's pastoral landscape.

Luton Hoo, another great Brown landscape, was also enriched in the early years of the century when it was acquired by the diamond magnate, Lord Wernher. The house was remodelled in 1903 and set on terraces descending to a marvellous rose garden with twin sculptured hedges and temples of Indian design at its outer corners. The huge hexagonal walled garden was built in 1906, and a superb rock garden with towering rocks, dark caverns, bridges and streams was made in the lower part of the valley.

Henry Pochin of Bodnant died in 1895, but his daughter, Lady Aberconway, and her son (later Lord Aberconway, President of the Royal Horticultural Society) continued to develop the garden. The great terraces were made between 1905 and 1914, and many new introductions by Wilson, Forrest, Kingdon-Ward and Rock were planted on the valley sides. Embothriums, eucryphias and

The Pin Mill at Bodnant.

other South American plants were also added. Their development continued until, with the re-erection of a Gloucestershire pin-mill as the focal point of the canal in 1939, the garden plan was essentially complete.

On a rather more domestic scale, Captain and Mrs Ronald Greville bought the elegant Regency villa of Polesden Lacey in Surrey in 1906 and Mrs Greville in particular remodelled both the house and garden to reflect her position as a leading society hostess. The walled rose garden with its pergolas and crazy-paving paths, the iris and lavender gardens, long herbaceous borders, croquet lawns and liberal accompaniment of classical statues made the garden an ideal extension of the house for lively weekend parties.

In many other gardens room was made for new flower borders and other formal features. In 1901 Edrick Hopkins built the terrace walk at Sharpitor, South Devon (now Overbecks). At Nymans, the walled garden was built in 1904, its quartering paths lined by wonderful colour borders and decorated with topiary. A walled garden was also made at neighbouring Borde Hill in 1906, primarily for vegetable cultivation though the many aspects of its high walls were soon exploited for the protection of many rare and tender plants. At Upton House, Warwickshire, terraces were built in 1927–9 for Viscount Bearsted and a rock garden for his wife.

On less formal lines, Arthur Soames began his planting around the lakes at Sheffield Park in 1909. At Trengwainton, Lt.-Col. E. H. W. Bolitho continued the tradition of his father and grandfather, taking to gardening in 1925 and sharing in the 1926 expedition of Kingdon-Ward sponsored by the owners of Trewithan and Hidcote. The tradition of woodland gardening with exotic plants was picked up in Windsor Great Park, where in 1932 Eric Savill began planting along the chain of settling ponds for Virginia Water to create the Bog Garden, renamed by command of George VI the 'Savill Garden'.

In 1903 Sir Thomas Hanbury acquired G. F. Wilson's garden, Oakbank, in the village of Wisley, and gave it to the Royal Horticultural Society who extended Wilson's woodland planting, created the rock garden, and gradually shaped the mecca for Fellows of the Society.

Some of the new gardens were highly individual creations. A rock garden was the chief feature of Friar Park near Henley. Sir Frank Crisp, a highly successful company lawyer, built a private railway to carry 4,000 tons of stone up from the Thames. The main rock garden, reached from the house by a tunnel, was built by Backhouse. This was supplemented by extensive outcrops of Pulham's artificial stone and topped by a 'snowy' (alabaster-covered) Matterhorn. Crisp also amassed a large collection of medieval manuscripts and began a book on medieval gardens.[25] He also went into partnership with the famous Waterer nursery at Twyford, to form Waterer Sons and Crisp Ltd.

From 1895 the garden of Myddleton House, Enfield, Middlesex, became notable. Edward Augustus Bowles was introduced to gardening by his father's associate, Canon Ellacombe. Bowles was remarkable as a scholar and plantsman in the mould of Ellacombe and Dean Hole rather than as a designer, and the garden developed in an incoherent but highly individual manner. Fossilized tree trunks, a lead ostrich and a 'lunatic asylum' of plant freaks were among the notable features. Like Crisp, one of Bowles's main interests was his rock garden, but his interest was less in its scenic than in its horticultural value. Most of the rockwork at Myddleton House was sunk into the bank to provide a cool root-run for his plants, and elaborate systems of underground irrigation through screes of crushed stone were devised to imitate the endless water supply of melting glaciers. Bowles wrote scholarly works on the crocus and colchicum, snowdrops and snowflakes, but is best known for his charming trilogy of books about his garden, a lighthearted but learned and informative near-autobiography. *My Garden in Spring, My Garden in Summer* and *My Garden in Autumn and Winter* appeared in 1914.[26]

The other outstanding gardener of the Ellacombe circle was Ellen Willmott. Like Gertrude Jekyll, Miss Willmott was one of the first recipients of the Victoria Medal of Honour in 1897, but this was one of their very few similarities. Miss Willmott, the daughter of a wealthy solicitor, was a haughty and forceful character, strikingly attractive but with few friends. In 1875 her father bought Warley Place in Essex and Miss Willmott took over the garden. In 1882 the new alpine garden was begun, constructed by James Backhouse of York as a sunken ravine rather than a raised mountain and leading into a subterranean fernery. Miss Willmott travelled widely (she had a notable garden on the Mediterranean as well as at Warley Place); she collected plants avidly and at one time employed 100 gardeners. Her book of photographs of *Warley Garden* (1909) shows her catholic taste for plants: the first plate shows huge exotic agaves in tubs with a newly-mown wild-flower and bulb meadow in the foreground. Her great love was roses, and

Warley Place: giant agaves border the bulb-strewn meadow.

her sumptuous *The Genus Rosa*, illustrated by Alfred Parsons, appeared in parts from 1910 to 1914. Unlike Miss Jekyll, Miss Willmott was a gardener first and foremost, but because of the scale on which she planted the garden scene at Warley Place was dramatic and the freedom of planting – allowing plants to seed at will – created just the degree of wilderness which Robinson preached but generally failed to achieve. Eventually Miss Willmott's enthusiasm overtook her income and she died, impoverished, in 1934.

If Warley Place represented the ultimate in wild gardening, contemporary formal splendour is nowhere better exemplified than at Port Lympne, Kent, designed by Herbert Baker *c.*1910 as a holiday house for Sir Philip Sassoon. The garden stretched below the house in a series of elaborate terraces: marble pools and colonnades, a gigantic staircase, separate terraces for asters and dahlias, a chess-board garden, a vineyard and matching figyard, water gardens, tennis courts (one orientated for morning and one for afternoon use) and vast herbaceous borders. Fifteen gardeners were employed throughout the year, with the number swelling to thirty in August when Sassoon was in residence.[27]

Americans abroad

The gradual fusion of classical, Old English and cottage garden ideals was greatly stimulated by the arrival in Britain of the 'Henry James Americans', people who, having made or inherited enormous fortunes in their New World, migrated back to the Old World to revel in its history and culture. This American influence did not express itself in specific features. Rather it resulted in the leavening of established British ideas with a unique blend of New World vigour and with a profound reverence for Italian history, Parisian sophistication and English cottage-garden simplicity.

In 1893 William Waldorf Astor bought Cliveden, the great Italianate villa built by Barry for the Duke of Sutherland, and embellished the garden with many genuine Italian works of art including the Villa Borghese balustrade acquired when Astor was American ambassador in Rome. In 1903 Astor gave Cliveden to his son and bought the moated castle of Hever in Kent. Here, with F. L. Pearson as architect and Joseph Cheal as landscape gardener, he restored the castle, built a new 'Tudor' village to house his many guests and made a remarkable schizophrenic garden, part Old

Geoffrey Jellicoe's parterre at Ditchley: fountains screen the bathing pool from view.

English and part Italian, to house his enormous collection of Italian and especially Roman sculpture.

In 1904 came Edith Wharton's *Italian Villas and Their Gardens*, the first of a flurry of such works. In 1925 the English architects Geoffrey Jellicoe and J. C. Shepherd published *Italian Gardens of the Renaissance*, in which the architectural accuracy of Inigo Triggs and the philosophical analysis of Sir George Sitwell were combined. This led to Geoffrey Jellicoe being commissioned by Ronald and Nancy Tree to design the garden for the Palladian mansion of Ditchley Park, Oxfordshire.[28] The garden, constructed by William Wood in 1935, was partly a restoration of the original eighteenth-century concept, partly a reflection of the Italian origins of Palladio and partly an acceptance of a modern way of life. A small temple was moved up from the lake to terminate the long grass terrace. An elaborate parterre ran parallel to the terrace walk and out to a semi-circular swimming pool with a water-curtain of innumerable fine jets. This not only created a subtle terminus to the parterre but partly concealed bathers from the house.[29] With the water turned off, a long vista through the park was revealed beyond the pool.

Another wealthy American, Mrs Gillson, bought Cornwell Manor, only five miles from Ditchley, in 1936, and she restored not only the house but the whole village of Cornwell. Her Italian sympathies found their expression in Clough Williams-Ellis, the architect and owner of Portmeirion. The garden included steep flights of steps down to a formalized stream and up to classical gate piers on the road, balustraded terraces and a charming, concealed swimming-pool garden.[30]

Ditchley attracted the Trees because of its classical grandeur. Cornwell Manor was on a lesser scale but had the added appeal of its Cotswold setting and its charming village. The steep hills, clear light and enchanting honey-coloured villages of the Cotswolds, sprinkled with handsome merchants' houses reflecting the wealth of the Tudor woollen trade, exerted a considerable appeal for other Americans. Broadway, Gloucestershire, in particular boasted a substantial colony of American Anglophiles, and it was just outside Broadway that the fusion of European elegance and Cotswold charm first occurred, with momentous consequences for the future of the English garden.

A cottage garden par excellence

In 1907 Gertrude Winthrop, wife of a wealthy New Yorker, bought the estate of Hidcote Bartrim, deep in the Cotswolds, for her son Lawrence Johnston. Born in Paris, Johnston studied history at Cambridge from 1894–7 and became a naturalized British citizen in 1900. The garden at Hidcote soon grew beyond its walled enclosure on to the windswept hilltop, so hedges were necessary for shelter. Johnston planted beech and hornbeam, yew and lime, 'tapestry' hedges of box, holly, yew and copper beech around a series of garden compartments. The compartments show some influence of Lutyens, although their apparently haphazard arrangement and the simple, almost crude, treatment of connecting steps and walls had none of Lutyens's elegance. The colour planning of the garden owed much to Gertrude Jekyll and to Johnston's closest woman friend, Norah Lindsay,[31] and the planting benefited from Johnston's association with a wide circle of distinguished gardeners. He thought of himself mainly as a collector of plants, and his enthusiasm for collecting took him to the Cape in 1927 with Collingwood Ingram, George Taylor (later Director of Kew) and Reginald Cory, and to Yunnan in 1931 with George Forrest.

The success of Hidcote, however, and its widespread renown resulted not so much from its plant collection but from its stunning versatility. The house sheltered just below the escarpment ridge, so Johnston created a long axis rising gently through the walled garden and red borders, up between twin gazebos to the hornbeam stilt garden, then through a gateway offering breathtaking distant views. From the gazebos, a second long axis swept at right angles down

The Bathing Pool Garden at Hidcote c. 1910, with trellis reinforcing the effect of the young hedges.

the hill and up again between high hedges to a second gate. On to these two dominant axes the clusters of smaller gardens were attached: the winter garden, the fuchsia garden, the bathing-pool garden, the pillar garden and the yellow garden, dedicated to Johnston's mother, Mrs Winthrop. Below these formal hedged enclosures was the stream garden, a completely informal woodland garden beginning behind the bathing-pool garden, extending across the Long Walk where a bridge and steps were so planned as to be invisible from the gazebo and extending on to merge into the surrounding countryside beyond a ha-ha.

Rare plants mingled with local cranesbills. Crisp hedges were softened by festoons of *Tropaeolum speciosum* or trails of *Vitis coignetiae*. Fiery sprays of alstroemeria blazed from the base of tall dark columns of tightly clipped yews. In the red garden, trees and shrubs, vines and roses, herbaceous plants and tender perennials combined to create the richness of red velvet while, behind the

hedge, a wide expanse of plain grass carpeted the theatre garden. By the side of Mrs Winthrop's garden a tunnel of pleached lime terminated in a view over the stream garden, recalling in miniature the views from a Renaissance loggia over the Italian campagna.

Mrs Winthrop's Garden c. 1920, named after Lawrence Johnston's mother.

Lawrence Johnston's example was widely emulated. In 1918 Mr and Mrs J. B. Muir moved to Kiftsgate, becoming Johnston's next-door neighbours, and Mrs Muir especially began to develop her garden, exchanging plants and ideas with Johnston. The old paved garden, Four Squares, was hedged in box and filled to overflowing with shrub roses, herbs, bulbs and herbaceous plants. Rare climbers and a huge *Rosa mutabilis* softened the walls of the house. The wide border, the yellow border, the white sunken garden and the long rose border followed, and in 1930 planting began on the steep, dry bank below the house. In 1938 the most notable of Kiftsgate's plants came from E. A. Bunyard's nursery, *Rosa filipes* 'Kiftsgate'.

In 1919 Charles Wade followed Johnston's example by buying an old Cotswold manor house and tumbledown farm buildings at Snowshill, Gloucestershire. Wade had professional advice on the planning of his garden from Baillie Scott, but he was determined not to be ruled by a professional gardener, as his father had been.

Preferring to have my own garden and not a gardener's garden in which I was allowed to walk ... I noted a labourer who was a good worker and very tidy ... and having asked him, I was satisfied that he knew nothing about gardening beyond cabbages and cauliflowers, so here was my very first man.[32]

Wade's garden was much smaller than Johnston's, a mere two acres, but it sloped steeply. He carved the hill into a series of small terraces, a delightful three-dimensional puzzle, and furnished the bones of the garden with the restrained but varied planting which Johnston had shown would flourish on the limestone soil.

In 1933 Captain F. E. and Mrs Phyllis Reiss bought Tintinhull House in Somerset, an early seventeenth-century manor house with a charming and distinguished façade added in the eighteenth century. Its garden was less than an acre in extent and completely flat, but it had already been divided into small formal gardens by Dr S. J. M. Price from 1900. Mrs Reiss lived for twenty-eight years at Tintinhull, embellishing the gardens with planting schemes which evolved over many years of patient experimentation. After

Tintinhull, a compact cluster of garden compartments. A view of the Eagle Court from the west front of the house.

the war the tennis court was converted into a flower garden in memory of a nephew killed in the war. The loggia, rectangular lily pool and twin flanking borders, one in strong, warm colours and the other in soft pastels, turned the axis of the garden and welded it into a varied but unified whole.[33]

'Without grandeur, but not without formality'

Lawrence Johnston's close friend, Norah Lindsay, also spread far and wide the Hidcote atmosphere which she had helped to develop. She described her own garden at Sutton Courtenay as 'without grandeur, but not without formality', and she worked to create a timeless, drowsy background for an old and sleepy house, a garden in which stray seedlings were welcomed for their charming spontaneity.[34] The garden merged from the grape-wreathed pergola of the Persian Garden to riverside walks through carpets of wild

Norah Lindsay's garden at Sutton Courtenay, 'without grandeur but not without formality'.

flowers. From its beginning the garden was planned as a bird sanctuary as well as a home for native and exotic flowers.

Mrs Lindsay also converted Fleming's ribbon borders in the Long Garden at Cliveden into flowing herbaceous borders within trim box hedges for the second Viscount Astor. Later she rearranged the fussy nineteenth-century parterre at Blickling Hall in Norfolk, concentrating the planting into four big square beds filled with herbaceous plants in soft colours near the house and strong oranges and yellows in the more distant beds. At Godmersham Park, Kent, she designed the borders around the swimming pool built in the old kitchen garden for Robert Tritton.[35]

One of the most remarkable visitors to Hidcote Manor was Vita Sackville-West. She and her husband, Harold Nicolson, began their own garden at Long Barn, Kent, in 1914. Born in 1892, an only child in the great house of the Sackvilles at Knole, she spent much of her childhood in romantic isolation exploring the ancestral home and its garden. The Nicolsons spent the first months of their marriage in Istanbul, in the diplomatic service, but returned to England and Long Barn in 1914. Here Vita was introduced to Gertrude Jekyll, Lutyens designed a Dutch garden for her, and she became a friend of William Robinson, who was fifty-four years her senior. In 1926 and 1927 she returned to the Middle East, to Persia, where her romantic character revelled in the secluded, formal paradise gardens filled with placid pools and brilliant, fragrant flowers. She loved Hidcote, too, for its abundance of flowers, its firm geometry, its native charm allied with an indefinable air of more southern sophistication. In 1949 she wrote a perceptive description of Johnston's garden in the *Journal of the Royal Horticultural Society*.[36]

Sleeping Beauty

By 1929 the Nicolsons were worried by sprawling development which threatened to engulf Long Barn. They began to look for a new home and in May 1930 they acquired the ruined, squalid but isolated remains of Sissinghurst Castle in Kent. Vita described it as 'Sleeping Beauty's Garden ... a garden crying out for rescue'.[37] For two years they camped in the castle, clearing centuries of filth, rubbish and clutter. In 1932 Harold began surveying the garden and gradually, despite his discovery that the garden and its 700-year accumulation of walls and moat contained not a single right-angle, he coaxed a network of orderly vistas which bound the

Sissinghurst, a view from the Tudor tower.

garden together. The meticulous renovations which transformed Sissinghurst Castle into a romantic, if unorthodox and inconvenient home were assisted by Albert Powys, Secretary of the Society for the Protection of Ancient Buildings. In 1935 Powys enclosed the west end of the former vegetable garden with a bold semi-circular bay of brick wall. Powys's Wall reflected the shape of the yew rondel which was in turn modelled on the traditional dimensions of Kentish oasthouses.

Vita Sackville-West poured herself and her poetry into the garden (she later poured her garden into poems and books), clothing the vistas with a 'profusion, even extravagance and exuberance' [38] of informal planting. She was as striking and flamboyant as Lawrence Johnston was shy and retiring. Her prolific literary output, her position at the centre of the Bloomsbury set and her unconventional family life at Sissinghurst earned for the garden a renown which has remained unequalled in the twentieth century.

The many compartments of the garden were planned – as in Miss Jekyll's garden at Munstead Wood – for seasonal effect: the lime walk of early spring flowers, the nut walk thickly under-planted with polyanthus, the Cottage Garden of summer flowers and billowing rose borders. Colour, too, was carefully disciplined: glowing yellow and orange against the Tudor brick walls of the Cottage Garden, velvety purple and blue of the shrub roses inter-planted with geraniums, alliums, clematis and violas, vibrant lemons and oranges of azaleas among pale spring foliage in the moat garden and, in the opposite corner of the garden, the luminous, aromatic tranquillity of the White Garden.

When, in May 1938, the garden was first opened to the public for the National Gardens Scheme, the brilliance of Sissinghurst, the perfect fusion of Harold Nicolson's classical mind and Vita Sackville-West's romantic heart, was magnified and its tranquillity intensified by the looming threat of war.

Sixteen months later war was declared. The Nicolson sons, Ben and Nigel, and the young head gardener, Jack Vass, went into the army. With them went a host of other young gardeners and a way of life which would never return.

II

The Modern Garden

A brave new world

In 1945 a new era dawned. The government had worked hard during the war to ensure that soldiers would return, this time, to a land fit for heroes. The New Towns Act (1946) established a new framework for protecting the countryside against suburban sprawl, for creating green and spacious New Towns modelled on Ebenezer Howard's 'Garden City' and for improving conditions within older cities. The National Parks and Access to the Countryside Act (1949) recognized, after seventy years of parliamentary debate, that Britain's finest scenery was worthy of protection and established nine National Parks. The Agriculture Act (1947) established a system of guaranteed prices for staple foods and grants for improvement and agricultural land and buildings, to ensure that England would never again be so dependent on imported food and at the mercy of enemy submarines.

To pay for such measures and for improved education, a National Health Service, pensions and other social benefits, taxes steadily increased, crippling the hereditary landed estates and family-owned industries on which the maintenance of great houses and the making of great gardens depends. Aristocratic gardeners had no place in the new Utopia.

Such gardens as continued to develop after the war were mainly informal woodland gardens. The few significant formal gardens were on flat sites where formality could be achieved with hedges and avenues. Terraced Italianate gardens requiring skilled craftsmen belonged to the past. Even where financial resources were available, building materials were strictly rationed.

At Bussock Mayne, near Newbury, Gerald Palmer found that rock was one of the few commodities not subject to rationing

(*Above*) Norah Lindsay's four squares of herbaceous plants in the West Garden at Blickling: the most recent overlay in a garden frequently modified since the house was started in 1619.

(*Right*) Knightshayes, with its combination of simple formality and rich plant collection, is one of the very few great gardens of post–war years.

(Above) Alternation of light and shade structures the interlocking compartments at Tintinhull. Dark holm oaks provide an ideal background for the white garden and frame the main vista.

(Left) Glowing orange, red and yellow flowers in the Cottage Garden at Sissinghurst harmonize with the Tudor brickwork all around.

(Opposite above) At Bressingham, Alan Bloom gradually amassed an extensive collection of herbaceous perennials for his informal 'island' borders.

(Opposite below) Graham Thomas's extensive planting at Killerton transformed the mundane topic of ground-cover planting into an art form.

(Above) Thomas Church's garden at
Sonoma, California: fluid forms of
the swimming pool and its sculpture
echo the lines of the natural landscape.

(Left) John Brookes's garden for
Penguin Books at Harmondsworth,
Middlesex, turned a Mondrian
painting into a living landscape.

(Left) East Lambrook Manor: Margery Fish's carefully planned muddle around her Somerset cottage provided a potent counter-attraction to the geometry of the Modern garden.

(Right) Historical influences which inspired the garden plan at Barnsley House, near Cirencester, extend into the ornamental kitchen garden or 'potager'.

(Above) The Tradescant Garden, in the churchyard where John Tradescant lies buried, designed by Lady Salisbury was modelled on seventeenth-century patterns for knot gardens.

(Left) Historical inspiration can also be seen in the 'English' roses bred by David Austin. The yellow rose in the foreground is 'Graham Thomas'.

(Opposite above) Beth Chatto's garden at White Barn, Essex: plants for ground-cover for sun and shade, for flower-arranging, in apparently casual profusion.

(Opposite below) Heathers and conifers in Adrian Bloom's garden at Bressingham: the twentieth-century equivalent of the Victorian pinetum with its impressive array of solid evergreens.

Cornfield annuals in a country park: using technology to re-create a landscape
which technology has all but destroyed.

and he commissioned Pulhams to make an extensive rock garden extending from the old farm pond below the house.[1] H. Milner White planned the more formal elements of the garden – the drive, rose garden and kitchen garden, in 1946/7.

Pusey, in Oxfordshire, and Heaselands, in West Sussex, were also typical of the new scale of gardening. At Pusey, bought by Mr and Mrs Michael Hornby in 1935, Geoffrey Jellicoe designed the terrace and steps in 1937 but most of the garden was developed after the war. There was a considerable emphasis on permanent shrubs, including shrub roses, but Pusey also retained one magnificent herbaceous border and much Robinsonian herbaceous planting at the water's edge.[2]

In the Savill Garden, building materials were provided as a symbolic gesture. In 1947 bricks from bombed houses in East London were used to build a high buttressed wall, an ideal home for climbers and tender wall plants. From this the raised beds of choice alpines, the rose garden and herbaceous borders merged into the pre-war woodland garden. Work was also begun in 1947 on more extensive woodland planting in the Valley Garden at Windsor overlooking Virginia Water. The garden was greatly extended in 1951 with a collection of species rhododendrons moved from Tower Court, Ascot.

Winkworth Arboretum near Godalming, like the Valley Garden, started to develop rapidly after the war. The tangle of birch scrub with scattered oaks and pines was enriched by Dr Wilfrid Fox with a special enthusiasm for maples, mountain ash and other plants of brilliant autumn colours.[3] At Wisley, too, similar developments were taking place with the planting of rhododendrons, camellias and magnolias on the newly acquired Battlestone Hill.

In 1948 work began on the 'Northern Wisley', the garden of the Northern Horticultural Society at Harlow Car, Harrogate. Although on a smaller scale than Wisley, the garden grew quickly to include all the features of a traditional garden: rose gardens and herbaceous borders, annuals and alpines, trial beds, water gardens and rhododendron woodland.

The planting at Anglesey Abbey in Cambridgeshire was on a totally different scale. The Elizabethan manor house, built on the remains of an Augustinian monastery, was bought by Lord Fairhaven and his brother in 1926, and work began on planting the vast, flat, fenland garden before the war, with avenues of seventeenth-century grandeur. In 1953 a circle of classical columns around Bernini's *David* celebrated the coronation of Queen Elizabeth II. Islands of coloured-leaved shrubs and trees were arranged

Anglesey Abbey: the colonnade celebrates the coronation of Queen Elizabeth II.

informally in grassy plots. The hyacinth garden, in which 4,000 bulbs are replaced by dahlias for summer, and a vast semi-circular herbaceous border provided more detailed and colourful interest nearer the house. Tree-planting continued until Lord Fairhaven's death in 1966, when the Abbey was bequeathed to the National Trust.

One of the most enchanting post-war woodland gardens began in the 1950s at Knightshayes Court, near Tiverton in Devon. The house was built in 1863 to the design of William Burgess, who also planned the terraces below the house. Sir John and Lady Heathcote Amory married in 1937, but the war and post-war industrial problems delayed their attempts to develop the garden. Once started, however, progress was rapid. Stereotyped flower-beds on the terraces were replaced by simpler patterns of low thymes and

THE MODERN GARDEN · 249

hardy borders. A paved garden with silver foliage and a lead tank was inserted into one yew-hedged enclosure by Graham Thomas in 1959, and the adjacent bowling green was replaced by a circular pool overhung by weeping silver-leaved pear. In the woodland, planted by Sir John's grandfather, glades were cleared, steps made and an exquisite garden of rhododendrons and magnolias, maples and other decorative-barked trees developed, richly underplanted with bulbs, trilliums and other herbaceous woodlanders.

In a more formal manner the gardens at Hidcote, Tintinhull and Sissinghurst continued to develop and to receive widespread admiration. Their deceptively simple formality overlain with a rich tapestry of shrubs, herbaceous plants, bulbs and climbers in close mixture showed what might be achieved on a more limited scale on flat sites and with closely confining rectangular boundaries. It helped, of course, to have a beautiful house, as at Tintinhull, or the historic remains of a romantic castle as at Sissinghurst, and these advantages were shared by two notable post-war gardens, Greys Court and Haseley Court, both in Oxfordshire. Greys Court

Flowering cherries at Greys Court.

Haseley Court: the chessmen.

showed much allegiance to Sissinghurst, with a white garden, a rose garden, a nut walk and a cherry garden inserted into the picturesque remains of a medieval flint castle.

Haseley Court is one of the most delightful of the Anglo-American gardens. Nancy and Ronald Tree, the restorers of Ditchley, were divorced after the war. Mrs Tree remarried, becoming Mrs Nancy Lancaster. In 1954 Mrs Lancaster discovered Haseley Court, a once-splendid Queen Anne house, roofless, decaying and threatened with demolition. She bought it, re-roofed it, and restored its surroundings. A new forecourt and steps were added, designed – as at Ditchley – by Geoffrey Jellicoe. The one remarkable survival at Haseley was a topiary chess-garden, planted *c.* 1850 and saved by an old man in the village who carefully trimmed the figures each year while the rest of the garden sank into oblivion. Mrs Lancaster added more yews. Bastions of yew compartmented a new border leading down to the remaining arm of a moat. Old irregular walls behind the house and a new hornbeam tunnel enclosed a quartered garden of box-edged borders. The hornbeams were thickly underplanted with spring bulbs, the borders were filled with old-fashioned flowers, and each of the quarters of the garden was planted in a different manner. The most intriguing quarter was the maze-like garden patterned on the Roman pavement at Torcello. Haseley Court became a blend of formal axes and informal planting, reason and romance, cottage garden charm and cosmopolitan *joie-de-vivre*.[4]

Gentlemen gardeners

The subtlety and richness of Haseley Court, as of Hidcote itself, resulted from the constant ministrations of a devoted owner and occasional guidance from a new generation of gentlemen garden consultants. Mrs Lancaster had assistance from Geoffrey Jellicoe and Norman Fowler. James Russell of Sunningdale Nurseries advised on the planning and planting of innumerable gardens for which his nursery supplied plants.

Graham Thomas, who trained at the Cambridge Botanic Garden and who, as a student, was one of the last visitors to Gertrude Jekyll's garden at Munstead Wood, joined Russell at Sunningdale. Here he began his notable collection of old roses and from here, with his combination of artistry and plantsmanship, he advised on many major gardens, including Knightshayes and Sezincote. In 1956 he became Gardens Adviser to the National Trust, a post he held until 1974 when he partially retired to the position of Gardens Consultant, in which capacity he has continued to contribute to National Trust gardens to the present day.[5]

Lanning Roper, an American by birth, first came to England as an ensign in the US Navy during the war and later returned to study at Kew and Edinburgh. In 1957 he became a freelance writer and garden designer, travelling widely and influencing a generation of garden owners with his restrained combinations of old roses, herbaceous perennials, herbs and shrubs with good foliage. Like most of his fellow 'gentlemen consultants', Lanning Roper worked mainly in the larger private gardens but, in 1972, he joined forces with Geoffrey Jellicoe to design the new canal garden south of the house at Wisley.[6] John Codrington, Beverley Nichols and Russell Page, all designers in the same tradition, planned gardens of luxuriant good taste, secure in the knowledge that their designs would be sustained by the attentions of their knowledgeable clients.[7]

The profession of garden design in the more traditional sense was almost solely maintained by Mawson's natural successor Percy Cane.[8] Much of Cane's work was carried out before the war – indeed he began to design even before the First World War – but

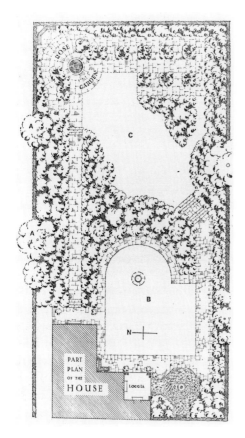

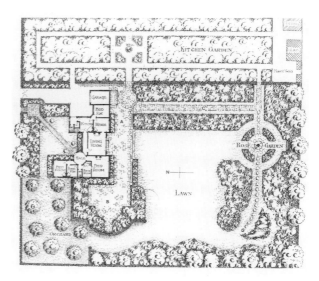

he continued to practise until 1973, when he retired at the age of ninety-one, two years before his death.

Cane redesigned the huge herbaceous borders of the Lutyens garden at Hascombe Court in Surrey, and designed a rock garden and Japanese gallery below the terraces. In 1945 he was called to the Elmhirsts' garden at Dartington Hall in Devon, where he cut wide vistas through the woodland and designed the long steps which are still a feature of the garden. In 1947 he replanned the gardens of Falkland Palace, emphasizing the plan of former palace buildings with rows of Lawson's cypress and adding long walks, terraces and huge herbaceous borders. One of his most interesting gardens, started in 1953, is Westfields in Bedfordshire. Westfields has all the ingredients of a Cane garden – the formal lily pool, rose garden, glade and rock garden with cascading pools – but arranged with unusual subtlety.[9]

Percy Cane's larger commissions were elegantly classical and reliably simple in their planting: roses, lilacs, *Viburnum tomentosum* 'Mariesii' and laburnums, flowering cherries, brooms and Pfitzer

Two gardens by Percy Cane; glades, rose gardens, lily pools and shrub walks compressed into every garden plan.

juniper became almost trademarks, but Cane also gave advice on smaller gardens through his periodicals and his three books, *Garden Design of Today* (1934), *The Earth is My Canvas* (1956), and *The Creative Art of Garden Design*, published in 1967 when he was eighty-six. However, his advice on small gardens was largely counter-productive. By skilfully squeezing a quart into a pint pot himself, he misled his readers into trying to squeeze a pint into a thimble and many post-war gardeners struggled in vain to achieve the impossible.

Gardens in peril

In 1956 a reviewer of *The Earth is My Canvas* recognized that 'Mr Cane's creation can have no place in the gardens of tomorrow. Changed economic circumstances will make every man his own garden-architect.'[10] Even when every man was his own garden architect the future for the larger garden looked increasingly grim. At Hidcote, Lawrence Johnston became increasingly concerned about the future of his garden as his memory began to fail. Lady Colefax persuaded him that he should give his garden to the National Trust. The Trust joined with the Royal Horticultural Society to form a Garden Fund, and in 1948 Hidcote became the first garden to be acquired by the National Trust as a garden in its own right.[11]

The National Trust, founded in 1895 to preserve the natural heritage of the Lake District and other threatened rural landscapes, gradually steered its activities to saving what it could of our cultural heritage. Gardens were accumulated incidentally as the appurtenances of fine houses. Barrington Court was acquired in 1907 and the garden was made by Sir Philip Lyle when he became the tenant. Montacute was given to the Trust in 1931 by the Society for the Protection of Ancient Buildings, who wished to preserve the building but were unable, under their Constitution, to own property. The garden borders were replanted by Vita Sackville-West and subsequently by Mrs Reiss from Tintinhull. Sharpitor and Wightwick came to the Trust in 1937 and Little Moreton Hall in 1938. By the end of the war Cliveden, Blickling, Packwood, Peckover, West Wycombe, Killerton and Polesden Lacey were added. Two or three major properties followed each year for more than a decade; Stourhead with its eighteenth-century landscape and Knole, childhood home of Vita Sackville-West in 1946, Peto's garden at Buscot in 1948, Snowshill in 1951, Tintinhull in 1953

Lutyens's Castle Drogo, acquired by the National Trust in 1974.

and eventually Sissinghurst itself in 1967. Knightshayes, essentially a post-war garden, was bequeathed by its maker, Sir John Heathcote Amory, in 1972, and Lutyens's Castle Drogo came in 1974.

The Garden Fund which accepted Hidcote in 1948 also acquired Bodnant in the following year. Nymans and Sheffield Park followed in 1954, Mount Stewart in 1955, Trengwainton in 1961, Knightshayes in 1972 and Studley Royal in 1980.

With the demise of a gardening aristocracy the impetus for plant exploration also declined. Frank Kingdon-Ward returned to Assam in 1946, spending four years there, and made his last expedition to Upper Burma in 1953. Frank Ludlow and Major George Sherriff also explored Bhutan, Tibet and Kashmir before the war, being joined by Dr George Taylor in 1938, and introduced or re-introduced many fine rhododendrons, gentians, lilies, meconopsis and primulas. In 1945 Ludlow and Sherriff returned to Asia and sent large consignments of living plants by air back to Taylor in

London. One of the most remarkable introductions of the post-war years was the Dawn Redwood, *Metasequioa glyptostroboides*. Known initially only from fossil records, living plants were discovered in China in 1941 and living material was collected from them in 1944. Seeds were sent to the Arnold Arboretum in 1947 and distributed in America and Europe in 1948.[12] Although new to science and extremely rare in the wild, the metasequoia proved thoroughly amenable to cultivation, and is now widely planted.

Brave new plants

The ease of world travel by air has greatly facilitated plant exploration but this ease of communication, the feeling that there could be few hardy plants left to be discovered and the absence of wealthy collectors or prestigious plant-collecting nurseries have combined to reduce the romance of plant introduction.

During the latter half of the twentieth century the emphasis has shifted from plant introduction to plant breeding. Mendel's pioneering work on inheritance was almost unknown until William Bateson read Mendel's paper of 1865 to a meeting of the Royal Horticultural Society in 1900.[13] In 1906 the word 'genetics' was coined and plant breeding became increasingly systematic. By 1960 the molecular structure of chromosomes and genes, the carriers of inherited characters, was unravelled, and breeding entered the space age of 'genetic engineering'. Micropropagation techniques, used to produce millions of plants from one small piece of stem or bud, have also had considerable impact on the production of garden plants and will continue to do so.

Much attention is focused, from time to time, on the more extreme ambitions which continue to elude breeders seeking blue roses, black tulips, red daffodils, golden sweet peas or yellow clematis, but many advances of a less sensational kind have been made. In roses the form of the hybrid tea and freedom of flowering of the polyantha roses have been combined in the floribunda rose. The colour range has been widened to include brilliant orange and subtle copper/amber. Fragrance, resistance to disease, compact habit and beauty of leaf are all increasingly important in the breeding programme. The Yakusimanum rhododendrons have brought year-round foliage interest to colourful and compact rhododendrons.

The Plant Varieties and Seeds Act 1964, by allowing breeders to protect their investment in plant breeding, gave a major boost to the development of new varieties of flowers and vegetables and lawn grasses. Among bedding plants especially, many F_1 hybrid varieties produce compact floriferous and colourful plants which are nearly as uniform as the vegetatively propagated cultivars they have largely replaced.

The interest shown by plant breeders in compactness, brightness and durability was symptomatic of the new market for plants: post-war Britain and post-war gardens belonged increasingly to Mr Everyman.

Everyman's garden

More than 4 million new houses were built between the wars, appealing to the national ideal of the small, individual cottage home.[14] After the war New Towns were established in the hope of providing more houses without creating suburban sprawl. The typical dwelling was a two-storey house with a fairly spacious plot. England had become a nation of garden owners.

The small garden represented a new problem for makers of gardens. Not surprisingly the vacuum was filled by technology before it was tackled aesthetically. William Wood's 1938 catalogue, which proudly illustrated the Ditchley garden, offered equipment for harrowing, brushing, spiking and rolling the lawn, rhinohide hoses and garden sprinklers, Karbo-Killegg winter wash, nicotine and lime sulphur. There was a 'Little Wonder' hedgetrimmer (operated by winding a handle, as for an egg whisk), a 'Stuart' centrifugal pump for fountains and waterfalls and a vast array of gadgetry.

After the war, with rapid advances in engineering and chemical industries, the range of products increased as their size, flexibility and cost diminished. DDT (1939) and hormone weedkillers (1942) revolutionized pest and weed control. The development of plastics, replacing steel in a wide range of products, led to further advances. Lightweight electric mowers appeared in the 1960s. The hover-mower was patented by Flymo in 1966, and in 1975 the nylon-cord grass cutter made it possible to trim long grass and edges in awkward corners.

Production of plants benefited, too, from technical advances. Mist propagation in the 1950s, peat and plastic pots in the 1960s, polythene tunnels, automatic and later computer control of the glasshouse environment, have made it possible to produce an ever wider range of plants of high quality at reduced cost. The main

CROCK BREAKING MACHINE

In Use at Many
of the Leading
Establishments

Renders
Invaluable
Service

" Crock " Breaking Machine

This Machine has become very popular amongst Orchid Growers and others who have long felt the need of a machine for breaking up Crocks.

The construction of the Star or Toothed Rollers is entirely novel and effective, and by a simple movement of the regulator they can be adjusted to break from dust to 2 in. Crocks. The whole of the gearing is encased, thus forming a neat and serviceable machine.

PRICE, complete as shown, **£4-9-6**

' LITTLE WONDER ' HEDGE CLIPPER

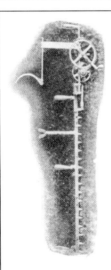

The All-British " Little Wonder " Hedge Clipper is manufactured in one size only, which makes a 40 in. cut. The machine (with attachment at 12/6 extra) is a one-man machine for side-cuts up to 4 ft. high in one operation, and one or two-man for top-cuts. It will clip tops as wide as 6½ ft. Sides as high as 9 ft. can be clipped by two men, without scaffolding.

Two men with a " Little Wonder " can do in one hour the work that two men with shears would do in an ordinary working day.

WE CLAIM that this clipper will clip the same thickness, and even more, than a pair of ordinary shears (excepting notch). The machine is guaranteed not to break—in the event of its meeting with a hard stump, the machine simply stops.

Price £6-18-6, including practical packing case in which Clippers can be kept when not in use, sharpening stone, spanner, and spare nuts and bolts. Carriage Paid in Great Britain and Ireland. All Spare Parts kept in stock. Attachment for use as a One-man Outfit, **13/9** extra.

A crock-breaker for potting orchids and a mechanical hedge-trimmer: indispensible equipment for the modern garden.

change for the consumer – the gardener – however, has been in distribution of plants: the availability of rapid door-to-door transport made it possible for nurseries – like the seed firms after the advent of the penny post – to develop national rather than local markets. Firms with a reputation for quality and variety flourished. Sunningdale, Waterer and Notcutt became household names.

Hilliers' Nursery, founded in Winchester in 1864, was already renowned for its range of plants when Harold Hillier took the reins in 1946, but Harold continued to extend the range of plants until some 14,000 different plants were listed.[15]

Gardening on impulse

By 1960 the private motor-car was also becoming commonplace. The more astute nurserymen turned this situation to their advantage by setting up shops on the nursery from which plants could be sold. 'Sundries' were added and the 'garden centre' was born. Throughout the 1960s nearly every nursery bordering on a main road, and many less fortunately placed, established a garden centre. Growing of plants in containers rather than in the field enabled customers to buy at any time of year. As container-productions used much less space than open-ground production, land was released for the all-important car park to allow customers to carry away their cumbersome purchases.

In the sundries section every conceivable device for furnishing, controlling and maintaining the garden is now displayed, skilfully packaged and presented to stimulate impulse purchases. With the availability of Plant Breeder's Rights to patent new varieties, such marketing techniques have extended also into plantsmanship. Roses are named after film stars or are sponsored by banks and building societies, whisky and tobacco manufacturers and stately homes. Even the plants themselves receive film-star treatment. *Potentilla* 'Red Ace' was the first 'superplant' to be so launched, in a blaze of publicity, in 1976.[16] *Scabiosa* 'Blue Butterfly' received national promotion on its début in 1985, and 'flavour of the month' plants are now being advertised nationally in many garden centres.

As in the 1860s with railways and manufacturing, so in the 1960s the motor-car and technology brought virtually unlimited opportunity for garden-making, but concepts of design lagged far behind. Scarcely anyone in the new democracy dreamed of consulting a professional designer: Capability Browns were for aristocrats. Gardening books and periodicals were written, of course, but for people already interested in gardening. In the new media for disseminating ideas – radio and television – producers decided very early on that broad accents and heavy boots were necessary to create an authentic atmosphere in the studio. In 1934, eight years after the foundation of the BBC, Cecil Middleton was engaged to broadcast a series of Sunday afternoon programmes, *In*

Your Garden. He continued, with great success, until his death in 1945, to be succeeded by Fred Streeter, Percy Thrower, Geoffrey Smith and many others, but the emphasis has remained firmly on plants and gardening. The overwhelming majority of gardeners continued to create gardens which were pale shadows of Chatsworth and other great Victorian gardens.

The main agreement about the design of gardens was that it should be labour-saving, and the three main approaches to labour-saving seemed to be mechanization, the use of shrubs and ground-cover planting.

Armchair gardening

Mechanization, and particularly the enormous improvement in powered mowers, cultivators, sprayers and hedge trimmers, saved many larger gardens from complete decay. As machinery became lighter and cheaper its use spread to smaller gardens: in the late 1980s, even the most minute lawn is usually mown with an electric mower.

In 1949 the *Journal of the Royal Horticultural Society* contained two articles on labour-saving gardens and Wisley held a 'Mechanical Appliances Demonstration'. E. R. Hoare[17] described mowers and powered diggers, hedge trimmers and sprayers, and the need to design the garden to suit them. F. E. W. Hanger,[18] the Curator of Wisley, concentrated on planting. His advice was to abandon bedding schemes, to use the new wealth of shrubs introduced from the Himalayas, China and Japan, and to concentrate on those shrubs which grow well on the local soil: rhododendrons, conifers, maples and magnolias on acid soil, viburnums, lilacs, philadelphus, spiraea and cherries on chalk. Hedges, the backbone of Hidcote, were out, except near the house where slow-growing holly and yew were admissible. Pergolas were 'a thing of the past'. The herbaceous border was deeply suspect, but carpeting plants were approved as undoubtedly great labour-savers! Automation in the greenhouse was discussed as a dream, suited only to the largest and most adventurous commercial growers, but in the vegetable garden there were to be no short cuts. The 'no digging practice' was scornfully dismissed.

In November of 1949 the *Journal* contained two articles on gardens. One was Vita Sackville-West's description of Hidcote Manor, on its passing into history as the first garden accepted by the National Trust.[19] The other was on 'My New Shrub Garden' by Michael Haworth-Booth, a nurseryman near Haslemere.[20] His garden was started in 1946 and among the objectives in its design was that 'the area gardened, excluding a small lawn area, had to be limited to that which could be maintained by one person spending only an hour a day at most'. The garden was almost exclusively of shrubs. To reduce weeding, any bare ground was mulched with a thick layer of June-cut bracken. Haworth-Booth did not refer specifically to ground-cover plants, but 'the evergreen Japanese Azaleas [were] interwoven with Genistas, Helianthemums, Cistus, Halimiums, Lithospermum and alpine Rhododendrons', so the ground was effectively carpeted.

Just as this garden was beginning, A. T. Johnson, a schoolmaster turned gardener-journalist, wrote a small booklet on *Labour Saving Plants*[21] in which he began: 'Garden economy is a matter which concerns us all ... It is with the object of reducing the weekly wage bill, or doing away with it altogether, as well as of relieving the owner-gardener of that fear of failure over upkeep which so frequently haunts his efforts, a grim shadow, that these pages are written.' Johnson advocated permanent plants and especially 'those which by their carpeting, or otherwise weed-smothering nature, absolve us from such work as weeding and hoeing'. The lovely hardy geranium 'Johnson's Blue' typifies his carpeting plant. Johnson's advice on the use of 'carpeting plants', hinted at by Francis Hanger and Michael Haworth-Booth, suggested a new, natural way of combating weeds, by blanketing the bare soil in which they would normally germinate.

In America the difficulty of growing grass in many states and the insistence on reducing garden maintenance to a minimum had already led to the use of low evergreen plants as grass substitutes. Ivy, vinca, pachysandra and horizontal junipers were favourites in American gardens, but Donald Wyman's *Ground Cover Plants*, published in 1956, listed many other suitable plants for the various climatic zones of North America.

'Ground cover' soon entered the English vocabulary, but the first English book on *Ground Cover Plants* put quite a new complexion on the use of such plants. The book was written by Margery Fish and published in 1964. Margery Fish was the post-war ideal of the cottage gardener personified; a more attainable ideal than the larger-than-life Vita Sackville-West at Sissinghurst. Mr and Mrs Fish stumbled on East Lambrook Manor, in Somerset, on the eve of war. As weekend gardeners they struggled to create a garden which was simple and sensible in its planning and filled to capacity with interesting plants both rare and commonplace. Mrs Fish's first book, the autobiographical *We Made a Garden* (1956), inspired many owners of weekend cottage gardens to similar efforts. In *Ground Cover Plants* Mrs Fish saw the use of such plants as offering a natural approach to gardening – there is no bare ground in nature – and portrayed ground-cover as a rich tapestry of weed-smothering herbaceous plants and shrubs rather than as large expanses of dull green uniformity.

Graham Thomas's *Plants for Ground-Cover* followed in 1970. Techniques of book illustration had advanced rapidly in the years between the two books, and the many illustrations of Graham Thomas's own garden showed the variety of effect which could be achieved within the concept of ground-cover planting. Intricate mixtures of pulmonarias, hostas and ferns, flourishing borders of day lilies and geraniums, patchwork quilts of heather at Ness and extensive sweeps of crown vetch (*Coronilla varia*) or juniper for institutional use, all characterized a system of gardening in which brain was used more than brawn to create a garden which was more a work of art than a scene of cultivation. Graham Thomas's borders at Killerton, an undulating sea of santolina, lavender, hypericums and yucca, created one of the most memorable modern planting schemes. When he moved to a smaller house and garden from the one illustrated in *Plants for Ground-Cover*, many of his plants were moved to Cliveden where they continue to adorn the Water Garden.

The garden at Great Comp in Kent is another excellent example of what can be achieved in the late twentieth century by extensive use of ground-cover plants and careful design for mechanized maintenance.[22] Started by Mr and Mrs R. Cameron in 1958, the seven-acre garden was maintained by them without assistance until increasing numbers of visitors and a flourishing nursery within the garden demanded part-time help.

A new English garden?

There is usually a substantial time-lag, often half a century, between the development of a new idea in gardening and its widespread adoption, but by 1960 the influence of Gertrude Jekyll's example of mixed planting and her emphasis on good foliage, translated into modern terms by Margery Fish, was beginning to make its mark in the English garden. The series of gardening handbooks published between 1959 and 1962 by Penguin Books in collaboration with the Royal Horticultural Society marked a watershed in the modern history of the English garden. Profuse illustration and attractive front covers in colour gave the series, which had many distinguished authors, an aura of modernity, but the topics were, in the main, far from modern. *Annual and Biennial Flowers, Chrysanthemums, Dahlias, Delphiniums* and *Roses, Rock Gardens* and *Water Gardens, Lawns* and *The Cool Greenhouse* were garden features as much Victorian as Edwardian. The treatment of most of the subjects, while making passing reference to small gardens and to changing circumstances, took their illustrations and attitudes from large, professionally maintained gardens.

In some of the contributions, however, signs of change were evident. In 1960 Lanning Roper's *Hardy Herbaceous Plants* was published. Much attention was given to delphiniums and lupins, iris, Michaelmas daisy, phlox and other denizens of the traditional herbaceous border, and the illustrations were of Hidcote, Sissinghurst, Tintinhull and other major gardens. In Chapter 2, though, Roper carefully referred to the herbaceous *garden* rather than herbaceous border, to indicate a wider use of herbaceous plants, and he recommended the mixed border 'in which hardy herbaceous plants are combined with shrub roses, flowering shrubs, and even spring bulbs and annuals ... ideal for small gardens'.[23] A section on 'Ground Covers' was also included, as were descriptive lists of herbaceous plants with fine foliage and plants for woodland gardens.

In the same series, Roy Hay's *Gardening the Modern Way* (1962) was largely devoted to mechanization in the larger garden and 'streamlining the garden to meet the exigencies of the modern age'.[24] It showed powered pruning-saws, pressure sprayers, mist-propagation units, thermostatically controlled electric warming cables and irrigation systems based on polythene piping. There were, however, thoughts on planting, on the use of plants which do not need staking, the use of 'ground-covering plants' and the need to suit plants to the soil of the garden.

Fourteen titles in the Penguin/RHS series were issued in three years. Four years later a final title was added, Kenneth Midgley's *Garden Design*. It was written specifically for the owners of fairly small gardens around very ordinary houses, and its publication marked an important step in the development, in England, of the modern garden. To understand clearly the origins and characteristics apparent in Midgley's book, though, it is necessary to look back briefly to the pre-war years and the development of the Modern (with a capital 'M') garden, an international phenomenon made possible by the ocean liners and aeroplanes which were themselves symbols of a new era.

The Modern garden

The development of steel, concrete and their hybrid, reinforced concrete, at the turn of the century led to much greater freedom in the design of buildings and a desire by a new generation of architects to shake off the heavy ornamentation of the Victorian era.

From 1919 the ideals and structural simplicity of modern architecture found great scope for expression in the rebuilding of Germany during the financial stringency of the post-war years.[25] In 1925, when the Bauhaus school of design moved to new buildings in Dessau, its new director, Walter Gropius, designed the new school buildings and much of the surrounding community with the guiding principle that 'form follows function': the form of a building should develop from and express its use. Cubism and abstract painting, in which reality was dissolved into studies of pure form and colour, had a profound influence on the new architecture: applied decoration became superfluous as the proportions and arrangement of building units became aesthetic compositions sufficient in themselves.

England was slow to adopt modernism. Perhaps because of the brilliant achievements of vernacular architecture in this country and the ideal of the English country cottage, the populace demanded Tudoresque or mild Gothic for the wave of speculative and public housing which swept across the country in the inter-war years. However, in 1926 Behrens designed a house for Mr Bassett-Lowke near Northampton. In 1927 Le Corbusier's *Vers une Architecture* was translated into English. In 1928 the Royal Horticultural Society opened their New Hall, in Greycoat Street, around the corner from Vincent Square, one of London's first modern buildings,[26] and in the same year *Country Life* published its first article on modern buildings, including the manager's house in Silver End Garden Village, Essex.[27] Modern buildings were born of high ideals. Christopher Hussey declared:

A new synthesis of needs, techniques, and materials has been evolved, capable of replacing the old to which we have clung for so long ... a

formula that will give unity to our lives, and while preserving beauty, enable our homes to be as simple, and comfortable and well founded as are already the car, the ship, the aeroplane . . .[28]

The dilemma of the 'Modern' garden: self-conscious geometry at Amyas Connell's High and Over.

For the new generation of landscape architects the Modern garden posed a major problem. If form followed function and decoration was to be eschewed, what form should the garden take when decoration had for so long been its major function? Behrens's house sat above a rockery bank flanked by a rustic pergola. Other modern houses looked across bleak lawns to lily pools surrounded by crazy paving and tulip beds. Some simply extended the severe geometry of the house into the garden.

Ironically, the solution to the dilemma of the Modern garden was precipitated by Adolf Hitler. Modern architecture was based on a pragmatism, idealism and rationalism deeply disturbing to dictators. It was banned in 1932 both in Germany and Russia and its practitioners fled Germany for England and America. Gropius was appointed Professor of Architecture at Harvard.

At the time of his appointment the American schools of architecture were still wallowing in the Beaux Arts tradition of heavy classical ornamentation. Gropius's maxim was 'less is more'. His pure geometry of glass, steel and concrete caused a ferment of excitement and, at Harvard in particular, home of the world's first landscape architecture course, the enthusiasm for modernism spread from building to landscape.

A new look at the Orient

In the cultural melting pot of Harvard the Modern garden evolved from a fusion of American ideas of use, European ideals of beauty and oriental philosophy. The period was vividly described by J. O. Simonds:

> Looking back I feel extraordinarily lucky to have been at the Harvard School of Design during 1936–9 in the tumultuous years of the rebellion. A fervour almost religious in quality seemed to sweep the school ... We determined we must seek a new philosophy ... I set out once again with a fellow student to wander in search of fundamentals through Japan, Korea, China, Burma, Bali, India and up into Tibet. In the contemplative attitude of Buddhist monks we would sit for hours absorbed in the qualities of a simple courtyard space [noting] the relationship of sensitive landscape planning to the arc of the sun, the direction and force of the wind and topographical forms.[29]

America was already developing its own interpretation of the relationship of man to nature, notably in Frank Lloyd Wright's prairie houses.

In California, especially, the climate was particularly suited to modern architecture, with glass walls opening like Japanese rice-paper screens on to the garden. There was a large Japanese population, too, infusing its spirit into the modern American lifestyle while the lifestyle itself solved the question of the function of gardens. A large rambling house, a driveway for several large cars, a swimming pool and a large terrace for barbecues, outdoor meals and parties easily utilized every piece of available ground at a time of increasing land values and smaller plots.

Gardens are for people

One of the key figures in shaping the Modern garden was Thomas Church.[30] Trained in landscape architecture at Berkeley and at Harvard, strongly influenced by the Cubists, by the Finnish designer Alvar Aalto and by the brilliant Brazilian painter/botanist/garden designer Roberto Burle Marx, and sensitive to the personalities and

requirements of his clients, Church evolved a new type of garden: carefully detailed, thoroughly practical and serenely simple. There was no division into compartments, no axial symmetry with planned vistas, little emphasis on plantsmanship unless the interest of a client demanded it. The garden was a single composition of fluid lines attractive from any angle. Church's gardens were as varied as his clients, but the garden at Sonoma for Dewey Donnell, begun in 1947, epitomizes the Modern garden.[31] Church's slim book *Gardens are for People*, published in 1952, suggested an entirely new way of thinking about gardens in America and in Britain, where it had been tacitly assumed for more than a hundred years that gardens were for plants.

In Britain, with its much stronger tradition of plantsmanship, the struggle to cast off outmoded ideas was a difficult one. Geoffrey Taylor's *The Modern Garden* (1936) began with illustrations and laudatory captions of stark, white, modern concrete houses, then, having dispensed with Modernism, wallowed in 200 pages of

Thomas Church's garden at Sonoma: sophisticated curves framed by indigenous trees.

A small modern garden by Thomas Church: wooden decking, concrete floor and low-maintenance planting.

cottage gardens, rose gardens, herbaceous borders, rock and water gardens and woodland gardens with illustrations garnered from the archives of *Country Life*, where Taylor was gardening editor.

Two years later came Christopher Tunnard's *Gardens in the Modern Landscape*. Tunnard was a landscape architect and an advocate of Modernism. A modern house needed a modern garden. Tunnard described 'the three sources of inspiration the modern designer has at his disposal – those of "functionalism", the oriental influence and modern art'.[32] Functions were harder to find in England than in California but he included seats, lawns, pools for children, flowering shrubs, views where possible and sitings for (modern) sculpture.

The oriental influence included the triumph of asymmetry, over the parallel and perpendicular of Western classical gardens and a deep reverence for the natural world.

> Our modern buildings are simple statements, but our gardens have a new mission – to fulfil the need for an affinity with Nature ... which even Rousseau could not have imagined ... We begin ... to use Nature as the Oriental has for centuries, not as a refuge from life, but as a sustainer of it.[33]

Of modern art in gardens Tunnard was less assured, but he suggested that ornamentation be abandoned in favour of the inherent beauty of the garden's materials.

Bold curves, massed planting and subtle detailing: the hallmarks of Roberto Burle Marx.

Tunnard's own garden at St Ann's Hill, Chertsey, and his garden for Serge Chermayeff's house at Hallands in Sussex carried his ideas into reality. High walls, severely rectangular pools and abstract rectilinear patterns of concrete paving were relieved by isolated trees, sculpture and bold foliage. It helped that both houses were set among large trees in open parkland! Fortunately Tunnard's suggestions for the garden at Claremont were not realized. Rather than 'spoiling' the garden by surrounding it with amorphous suburbs, he suggested 'improving' it with modern tower blocks and ribbon terraces so that 6,000 residents could benefit from the open landscape.[34] In 1939, on the eve of war, Tunnard left for America and spent the rest of his life teaching landscape architecture at Harvard.

The English experience

After the war modern architecture resumed its progress. Its simple forms and economical use of new materials suited the austerity and hurried rebuilding of the post-war years. Landscape architects were deeply involved in the post-war reconstruction too. New Towns, new factories, roads, power stations and reservoirs left little opportunity to work on frivolities such as private gardens but, in 1951, the centenary of Paxton's triumphant Great Exhibition provided an excuse for the nation to shrug off its cares and revel in the Festival of Britain. The Festival Hall was the centrepiece of a site crowded with lighthearted modern buildings set among informal gardens designed under the direction of Frank Clark. Water, irregular boulders and striking foliage created maximum impact with minimal resources.

The Festival gardens vanished as quickly as they had come but their spirit lived on in a flurry of books on modern gardens. Peter Shepheard's *Modern Gardens* (1953), Marjory Allen and Susan Jellicoe's *The New Small Garden* (1956) and Sylvia Crowe's *Garden Design* (1958) were important additions to American books by Thomas Church, James Rose and Garret Eckbo. In 1952 Frank Clark wrote (jointly with Margaret Jones) a small book on *Indoor Plants and Gardens* illustrating some of the planting schemes in the Festival buildings and many others from Scandinavia, where the Robinson/Jekyll tradition of foliage plants had been eagerly adopted and adapted to indoor planting to relieve long, severe winters. Indoor plants and gardens were also becoming popular in America. In 1955 and 1957 two books were written on growing indoor plants under artificial lighting.[35]

The English books were mainly by designers for designers and their immediate influence did not spread outside a small professional circle, although the authors and their contemporaries in the Institute of Landscape Architects were involved to some extent in the design of private gardens in addition to their major public commissions. Geoffrey Jellicoe's rose garden, designed for Lord Astor at Cliveden in 1959, was strongly influenced by the bold curves of Roberto Burle Marx's work in Brazil,[36] an influence even more obvious in his roof-garden on Harvey's store in Guildford, completed a year earlier.[37]

In 1962 Brenda Colvin moved her landscape architectural practice from London to the Cotswold village of Filkins. Her own garden, which grew around the old cottage in which reservoirs, motorways and power stations were planned, was not obviously designed but it combined the effortless curves of Church's garden in Sonoma with the controlled muddle of an English cottage garden.[38] The same restrained inevitability of shape with rather simpler planting could be seen in many of Brenda Colvin's gardens, at St Peter's House in Filkins[39] and the Manor House at Sutton

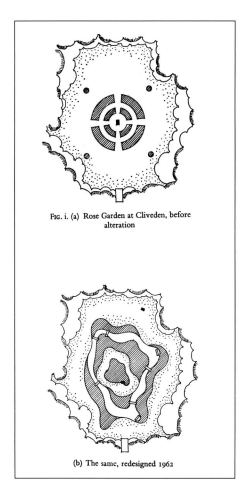

FIG. i. (a) Rose Garden at Cliveden, before
alteration

(b) The same, redesigned 1962

*Geoffrey Jellicoe's rose garden
at Cliveden, an exploration of
the psyche.*

Courtenay, but the subtlety of these gardens led to their being
overshadowed by the more flamboyant and overtly modern
gardens of the times.

Room outside

Although the books on modern gardens had a limited circulation,
the new glossy magazines fed the creed of modernism, in small
monthly doses, to a much wider audience. The new Elizabethan
age dawned with illustrations of sleek cars, Scandinavian furniture
and a host of labour-saving gadgets. In July 1953 *House and Garden*
featured the noble garden of Cranborne Manor in Dorset, the
ancient art of topiary (maintained by new electric trimmers), outside-
inside furniture and Terence Conran cooking hot-dogs on a

barbecue. Even Cranborne Manor had its lessons for the small garden, with 'a permanent planting of rosemary ... and Senecio Greyi, making a weed-free ground cover, which looks pleasant the whole year round'.[40]

House and Garden and its contemporaries appealed especially to young people who were interested in the quality of their surroundings, in the garden but not necessarily in gardening. Gradually the realization dawned that culture rather than climate prevented the English using their gardens as the Americans did. The main stumbling block to a usable garden was a dewy lawn underfoot. Concrete slabs gradually replaced the tiny lawn and the word 'patio', quite wrongly used, crept into the English garden vocabulary.

In 1960 the Cement and Concrete Association published a booklet on *Concrete in Garden Making*. Most of the examples were traditional: pergolas, formal steps and lily ponds, but there were two views of a garden designed by Derek Lovejoy with patterned screen-walls, a simple overhead framework and a random pattern of stepping stones across a large rectangular pool. The Association went on to demonstrate the use of concrete in the garden by commissioning work from other leading landscape architects. Geoffrey Jellicoe designed a modern pergola on a concrete-paved terrace. Sylvia Crowe designed a town garden with concrete paving, pools and screens. Storage buildings along the edge of the sports field were extended southwards to make sheltered arbours, and the north-facing recesses between the arbours accommodated a superb planting scheme of shade-tolerant plants by Susan Jellicoe.

In 1969 John Brookes's *Room Outside* marked a turning point in the publication of popular garden books. The message in *Room Outside* was clear. 'Gardens are for plants' was a historically brief and revocable concept. Gardens are now for people, even for people who do not always enjoy gardening. The small garden could function as an extension of the too-small house, as a room outside, and the small, useful garden should be designed as one might design a room. Bravely for an English market, there was more emphasis on how to lay a patio than how to double-dig the border. The modern garden had arrived.

Room Outside clearly characterized the Modern garden. It was small so there was seldom room for compartmentation. The terrace (or patio), lawn, beds and borders, sandpit and summerhouse, roses and rockplants, all had to be assembled into a single composition. The garden plot came inevitably with the house. Whereas earlier writers such as Mawson and Milner spent whole chapters on the selection of a site for house and garden, for Brookes the reality was that people bought a house by balancing location and price. The garden was the patch of land which came with the house and one often had to make the best of a very bad job, whether it be heavy clay, shade from neighbouring trees or unsightly views.

The garden was part of the house. Flourishing pot-plants in centrally-heated rooms merged the house into the garden with help from large, sliding glass doors and the inevitable patio. For outdoor use privacy was important: fence panels sold as well as paving slabs in the garden centres and many nurseries produced – or seemed to produce – nothing but the ubiquitous Leyland cypress for instant seclusion.

The Modern garden was on view all the year round, at close range through the picture windows. Plants had to be chosen for permanent or long-lasting effect. The exciting new foliage plants of the Festival of Britain gardens became clichés. *Viburnum davidii, Mahonia japonica, Phormium tenax* and Miss Jekyll's favourite bergenias were everywhere.

To compensate for lack of size and lack of plants the garden had to generate interest in other ways: a strong ground pattern, raised beds, millstone fountains, pools and containers.

Man in the dock

Ironically *Room Outside* marked almost the end, as well as the beginning, of the Modern garden. The 1960s was a decade of rapid development, but development brought problems. Modern farming meant removal of hedgerows, draining of wetlands, ploughing of ancient meadows. Modern forestry resulted in millions of acres of coniferous blanket laid mechanically over the finest landscape. Motorways, reservoirs and other major developments eroded the countryside while urban renewal became a euphemism for replacing people's homes by high-rise offices, inhuman blocks of flats and urban motorways. In 1962 Rachel Carson's *Silent Spring* pointed to the peril of concentration of pesticides in the food chain with man at the peak.

Space travel, the most advanced arm of technology, cast man's activities into a new perspective. The space voyages of Yuri Gagarin in 1961, John Glenn in 1962 and the moon landing of Neil Armstrong in 1969 effectively shrank the globe, in the same way that the railways had shrunk Britain, making it easily possible to comprehend the Earth as a single, quite small unit. What had been considered as technological progress only a few years before could be seen quite clearly from space. Conservationists likened it to a bad attack of scab on an apple or a cancerous growth over the fertile green face of nature. By 1970, European Conservation year, the words 'ecology' and 'conservation' were on everyone's lips. Ecology was no longer something confined to ancient meadows or bluebell woods. It included man.

During the succeeding decade there was a widespread move to soften the urban environment. Ecological parks and urban farms were established on derelict sites. Interior planting in open-plan offices became widespread, with specialist contractors such as Paul Temple recreating the luxuriance of a Victorian conservatory and the elegant tracery of plants in the Festival Hall.

Gateway House, Basingstoke, a multi-tiered roof garden designed for Wiggins Teape Ltd.

Roof-gardens, too, became an increasingly popular adjunct of modern architecture. The two-acre roof-garden above the Derry and Toms store in London, opened in 1938, and Geoffrey Jellicoe's

garden above Harvey's in Guildford (1958) were isolated examples to attract and amuse discerning shoppers to lunch and relax in the sky. When Wiggins Teape moved their headquarters from the City of London to the green edge of Basingstoke in 1976 the new building relied heavily on interior planting and its multi-tiered roof garden, designed by Ove Arup and Partners with James Russell, to create an ideal and efficient working environment. Paradoxically, of course, it was advances in the technology of lighting, heating and ventilation, waterproofing membranes, hydroponic cultivation and automated irrigation systems which made it increasingly possible to create these plant-filled paradises.[41]

In 1970 conservationists formed a vocal minority, but the oil crisis, sudden inflation, strikes by lorry drivers, coal miners, bakers and others threw the country into turmoil. Bread queues, jostling for sugar in the supermarkets, cooking on camp-stoves by candle-light became a new feature of the modern age. As if that were not enough, the early 1970s saw the devastating spread of Dutch elm disease. The prolonged drought of late 1975 and 1976 and growing concern about pesticides and artificial fertilizers combined to fuel the widespread dismay about the effects of man's tampering with the environment.

In a period of general disenchantment with 'progress', the slick commercialism of garden centres inevitably caused a reaction. The garden centres responded, wisely, by widening their range of plants and embracing the organic movement, marketing herbs, health foods and aids to organic gardening carefully packaged in dull green and earthy brown wrappers.

Similarly, the idea of the house as a 'machine for living', and the garden as a Cubist paving pattern with a fatsia or two, also repelled. When John Brookes wrote *Improve Your Lot* as a sequel to *Room Outside* in 1977 he took pains to emphasize that *he* had a garden with plants in, that he *enjoyed* planting and pruning and weeding. He underlined a point made but sometimes overlooked in the earlier book: '*Plants are important, of course,* but the first consideration should be the fitness of the garden for family use'.[42]

Old is beautiful

When the future is uncertain man usually retreats into the past, and the 1970s were no exception. A major theme for the decade was an emphasis on preservation, restoration and conservation – of historic buildings and gardens as well as of natural habitats.

Loosely speaking, the formal gardens at Blenheim between the wars might be considered restoration. In 1932 Sir David Bowes-Lyon began restoring the original lines of his eighteenth-century garden at St Paul's Walden Bury in Hertfordshire.[43] After Graham Thomas's appointment as Gardens Adviser to the National Trust, formal parterres, newly devised, but historically correct, were planted at Ashdown, Berkshire (1956), and Moseley Old Hall, Staffordshire (1963).[44]

In 1964 Peter Hunt's *The Shell Gardens Book* was published for Shell-Mex and BP Ltd. Its intention was to inform the one or two million people who visited gardens each year (in petrol-consuming cars) of the origins and features of the gardens they were looking at. The practice of visiting gardens, historic and otherwise, was a major factor in generating support for garden restoration and funds for garden maintenance and development. The opening of private gardens under the National Gardens Scheme and Gardeners' Sunday also provided inspiration to millions of garden visitors and,

Restoration of the garden at Erddig.

The terraces at Tatton Park with the elegant flower beds newly reshaped.

through plant-stalls, brought into increasing circulation many of the old-fashioned and reliable garden plants which garden centres chose not to handle.

The Shell Gardens Book had an historical introduction by Miles Hadfield, and a directory of garden features and styles. 'Modern gardens' included Hidcote, Nymans and Sissinghurst. Hunt found such a dearth of knowledge in preparing the book that he determined to form a society for the study of gardens, and in 1965 the Garden History Society was founded.[45] By arranging lectures, meetings, visits, publications and advice it had a major influence on the conservation of historic gardens.

Studley Royal was acquired by West Riding County Council in 1966, transferred to the new North Yorkshire County Council in 1974 and to the National Trust in 1983.[46] It has been gradually restored. Westbury Court was given to the Trust by Gloucestershire County Council in 1967 to save it from destruction.[47] Erddig was a much larger restoration in 1973, made possible by selling a corner of the estate for building development to raise the necessary endowment.[48]

Restoration also began in 1973 at Hestercombe Manor. Hestercombe had been acquired as the headquarters of the Somerset Fire Brigade, and Gertrude Jekyll's planting plan for the magnificent Lutyens garden was discovered intact in the potting shed. The landscape architects of the County Council prepared a five-year programme, and Cannington College propagated the plants for a complete restoration.[49]

To mark the growing awareness of cultural heritage, 1974 was declared European Architectural Heritage Year. The Garden History Society formed a Conservation Committee to co-ordinate requests for the Society's advice on garden restoration, while the Town and Country Amenity Act of 1974 included provision for the grant-aiding of such restoration – but provided no funds! In that same year John Sales was appointed Gardens Adviser to the National Trust, to share with Graham Thomas the rapidly increasing responsibility for the Trust's gardens. Ham was restored by the Trust in 1974,[50] and the restoration of Claremont followed in 1975.[51]

Painshill, one of the greatest eighteenth-century gardens, was compulsorily purchased by Elmbridge District Council in 1975 to save it from destruction; restoration there, just across the A3 from Claremont, is continuing steadily, after painstaking archaeological excavation of original features.[52]

In 1980 the Sussex Historic Gardens Restoration Trust was formed to assist and grant-aid restoration in the county.[53] Hampshire followed in 1982, thanks largely to the initiative of Mrs Drummond whose diminutive (seven-acre) Capability Brown landscape at Cadland was restored in 1983, to commemorate the

The Chinese bridge and lawns reclaimed from dense woodland, Painshill.

bicentenary of Brown's death.[54] In that same year Brown's memory was honoured at Blenheim, where Cobham Resource Consultants completed their management plan for the next 200 years.[55] Also in 1983 Paul Edwards oversaw the restoration of a charming rose garden designed by Robert Marnock at Warwick Castle.[56]

Restoration began with very simple tasks – a knot garden here and there in a suitably historic setting – but in the 1980s it has become increasingly complex. The 100-year plan for Stourhead, prepared by the National Trust in 1978, delicately balanced the conservation needs of many overlapping historical layers of the garden from 1720 to 1947.[57] In 1980 Travers Morgan were commissioned to begin a series of surveys of the Royal Parks by the Department of the Environment. Computer data-logging and graphics, tree-dating and other techniques have been co-ordinated to allow sophisticated analysis of these historically important landscapes.[58]

Other bodies, too, have been actively involved in garden conservation. In 1978 the National Council for the Conservation of Plants and Gardens was established under the aegis of the Royal Horticultural Society, to locate, propagate and distribute cultivated plants threatened with extinction. In 1982 the York Centre for the Conservation of Historic Parks and Gardens was set up, with financial support from the Countryside Commission, as an archival and educational centre. The reprinting of historical books, too, has proceeded apace, from the 20-pence leaflet on *Labour Saving Plants* by A. T. Johnson[59] to the lavish reproduction of Repton Red Books;[60] from the ninth-century *Hortulus*[61] to Reginald Farrer on rock gardening,[62] reflecting a rapidly increasing interest in the literature of garden history.

One of the most delightful results of this interest has been the making of the garden at Barnsley House, near Cirencester, Gloucestershire.[63] In 1967 Rosemary Verey was given a book on the mysterious properties of mandrake. This sparked a lifelong search for historical garden books, and the literary interest overflowed into the garden. David Verey was an architect and architectural historian, and the partnership between husband and wife led to a garden firmly organized and richly planted, a garden characteristic of the Hidcote/Sissinghurst tradition except for its many direct references to history. Knot gardens, herb borders, a splendid *potager*, lime walks and other features taken from historical sources are worked into a superb twentieth-century garden.

On 1 April 1984, ten years of work by the Garden History Society's Conservation Committee, influenced especially by the

Society's Secretary Mavis Batey,[64] bore its finest fruit. The National Heritage Act (1983) established the Historic Buildings and Monuments Commission – with its user-friendly synonym 'English Heritage' – to complete the County Registers of gardens begun by the Garden History Society, to notify owners and local authorities of the importance of historic gardens within their care and to grant-aid restoration.

Nature knows best

The recognition, conservation and re-creation of historically important gardens have been major triumphs of the last quarter-century, but ecology, conservation and nostalgia have pervaded all aspects of English gardening.

In smaller gardens the post-war vision of the labour-saving shrub garden lasted only as long as it took the forsythias and viburnums, hydrangeas and deutzias to extend their ever-increasing bulk across the lawns and paths. In *Gardening the Modern Way*, Roy Hay underlined the weakness of the all-shrub garden. 'Many garden owners have, in fact, found that a skilful combination of trees and shrubs, with a few long-lived and undemanding perennial plants, has largely solved their problems of maintenance.'[65] Alan Bloom had already recognized the value of the 'undemanding perennial

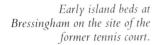

Early island beds at Bressingham on the site of the former tennis court.

plants' and at Bressingham Hall Farm in Norfolk, bought in 1946, he began to build up a nursery specializing in herbaceous perennials. To overcome the traditional image of the labour-intensive herbaceous border he advocated other ways of using herbaceous plants, especially in free-standing, double-sided or 'span-type' borders. 'There would be great scope for the planner who wished to fill a large square or circle with perennials [and] informal borders are quite feasible.'[66] Bloom lived only thirty miles from Blickling and must have known of Norah Lindsay's great herbaceous squares, but he can scarcely have envisaged the influence of his 'irregular borders' when he wrote: 'Nowadays the leanings are towards informality, though the shape of a modern garden plot, with its straight-line boundaries, is seldom conducive to it.' By 1964, when Alan Bloom lectured to the Royal Horticultural Society,[67] his 'island beds' were established at Wisley and in the gardening vocabulary.

While Alan Bloom was extending his Dell Garden, started in 1958, with great sweeps of subtle herbaceous plants, his son Adrian began to develop his own interest in another form of ground-cover planting – heathers and dwarf conifers. In 1966 he started his own garden, Foggy Bottom,[68] and this has grown to rival the Dell Garden in popularity. The stiff outlines, generally unchanging foliage and sharply contrasting blues and gold of the conifers could hardly differ more from the drifts of geraniums, hostas and hemerocallis of his father's garden, but the two men ensured that everyone could find something to please them in the Bressingham catalogue and gardens.

In 1960 Mrs Beth Chatto began her small garden around the new bungalow on her husband's fruit farm in Essex.[69] Nettles and elders were bulldozed away, lakes were made and plants arranged with great artistry, usually in bold triangular blocks of contrasting form and texture. Although the garden eventually expanded over several acres in the Essex countryside it had one feature in common with the typical small town garden: difficult micro-environments.

Much post-war building had been on flat clay soils or on poor sands unsuitable for farming. A new house on a small plot inevitably meant shade on one side, probably scorching sun on the other with a treasure-trove of builders' rubble. Mrs Chatto's garden near the house was hot and dry – her Mediterranean garden. The lakeside planting was on sticky clay and sometimes under the shade of large trees. Mrs Chatto found plants to flourish in these diverse environments and her catalogue was arranged with lists of plants for difficult situations. In 1976 she arranged an exhibit of her plants at the Chelsea Flower Show. The catalogue entry, 'Unusual garden plants arranged for shade, sun and damp conditions', was the greatest understatement of the century. The exquisite array, carefully blending from Mediterranean grey-leaved plants to soft greens of shade-tolerant and moisture-loving plants, a restful antithesis to the mountains of roses, orchids, tulips and begonias on all sides, caused a sensation.

The flower-arranger's garden

Another reason for Beth Chatto's amazing success was her recognition of one of the most important of all post-war influences on gardening: flower-arranging. The practice of decorating the dinner table with fruit, pot plants and flowers spread during the Victorian era but the arrangements, usually by the head-gardener, were elaborate and stiffly formal.[70] Josiah Conder wrote a book on flower-arranging in Japan in 1891, but it was Gertrude Jekyll's *Flower Decoration in the House* (1907) which established flower-arranging as an art in Britain.

Miss Jekyll's ideas on flower decoration were adopted and developed by Constance Spry, whose first shop, opened in 1928 in Belgrave Road, was called 'Flower Decorations'.[71] Like Gertrude Jekyll, Constance Spry's taste in plants was catholic. For the white interiors of Syrie Maugham's Chelsea salons she created masterpieces of white lilies and orchids, arums and eucalyptus, but she

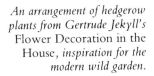

An arrangement of hedgerow plants from Gertrude Jekyll's Flower Decoration in the House, *inspiration for the modern wild garden.*

loved, too, rose-hips, dried bracken and trails of old man's beard, seed heads of onions, carrots and hydrangeas scavenged from the hedgerow, the vegetable plot or bonfire heap. As a result of her example, her school at Winkfield, her stream of books and articles and innumerable lectures, Constance Spry's devotion to flowers became a national phenomenon. In 1949 the first flower-arranging society was formed in Dorchester, Dorset. Others followed in London, Leicester and Colchester, and in 1951 these four societies staged a major display at the Royal Horticultural Society's New Hall. In 1956 a flower-arrangers' tent was included at Chelsea. In January 1959, a year before Constance Spry's death, the National Association of Flower Arranging Societies of Great Britain was formed, and within thirty years membership of the Association exceeded 100,000.

Styles have changed since Constance Spry's death, particularly towards an enthusiasm for the Japanese methods criticized by Gertrude Jekyll and disliked by Mrs Spry, but the demand for those flowers – and more particularly the leaves and seed heads – most admired by Mrs Spry has had a major impact on the demand for garden plants. Beth Chatto's catalogue, *Unusual Plants*, in addition to its emphasis on plants for hot and dry, waterside, clay, and dry shady situations, has three long lists of plants with flowers for cutting, handsome foliage and seedheads.

Other indications of the Spry influence can be seen in the enthusiasm for unusual and subtle colours in flowers such as Rembrandt tulips, smoky hellebores, black iris and green gladioli, in grey foliage and herbs, coppery and golden foliage, bold hostas and bergenias. It can be seen too in the rediscovery of old roses.

Old roses had fallen from favour between the wars in competition with the repeat-flowering, brightly coloured and elegantly pointed hybrid tea roses. In 1939 the large collection of roses gathered by E. A. Bunyard was sold, and the other major supplier of old roses, Beckwith and Son of Hoddesdon, ceased trading soon after.[72]

Graham Thomas did much to save these old roses, acquiring Beckwith's plants, propagating and comparing roses from Constance Spry's garden with those from Sissinghurst, Nymans, Highdown and Sutton Courtenay, and publishing his descriptions of romantic old varieties in *Old Shrub Roses* (1955). Flower-arranging enthusiasts needed little persuasion of the delights of these old roses and their popularity grew steadily in the years that followed. In 1970 Graham Thomas found a new home for his collection of old roses in the walled garden at Mottisfont Abbey, Hampshire.[73]

David Austin began crossing the old roses with repeat-flowering hybrid teas to produce a new range of English roses. Appropriately his first new rose, in 1961, was called 'Constance Spry'. The dark purple/crimson 'Chianti' followed, and gradually Austin produced an ever-widening range of hybrids in which the quartered, heavily scented flowers and robust habit of the old shrub roses were combined with repeat flowering and disease resistance. Significantly, in 1982, David Austin also produced a paeony handbook in addition to his rose catalogue, bringing back into prominence another favourite Spry flower.

Modern roses have also been produced to satisfy the flower arranger's craving for muted colours: 'Lavender Pinocchio' (1948), 'Magenta' (1953), 'Lavender Lassie' (1959) and 'Blue Moon' (1964) are all mauve/blue in colouring, while 'Café' (1956), 'Brownie' (1969) and 'Brown Velvet' (1983) are remarkable blends of brown and cream.

The phenomenal popularity of Constance Spry's graceful flower arrangements highlights many characteristics of the modern garden: the emphasis on good foliage, herbaceous plants, the luxuriant tapestry of ground-cover plants and soft, subtle colouring in roses and other flowers. Her interest in simple wild flowers, branches and fruits from the hedgerow, whether fresh or in their dried winter state, also underlines the link between the garden and the development of nature conservation in the wider landscape.

The flowery mead – again

From classifying plant communities, studying their development and charting their alarming disappearance, many ecologists have moved on to re-creating diverse ecosystems in New Towns, country parks, roadsides and wherever opportunity arises.

Terry Wells began his work on the establishment of species-rich grassland for the Nature Conservancy Council at Monks Wood in 1972. His recommendations for seed mixes and for management of grassland were published in 1981,[74] by which time the interest in creating wildlife habitats was firmly established. John Chambers, manager of the Horticultural Division of Mommersteg International Seeds, and Geoffrey Taylor, the technical officer of W. W. Johnson and Son Ltd, were among the first to sense this interest and began cultivating wild flowers for seed. In 1980 Chambers issued his slim pamphlet of wild flower, herb and ornamental grass seeds.

In the post-war years of advancing technology, weeds in the lawn were almost as socially undesirable as bad breath; by the mid 1970s, however, daisies could be claimed as evidence of environmental awareness rather than laziness, and gardeners started to clamour for wild flower seeds.

John Chambers's catalogue grew in size each year. Johnsons, Emorsgate and a handful of other specialist suppliers of British wild flower seed developed and added tempting colour illustrations to their new catalogues. In 1984 Chambers exhibited for the first time at Chelsea: the delicate tracery of dandelion 'clocks' in the hallowed marquee of the Royal Horticultural Society's major show caused much comment and much congestion in the surrounding gangways.

In the past few years the retail seedsmen – Dobies, Suttons, Thompson and Morgan and others – have all added wild flower seeds to their catalogues, and small plants of a few wild flowers are now being offered alongside salvias and bedding geraniums.

Wild flower meadows had long been an inevitable part of large private gardens, in orchards, on rough banks and where the naturalizing of daffodils necessitated infrequent cutting of grass. They were encouraged, too, by Robinson's wild-gardening ideas. Grassland strewn with wild orchids and other beautiful wild flowers still provides a delightful foil to exotic planting at Sissinghurst, Bodnant, Savill, Leonardslee and a hundred other great gardens. In 1976 Christopher Lloyd described the cultivation and delight of his own flowery meadows at Great Dixter in Sussex in *The Garden*.[75]

A garden philosopher

In recent decades Christopher Lloyd has unconsciously assumed Miss Jekyll's mantle as England's leading garden philosopher and writer. Like Miss Jekyll, Christopher Lloyd lives in a Lutyens house, or rather two farmhouses spliced together by Lutyens, at Great Dixter. The garden, too, was largely planned by Lutyens but planted by Lloyd's mother.

Interestingly, the Long Border at Great Dixter is almost identical in size to the main border at Munstead Wood and, like the Munstead border, it has a backdrop of shrubs as a foil to the splendid summer display of flowers, perennial and annual. Unlike Miss Jekyll, Christopher Lloyd studiously avoids colour-graded drifts in favour of a finer textured tapestry of planting. Creative pragmatism is the hallmark of the garden, but there are many similarities between

The main border of Christopher Lloyd's Great Dixter.

Miss Jekyll and Mr Lloyd, notably a catholic interest in plants, a willingness to work to achieve results and the use of the pages of *Country Life* to disseminate their ideas.

In his classic *The Well-Tempered Garden*, published in 1970 and revised in 1985, Christopher Lloyd praised the scarlet verbena and black veratrum, hybrid tea roses and wild spotted orchids, globe artichokes and laburnums. Many half-hardy and tender plants are raised from cuttings each year to supplement the Long Border and to fill pots and flower-beds. In the preface to *The Well-Tempered Garden* he wrote:

> Sometimes the reader may exclaim: 'What a lot of trouble!' ... But however labour saving you make your hobby, you will never get out of it more than you put in. Now and again it seems worth taking that extra bit of trouble that brings in its train some rather exciting result.

The phraseology is different, but the sentiment is identical to that expressed by Gertrude Jekyll.[76]

Ecological landscapes

The wildflower meadow is the most obviously decorative aspect of ecological gardening for small gardens, but it is not the only one. In 1971 the Royal Society for the Protection of Birds published an attractive slim booklet on *The Birds in Your Garden*, to encourage gardeners to replace some of the disappearing habitat in their own gardens. Books and articles on butterfly gardening and frog ponds also appeared. In 1984 the Greater London Council published *A guide to habitat creation*, written by Chris Baines and Jane Smart, to advise on the establishment and management of grassland, woodland, wetlands and wasteland for wildlife conservation and human enjoyment. Chris Baines's efforts to conserve Britain's wildlife – and in doing so to preserve man's sanity – achieved national recognition when his television programme *Bluetits and Bumblebees* was broadcast on television in January 1984. In April 1985 his book *How to Make a Wildlife Garden* was published, and in May his wildlife garden at the Chelsea Flower Show received a Silver Flora medal.

Ironically the enthusiasm for wildlife gardens and ecological landscapes soon reached such proportions that it engendered a

Chris Baines's wildlife garden.

reaction. In 1983 Stephen Rettig criticized the 'Ecological Approach' to landscape design in terms strongly reminiscent of Reginald Blomfield's *Formal Garden in England*.[77] Other landscape architects have been vociferous in their condemnation of ecological landscape, seeing in it an abdication of responsibility for design by making poor copies of nature rather than works of art.

A new synthesis

The last battle, between Robinson and Blomfield, was solved by the partnership of Gertrude Jekyll and Edwin Lutyens, a partnership which flourished in Edwardian England but which has emerged again as the last and perhaps most significant influence on the twentieth-century garden, drawing together the many strands of development of the modern garden.

In 1953 Christopher Hussey described Lutyens as the last architect of his era, a romantic idealist unable to function in a bureaucratic democracy, but as modernism palled, architects and the general public alike began to recognize Lutyens's timeless genius, the wit, warmth and human scale of his buildings. Admiration culminated in a major exhibition of his work at the Hayward Gallery, from November 1981 to January 1982.

Miss Jekyll never fell suddenly from favour. Her ideas on woodland gardening in particular remained of interest throughout the suburbanization of southern England. Her ideas on colour and form, her organization of the garden for seasonal interest and variety of character, strongly influenced the design of Hidcote and Sissinghurst. Her thoughts on flower decoration inspired Constance Spry. A vague Jekyll influence could be discerned in many aspects of modern gardening – her delight in wild flowers, her love of cistus, heathers and other plants of the hills interpreted in modern prosaic terms as ground-cover plants – but Miss Jekyll herself seemed irrelevant. In the late twentieth century, few people gardened on fifteen acres and, of those who did, fewer still could sit for days dividing polyanthus while 'a boy feeds me with armfuls of newly dug-up plants, two men are digging – in the cooling cow-dung at the farther end, and another carries away the divided plants tray-by-tray and replants them'.[78]

However, Miss Jekyll's writing had a deceptively simple period charm. Those who read her books soon became aware of a deep sense of purpose beneath the easy flow of words and, although she wrote from a substantial Lutyens 'cottage' in fifteen acres of garden, it became increasingly obvious that her ideas, the vignettes portrayed in her many photographs, were just as appropriate to the small modern garden.

Miss Jekyll died in 1932. Copyright of her books expired in 1982, by which time second-hand copies were eagerly sought after at high prices. As facsimile reprints and modern adaptations proliferated for a new readership, a new dimension was revealed in her writing. Her whole philosophy and that of the Arts and Crafts movement became more, not less, relevant as the computer age advanced. Workers in the Arts and Crafts movement looked back to a pre-Raphaelite era in an attempt to solve new problems. They were dismissed as reactionary but, after a tidal wave of modernism, progress and misapplied technology, reactionaries of the 1980s also looked back, to the Arts and Crafts and further, to the pre-Raphaelite, medieval era, where they found ideas remarkably in tune with the oriental philosophy which had wielded such influence in the modern movement.

In 1882, in the preface to *Landscape Gardening in Japan*, Josiah Conder wrote:

Some may ... hold that landscape gardening should be typical of the scenery of the soil, and regard the servile imitation of a foreign style as unnatural and purposeless. To this class the abstract principles of the Art [of Japanese gardening] may prove not totally unworthy of attention, and may even supply suggestion for a modified form of Western gardening ... the Japanese method reveals aesthetic principles applicable to the gardens of any country, teaching, as it does, how to convert into a poem or picture or composition, which, with all its variety of detail, otherwise lacks unity of intent.[79]

In 1961 John Simonds summarized what he had learned from his sojourn in the Far East.

All at once it came to me: what must count is not primarily the planned approach, the designed shapes, spaces and forms. What counts is the experience. The older, wiser cultures of the Orient have shown us that, because of the dynamic nature of their philosophies, the Taoist and Zen conceptions of perfection lay more stress upon the process through which perfection is sought than on perfection itself.[80]

For fifty years, from 1881 to 1932, Miss Jekyll wrote, in a manner simultaneously practical and mystical, about the character, the experience, the atmosphere of her garden, striving to reach per-

Japanese maple and Japanese white pine at a Royal Horticultural Society fortnightly show, 1970; an early display of Bonsai.

fection while knowing she would never attain it, but she was ahead of her time.

By 1982 a deeper oriental influence pervaded many aspects of English life. Gurus, acupuncture and yoga were called to the aid of distressed minds and bodies. At Chelsea, bonsai growers outnumbered rosarians, and the makers of traditional garden ornaments and classical balustrades added lanterns and lightweight rocks to their stock in trade. Modern gardens and modern flower-arranging had completely absorbed Japanese principles of asymmetrical balance. Chelsea in 1985 featured a Japanese garden complete with viewing pavilion, and the interest was so great that the crush inside the pavilion resembled a Tokyo train in the rush hour.

The garden: a way of life?

It gradually became clear, with the renewed availability of Gertrude Jekyll's books, that she had evolved a philosophy of life, a way of gardening, remarkably similar to that of Japan and yet entirely English. The simple ritual of dividing polyanthus or of making carnation-pegs from bracken, the appreciation of the finest detail in every plant, the deep reverence for nature and its changing moods, the earnestness with which she sought perfection knowing that perfection would never be achieved – ideas which could only be taken at face-value when they were written – took on a new significance in an age attuned to oriental philosophy. With fifteen acres of garden at her disposal and the Surrey countryside beyond, Miss Jekyll could still derive pleasure from a tuft of bell-flower and a patch of wild thyme growing in a crevice of the garden steps.[81] She even had a Thunder House, a very English one designed by Lutyens, from which she could contemplate storms playing over the Surrey hills.[82]

As the 1980s draw to a close, the many disparate strands of development of the modern garden are beginning to coalesce into a new unity of expression. Nowhere is this fusion better displayed than in Geoffrey Jellicoe's garden for Stanley Seager at Sutton Place, Surrey, with its modern interpretation of a Lancelot Brown lake, a paradise garden, a contemplative moss-garden, impressionist borders and a wildflower meadow.[83] Sadly, Sutton Place also demonstrates modern insecurity: a garden begun in 1980 was abandoned by its owner in 1986.[84]

In the smaller garden, however, the fusion of ideas has brought great promise. From Jekyll and Lutyens, Thomas Church, Brenda Colvin, John Brookes and Christopher Lloyd, Beth Chatto and Chris Baines, it becomes clear that a small garden can be designed *and* interesting. Ground-cover plants, plants with decorative stems or seedheads, old-fashioned cottage garden plants and even older herbs and flowery meadows can take their part in the design and provide year-round interest in the small garden. For the more industrious, salads and the more decorative vegetables and fruits can be cultivated among the flowers and herbs, in a pre-Lawson muddle or in a decorative *potager*. For the tidy-minded, multi-

Broadway Shopping Centre, Bexleyheath, a striking interior landscape.

Medieval and oriental influences in a new context: the Labyrinth at Stoke Garden Festival.

coloured heathers and dwarf conifers provide that firmness and delight so admired in the seventeenth century, while offering a very distant reminder of our heather-clad hills and the more rugged wilderness explored by David Douglas.

The closing decades of the twentieth century will, more than ever before, be the age of the small garden and, in recent years, there has been growing interest in the design of small gardens. Mr Everyman *can* consult his own Capability Brown and is increasingly keen to do so.

In 1929 a group of between thirty and forty garden designers met in the marquee at the Chelsea Flower Show to form a British Association of Garden Architects, but the Association quickly changed its name to the Institute of Landscape Architects and its horizons from the private garden to the public landscape of roads, reservoirs, New Towns and new forests. Among landscape architects there are, of course, many who enjoy garden design. Anthony Pasley, the late Kenneth Booth, Michael Branch, Gordon Patterson and Preben Jakobsen represent the diversity of such designers, their works ranging from traditional herbaceous borders to boldly

Cubism explored in a North London garden by Preben Jakobsen.

modern sculptural planting. In 1982 a Society of Landscape and Garden Designers was formed, to bring together practitioners for whom garden design is the major or sole occupation.

In the public sector, too, there has been growing interest in the value of good landscape as a civilizing and humanizing influence. Beginning with Liverpool in 1984, garden festivals have become as much a part of life as palm-filled office courtyards, and an invaluable focus for experimentation in garden design.

The Modern movement in garden design began with attempts to find the right shapes and forms for the garden of a 'Modern' house, and in particular instances the shapes and forms were wonderfully successful. The post-Modern garden, though, recognizes that gardens are for people, and that people come in all shapes and psyches and live in widely different circumstances. Design is about creating a private paradise to suit each individual, and not about squeezing currently fashionable shapes or contents of a garden into inappropriate sites.

Unlike post-Modern architects, who seem intent on satirizing historical details in a vain attempt to create history, one can only hope that garden designers, professional and amateur, will be content to rejoice in the diversity of opportunity, to solve individual design problems in individual ways and to leave the question of the 'style' of gardens at the end of the millennium to the next generation of historians.

Notes

[Details of books mentioned in the Notes are given in full in the Bibliography on p. 300.]

Chapter 1: In the Beginning (pp. 5–8)
1. George W. Johnson, *A History of English Gardening*, 1829, p. 3.
2. Marie Luise Gothein, *A History of Garden Art*, 1928, p. 30.
3. ibid., p. 103.

Chapter 2: The Medieval Garden (pp. 9–28)
1. John Harvey, *Mediaeval Gardens*, 1981, p. 29.
2. Walahfrid Strabo, *Hortulus*, Pittsburgh, Pennsylvania, 1966.
3. ibid., p. 29.
4. ibid., p. 31.
5. ibid., pp. 35, 37.
6. ibid., p. 45.
7. ibid., p. 63.
8. ibid., p. 53.
9. ibid., p. 61.
10. ibid., p. 33.
11. ibid., p. 43.
12. ibid., p. 47.
13. ibid., p. 57.
14. ibid., p. 59.
15. ibid., p. 43.
16. Harvey, op.cit., pp. 40 and 50.
17. Alicia Amherst, *A History of Gardening in England*, 1896, p. 67.
18. Harvey, op.cit., p. 67.
19. Amherst, op.cit., p. 67.
20. Teresa McLean, *Medieval English Gardens*, 1981, p. 99.
21. Harvey, op.cit., p. 3.
22. Amherst, op.cit., Ch. 2.
23. ibid., p. 43.
24. ibid., pp. 71–74.
25. Strabo, op.cit., p. 29.
26. Amherst, op.cit., p. 64.
27. John H. Harvey, 'Mediaeval Plantsmanship in England: the Culture of Rosemary', in *Garden History*, Vol. I, 1, pp. 14–21.

Chapter 3: Tudor Gardens (pp. 29–50)
1. Miles Hadfield, *Gardening in Britain*, 1960, p. 42.
2. Ronald Webber, *The Early Horticulturists*, 1968, pp. 15–16.
3. Mavis Batey, 'Autumn Visit to Harrington and Holdenby', in *Garden History*, Vol. V, 3 (Winter 1977), p. 9.
4. Alicia Amherst, *A History of Gardening in England*, p. 83.
5. Geoffrey Taylor, *The Victorian Flower Garden*, 1952, pp. 109–10.
6. Alice M. Coats, *Garden Shrubs and their Histories*, 1963, p. 297.
7. ibid., p. 270.
8. John Parkinson, *Paradisi in Sole, Paradisus Terrestris*, 1629; facsimile edition, 1904, p. 516.
9. John Harvey, *Early Nurserymen*, 1974, p. 23.
10. A new edition of *The Gardener's Labyrinth* was published by Oxford University Press, 1987.
11. Amherst, op.cit., p. 116.
12. William Lawson, *A new orchard and garden*, 1660 edition, p. 13.
13. Hadfield, op.cit., pp. 50–51.
14. J. M. Steane, 'The development of Tudor and Stuart garden design in Northamptonshire', in *Northamptonshire Past and Present*, Vol. V, no. 5.
15. Christopher Thacker, 'Fountains: Theory and Practice in the Seventeenth and Eighteenth Centuries', in Garden History Society's *Occasional Paper 2*, 1970, p. 23.
16. Stephen Switzer, *Ichnographia Rustica*, 2nd edition, 1741, Vol. III, p. 122.

17. Amherst, op.cit., pp. 87–88.
18. ibid, p. 88.
19. Hadfield, op.cit., p. 37.
20. Amherst, op.cit., p. 79.
21. Steane, op.cit., p. 15.
22. ibid., p. 4.
23. Thomasina Beck, 'Gardens in Elizabethan Embroidery', in *Garden History*, Vol. III,1 (Autumn 1974), pp. 44–56.
24. Steane, op.cit.

Chapter 4: Stuart Gardens (pp. 51–74)

1. William Lawson, *A new orchard and garden*, 1660 edition, pp. 54–5.
2. ibid., p. 44.
3. Facsimile editions were published in 1904 and 1975.
4. Prudence Leith-Ross, *The John Tradescants*, 1984.
5. Isaac de Caus, *Wilton Garden*, *c*. 1645, reprinted in Vol. 4 of *The English Landscape Garden* (ed. J. D. Hunt), 1982.
6. Miles Hadfield, 'William, Mary and Westbury', in *Garden History*, Vol. II,2 (Spring 1974), pp. 27–33, and John Sales, 'Westbury Court Gardens' in *National Trust Magazine* 15 (Autumn 1972), pp. 8–9.
7. Steane, 'The development of Tudor and Stuart garden design in Northamptonshire', in *Northamptonshire Past and Present*, Vol. V, no. 5, p. 20.
8. ibid., p. 19.
9. The garden at Kirby is now undergoing comprehensive restoration by English Heritage.
10. David Jacques, 'John Evelyn and the idea of Paradise', in *Landscape Design*, Nov. 1978, pp. 36–8.
11. ibid., p. 37.
12. Kenneth Lemmon, *The Covered Garden*, 1962, p. 22.
13. ibid., pp. 26–7.
14. David Green, *Gardener to Queen Anne: Henry Wise (1653–1738) and the Formal Garden*, 1956, p. 79.
15. Stephen Switzer, *Ichnographia Rustica*, 2nd edition, 1741, Vol. I, p. 81.

Chapter 5: The English Landscape Garden (pp. 75–105)

1. 29 September.
2. *The Spectator*, No. 414, 25 June 1712.
3. Robin Chaplin, 'Garden History and Local Studies: a symposium on source material for garden history at Oxford', in *Garden History*, Vol. IV,2 (Summer 1976), pp. 7–9.
4. Gervase Jackson-Stops, 'Formal garden designs for Cliveden: the work of Claude Desgots and others for the First Earl of Orkney', in *National Trust Yearbook 1976/7*, p. 101.
5. Stephen Switzer, *Ichnographia Rustica*, 2nd edition, 1741, Vol. III, pp. 113–27.
6. J. Addison in *The Spectator*, 414, 25 June 1712: see

John Dixon Hunt and Peter Willis, *The Genius of the Place*, 1975, p. 142.
7. ibid.
8. Switzer, op.cit., Vol. III, p. 88.
9. ibid., Vol. III, pp. v–vi and Ch. IV.
10. P. Willis, *Charles Bridgeman*, 1977.
11. ibid., pl. 116.
12. ibid., p. 108.
13. Richard Bisgrove, *Gardens of Britain 3*, 1978, pp. 146–7, and Willis, op.cit., pl. 47b.
14. Hunt and Willis, op.cit., p. 19.
15. Kenneth Lemmon, 'Wentworth Castle: a forgotten landscape' in *Garden History*, Vol. III,3 (Summer 1975), pp. 50–57.
16. John Serle, *A Plan of Mr Pope's Garden*, London, 1745; see Hunt and Willis, op.cit., pl. 81 (p. 248); also reprinted by Garland, 1982.
17. Christopher Hussey, *English Gardens and Landscapes 1700–1750*, 1967, p. 45.
18. Mavis Batey, 'The way to view Rousham by Kent's gardener', in *Garden History*, Vol. 11,2, pp. 125–32.
19. R. W. King, 'The "Ferme Ornée"; Philip Southcote and Wooburn Farm', in *Garden History*, Vol. II,3 (Summer 1974), pp. 27–60.
20. ibid., p. 37.
21. Isabel Chase, *Horace Walpole: Gardenist*, 1943, p. 37.
22. National Trust, *Conservation of the Garden at Stourhead*, 1978.
23. N. and B. Kitz, *Pains Hill Park*, 1984. The garden is now being restored by Painshill Park Trust.
24. D. Stroud, *Capability Brown*, 2nd edition, 1975, p. 58.
25. ibid., 1st edition, p. 15.
26. Reginald Blomfield, *The Formal Garden in England*, 1892, p. 85.
27. Christopher Tunnard, *Gardens in the Modern Landscape*, 1938, p. 22.

Chapter 6: Eighteenth-century Plant Introduction (pp. 106–19)

1. E. J. Willson, *James Lee and the Vineyard Nursery, Hammersmith*, 1961.
2. H. R. Fletcher, *The Story of the Royal Horticultural Society 1804–1968*, 1969, pp. 63–4.
3. Richard Gorer, *The Flower Garden in England*, 1975, pp. 49–53.
4. Kenneth Lemmon, *The Golden Age of Plant Hunters*, 1968, p. 17.
5. ibid., pp. 42–73.
6. Kenneth Lemmon, *The Covered Garden*, 1962, p. 27.
7. ibid., p. 54.
8. John Harvey, *Early Nurserymen*, 1974, p. 5.
9. Lemmon, *The Golden Age of Plant Hunters*, pp. 79–106.
10. Harvey, op.cit., pp. 6, 7.

Chapter 7: Into the Nineteenth Century (pp. 120–53)

1. H. R. Fletcher, *The Story of the Royal Horticultural Society 1804–1968*, 1969, p. 61.

2. Batty Langley, *The Builder's Chest Book*, 1727.

3. Thomas Wright, *Arbours and Grottos*, (ed. Eileen Harris), 1979.

4. John Harris, *Gardens of Delight, the Rococo English Landscape of Thomas Robins*, 1978.

5. Boyd Alexander, 'Fonthill Wiltshire II: The abbey and its creator', in *Country Life*, 160 (1 December 1966), pp. 1430–34.

6. Mavis Batey, 'Gilpin and the schoolboy picturesque', in *Garden History*, Vol. II,2 (Spring 1974), p. 24.

7. Mavis Batey, 'Oliver Goldsmith: an indictment of landscape gardening', in P. Willis (ed.), *Furor Hortensis*, 1974, p. 65.

8. R. P. Knight, *The Landscape, a didactic poem*, 1795, Books II and III.

9. Letter from Humphry Repton to Edward Chamberlayne, in George Carter *et al.*, *Humphry Repton Landscape Gardener 1752–1818*, 1982, p. 8.

10. Three of the 'Red Books' were republished in facsimile by Basilisk, 1976.

11. Carter, op.cit., p. 26.

12. Humphry Repton, *Sketches and Hints on Landscape Gardening* (collected with Repton's other works in *Repton's Landscape Gardening and Landscape Architecture*, ed. J. C. Loudon, 1840), pp. 102–3.

13. Humphry Repton, *Observations on the Theory and Practice of Landscape Gardening* (Loudon edition), p. 215.

14. Humphry Repton, *Inquiry into the Changes of Taste in Landscape Gardening* (Loudon edition), pp. 339–40.

15. The canal garden below the Conservatory is a twentieth-century addition, designed by Graham Thomas.

16. Repton, *Inquiry* . . . (Loudon edition), p. 364.

17. Humphry Repton, *Fragments on the Theory and Practice of Landscape Gardening* (Loudon edition), p. 559 and illustration, p. 561.

18. ibid., pp. 557–8.

19. ibid., p. 558.

20. A. P. Wylie, 'The history of garden roses', in *Journal of the Royal Horticultural Society*, Vol. 79, December 1954, pp. 560–61.

21. Ernest Smith, *History of Whiteknights*, 1957.

22. Fletcher, op.cit., p. 44.

23. ibid., p. 19.

24. ibid., pp. 92–4.

25. Curtis's *Botanical Magazine*, title page, Vol. 1, 1787; see Ray Desmond, 'Victorian gardening magazines', in *Garden History*, Vol. V,3 (Winter 1977), p. 47.

26. J. C. Loudon, *The Villa Gardener*, 1850, pp. 35–6.

Chapter 8: The High Victorian Garden (pp. 154–91)

1. See H. R. Fletcher, *The Story of the Royal Horticultural Society 1804–1968*, 1969, and Kenneth Lemmon, *The Golden Age of Plant Hunters*, 1968, for extensive accounts of plant hunters.

2. Fletcher, op.cit., p. 101.

3. Geoffrey Taylor, *Some Nineteenth Century Gardeners*, 1951, p. 66.

4. Fletcher, op.cit., p. 152, and Taylor, op.cit., p. 67.

5. *Quercus* x *hispanica*, a hybrid between the Turkey oak (*Q. cerris*) and the cork oak (*Q. suber*).

6. Alice M. Coats, *Flowers and their Histories*, 1956, p. 69.

7. A. P. Wylie, 'The History of Garden Roses', in *Journal of the Royal Horticultural Society*, Vol. 79 (December 1954), pp. 555–71.

8. Fletcher, op.cit., p. 176.

9. Taylor, op.cit., pp. 70–79.

10. John Parkinson, *Paradisi in Sole, Paradisus terrestris*, 1629; facsimile edition 1904, p. 11.

11. Coats, op.cit., p. 239.

12. David Green, *Gardener to Queen Anne: Henry Wise (1653–1738) and the Formal Garden*, 1956, pl. 52.

13. Coats, op.cit., pp. 259–60.

14. Brent Elliott, *The Victorian Garden*, 1986, pp. 50–51.

15. See Fletcher, op.cit., p. 560, and James Herbert Veitch, *Hortus Veitchii*, 1906, for detailed accounts of the Veitch nurseries.

16. 'A Cut Above the Rest', exhibition at the Museum of English Rural Life, University of Reading, 22 November 1977–8 April 1978.

17. Mark Girouard, 'The conservatory and the Victorian country house', paper given to joint meeting of Victorian Society and Garden History Society on *Victorian Conservatories*, 25 October 1980.

18. Fletcher, op.cit., p. 311.

19. Priscilla Boniface (ed.), *In Search of English Gardens*, 1987, pp. 75–6.

20. Elliott, op.cit., p. 155.

21. ibid., p. 156.

22. John Arthur Hughes, *Garden Architecture and Landscape Gardening*, 1866.

23. Elliott, op.cit., pp. 37–8.

24. National Trust guide *Penrhyn*.

25. Elliott, op.cit., pp. 61–2.

26. Graham Stuart Thomas, *Gardens of the National Trust*, 1979, p. 224.

27. John Sales, 'High Victorian horticulture: the garden at Waddesdon', in *National Trust Studies 1979*, p. 81.

28. Miles Hadfield, *Gardening in Britain*, 1960, p. 229.

29. Boniface, op.cit., pp. 82–4, and illustration, pp. 86–7.

30. Mavis Batey, 'Edward Cooke, landscape gardener . . . a Victorian par excellence', in *Garden History*, Vol. VI,1 (Spring 1978), pp. 18–24, and Peter Hayden,

'Edward Cooke at Biddulph Grange', ibid., pp. 25–32.

31. Fletcher, op.cit., p. 203.

32. See George F. Chadwick, *The Works of Sir Joseph Paxton*, 1961, and Violet R. Markham, *Paxton and the Bachelor Duke*, 1935.

33. Markham, op.cit., p. 30.

34. Taylor, op.cit., pp. 76–7.

35. John Fleming, *Spring and Winter Flower Gardening*, 1870, p. 22.

36. ibid., p. 4.

37. ibid., p. 28.

38. Elliott, op.cit., p. 72.

39. Fletcher, op.cit., pp. 197–210.

40. Frederic Morton, *The Rothschilds*, Greenwich, Conn., 1961, p. 153.

41. Barron's tree mover has been restored and can be seen at the Royal Botanic Gardens, Kew.

42. J. C. Loudon, *The Suburban Gardener and Villa Companion*, 1838, pp. 34–6.

43. Edward Kemp, *How to Lay Out a Garden*, 2nd edition, 1860, p. 92.

44. J. A. Hughes, *Garden Architecture and Landscape Gardening*, 1866, p. 49.

Chapter 9: The Battle of Styles (pp. 192–217)

1. Brent Elliott, *The Victorian Garden*, 1986, pp. 153–4.

2. William Robinson, *Parks, Promenades and Gardens of Paris*, p. 27.

3. ibid., pp. 52–4.

4. William Robinson, *The Wild Garden*, 5th edition, 1903, p. xiii.

5. ibid., p. 28.

6. ibid., p. 8.

7. Robinson, *Parks, Promenades and Gardens of Paris*, p. 239.

8. ibid., p. 242.

9. Robinson, *The Wild Garden*, pp. xiii–xiv.

10. Robinson, *Parks, Promenades and Gardens of Paris*, p. 240.

11. ibid., p. 240.

12. For a more detailed account of geology and gardens in the South-East of England see T. Wright, *Gardens of England 4*, 1978.

13. Mavis Batey, 'Edward Cooke, landscape gardener ... a Victorian par excellence', in *Garden History*, Vol. VI, 1 (Spring 1978), p. 23.

14. Elliott, op.cit., p. 201.

15. ibid., p. 200.

16. Richard Bisgrove, *Gardens of Britain 3*, 1978, pp. 74–5.

17. Graham Stuart Thomas, *Gardens of the National Trust*, 1979, p. 225.

18. Bisgrove, op.cit., p. 80.

19. S. Reynolds Hole, *Our Gardens*, 1901, p. 85.

20. ibid., p. 86.

21. William Robinson, *The English Flower Garden*, 12th edition, 1914, p. 11.

22. ibid., pp. 11–12.

23. H. E. Milner, *Art and Practice of Landscape Gardening*, 1890, p. 22.

24. Biographical information is given by E. F. Russell as a Memoir in J. D. Sedding's *Garden Craft Old and New*, 1891.

25. ibid., p. 129.

26. ibid., p. 180.

27. Reginald Blomfield, *The Formal Garden in England*, 1892, p.ix.

28. ibid., pp. 4–5.

29. William Robinson, *Garden Design and Architects' Gardens*, 1892, pp. 66–7.

30. Reginald Blomfield, *The Formal Garden in England*, 2nd edition, pp. v–vii.

Chapter 10: The Edwardian and Neo-Georgian Garden (pp. 218–45)

1. For biographical details of Gertrude Jekyll see Betty Massingham, *Miss Jekyll, Portrait of a Great Gardener*, 1966, and Jane Brown, *Gardens of a Golden Afternoon*, 1982.

2. Massingham, op.cit., p. 59. Brabazon became an overnight celebrity at the age of seventy-one after an exhibition of his watercolours.

3. Charles Newton was Keeper of Greek and Roman Antiquities at the British Museum.

4. A complete list of Miss Jekyll's publications is given in Michael J. Tooley (ed.), *Gertrude Jekyll, Artist, Gardener, Craftswoman*, 1984, pp. 135–51.

5. H. R. Fletcher, *The Story of the Royal Horticultural Society 1804–1968*, 1969, pp. 240 and 243, and Massingham, op.cit., p. 65.

6. Brown, op.cit., pp. 104–5.

7. C. Hussey, *The Life of Sir Edwin Lutyens*, 1953, p. 96.

8. Gertrude Jekyll, *Wood and Garden*, 1899, p. 1.

9. See R. Bisgrove, 'Gertrude Jekyll, a gardener ahead of her time', in Tooley, op.cit., pp. 51–60.

10. A plan of Arley Hall dated 1846 shows two herbaceous borders.

11. 'Drift' was a word suggested by Miss Jekyll for a long, thin group of plants. (*Colour Schemes for the Flower Garden*, 1914, p. 26.)

12. Reef Point Garden archive of Jekyll plans, folder 128.

13. ibid., folder 17.

14. ibid., folder 87 (Stilemans), folder 73 (Upton Grey) and folder 224, item 15 for embroidery pattern.

15. Massingham, op.cit., pp. 56–7.

16. Several letters from potential clients refer to poor designs from nurseries when asking Miss Jekyll for advice.

17. Several examples of Mallows's work were included

in Gertrude Jekyll and Lawrence Weaver, *Gardens for Small Country Houses*, 1912.

18. David Mawson, 'Thomas H. Mawson, 1861–1933', in *Landscape Design*, 127 (August 1979), pp. 30–33.

19. Although his gardens were smaller than those of Milner, Mawson became increasingly involved in civic design on a large scale and was appointed to Britain's first chair in Town Planning, at the University of Liverpool. See Mawson, *Civic Art*, 1911.

20. Miles Hadfield, *Gardening in Britain*, 1960, pp. 378–9.

21. Fletcher, op.cit., pp. 309–10.

22. W. J. Bean, *Trees and Shrubs Hardy in the British Isles*, 8th edition, Vol. III, 1976, pp. 912–3.

23. A. P. Wylie, 'The History of Garden Roses: part 2', in *Journal of the Royal Horticultural Society*, Vol. 80 (January. 1955), pp. 8–24.

24. G. S. Thomas, 'The influence of Gertrude Jekyll on the use of roses in gardens and garden design', in *Garden History*, Vol. V,1 (Spring 1977), pp. 53–65.

25. F. Crisp, *Mediaeval Gardens*, 1924.

26. Republished in 1972.

27. M. Andrews, 'Port Lympne, near Hythe, Kent', in *Landscape Design*, Vol. 143 (June 1983), pp. 31–3.

28. Sir Geoffrey Jellicoe, 'Ronald Tree and the gardens of Ditchley Park: the human face of history', in *Garden History*, Vol. 10,1 (Spring 1982), pp. 80–91.

29. William Wood and Sons Ltd, catalogue for 1938.

30. Richard Bisgrove, *Gardens of Britain 3*, 1978, pp. 63–4 and pl. 9.

31. Alvilde Lees-Milne, 'Lawrence Johnston, creator of Hidcote Garden', in *The National Trust Yearbook 1977–8*, pp. 18–29.

32. From National Trust guidebook.

33. Sylvia Crowe, *Garden Design*, 1958, pp. 181–4, considers the garden at Tintinhull to be one of the finest twentieth-century designs.

34. Norah Lindsay, 'The Manor House, Sutton Courtenay, Berkshire', in *Country Life*, Vol. 69 (16 May 1931), p. 610.

35. T. Wright, *Gardens of England 4*, 1978, p. 45.

36. *Journal of the Royal Horticultural Society*, November 1949, pp. 476–81.

37. V. Sackville-West, 'The garden at Sissinghurst Castle, Cranbrook, Kent', in *Journal of the Royal Horticultural Society*, Vol. 78,11 (November 1953), pp. 400–408.

38. Alvilde Lees–Milne, 'Sissinghurst Castle Gardens, an appreciation', in *Journal of the Royal Horticultural Society*, Vol. 91,9 (September 1966), p. 371.

Chapter 11: The Modern Garden (pp. 246–92)

1. Gerald Palmer, personal communication, see Bisgrove, *Gardens of Britain 3*, 1978, pp. 50–51.

2. Bisgrove, op.cit., pp. 147–8.

3. G. S. Thomas, *Gardens of the National Trust*, 1979, pp. 257–8.

4. Peter Coats, *Great Gardens of Britain*, 1967, pp. 272–81, and Bisgrove, op.cit., pp. 90–91.

5. G. S. Thomas, *Three Gardens*, 1983.

6. Jane Brown, *Lanning Roper and His Gardens*, 1987.

7. Jane Brown, *The English Garden in Our Time*, 1986, pp. 173–82.

8. Ronald Webber, *Percy Cane, Garden Designer*, 1975.

9. Arthur Hellyer, 'A Percy Cane period piece: the garden at Westfields, near Bedford', *Country Life*, 170 (2 July 1981), pp. 26–8.

10. Morton, *Journal of the Royal Horticultural Society*, Vol. 81,8 (August 1956), pp. 372–3.

11. The Earl of Rosse, 'The National Trust Gardens Scheme', in *Journal of the Royal Horticultural Society*, Vol. 74 (October 1949), pp. 432–9.

12. W. J. Bean, *Trees and Shrubs Hardy in the British Isles*, 8th edition, Vol. II, 1973, pp. 735–6.

13. H. R. Fletcher, *The Story of the Royal Horticultural Society 1804–1968*, 1969, p. 250.

14. Hugh Casson, 'Dreams and awakenings' in BBC, *Spirit of the Age*, 1975, pp. 216–17.

15. *Hillier's Manual of Trees and Shrubs*, 1971.

16. *The Garden*, Vol. 101,5 (May 1976), pp. 252–3.

17. E. R. Hoare, 'The Engineer Helps Horticulture', in *Journal of the Royal Horticultural Society*, Vol. 74 (August 1949), pp. 342–6.

18. F. E. W. Hanger, 'The Labour-Saving Garden', in *Journal of the Royal Horticultural Society*, Vol. 74 (June 1949), pp. 233–41.

19. *Journal of the Royal Horticultural Society* (November 1949), pp. 476–81.

20. ibid., pp. 492–7.

21. A. T. Johnson, *Labour Saving Plants* (n.d.), reprinted by Landsman Bookshop, Hereford.

22. R. Cameron, 'Great Comp and its garden', in *The Garden*, 1981, pp. 89–96.

23. Lanning Roper, *Hardy Herbaceous Plants*, 1960, p. 16.

24. Roy Hay, *Gardening the Modern Way*, 1962, p. 13.

25. See J. M. Richards, *An Introduction to Modern Architecture*, 1940, pp. 76–7 and 81.

26. Miles Hadfield, *Gardening in Britain*, 1960, p. 397.

27. Christopher Hussey, 'Some houses at Silver End Garden Village, Essex', in *Country Life*, Vol. 64 (27 October 1928), pp. 601–2.

28. Christopher Hussey, 'Yaffle Hill, Dorset', in *Country Life*, Vol. 74 (8 July 1933), p. 15.

29. J. O. Simonds, *Landscape Architecture*, 1961, pp. 221–5.

30. Michael Laurie, 'Thomas Church and the Evolution of the California Garden', in *Landscape Design*, 101 (February 1973), pp. 8–12.

31. Thomas Church, *Gardens are for People*, 1952, pp. 11, 42 and 231–5.

32. Christopher Tunnard, *Gardens in the Modern Landscape*, 1938, p. 69.

33. ibid., p. 87.

34. ibid., pp. 150–51.

35. Peggie Schultz, *Growing Plants under Artificial Light*, 1955, and F. H. and J. L. Kranz, *Gardening Indoors under Light*, 1957.

36. G. A. Jellicoe, *Studies in Landscape Design*, Vol. II, pp. 4–6. (See also pl. 1 after p. 16.)

37. ibid., pp. 28–31 and pl. 24 (opp. p. 33).

38. See Hal Moggridge and Chris Carter, 'Colvin and Moggridge', in *Landscape Design*, 164 (December 1986), p. 20.

39. Bisgrove, op. cit., p. 44.

40. *House and Garden*, July 1953, p. 40.

41. Arup Associates, 'Gateway House Basingstoke', in *The Architects' Journal*, 24 August 1977, pp. 343–58.

42. John Brookes, *Improve Your Lot*, 1977, p. 5.

43. Christopher Hussey, 'A grand garden in miniature', in *Country Life*, Vol. 109 (22 March 1956), pp. 532–5.

44. Thomas, op. cit., p. 21 (illustration) and p. 173.

45. Kay Sanecki, 'Memories of the Founding of the Society', in *The Garden History Society: Newsletter 15*, Autumn 1985, pp. 12–14.

46. Mary Keen, 'Studley Royal', in *The Garden*, Vol. 108, 8 (August 1983), pp. 301–5, and Martin Beckett, 'Fountains Abbey and Studley Royal – why the cost?', in *National Trust Magazine 40*, Autumn 1983, pp. 17–19.

47. 'Recent acquisitions' in *National Trust Newsletter 1*, p. 5.

48. Merlin Waterson, 'The Yorkes of Erddig', in *National Trust Magazine 18*, Autumn 1973, p. 8.

49. Andrew Paul, 'The restoration of Hestercombe', in *Landscape Design*, 133 (February 1981), pp. 26–7.

50. Paul Miles, 'The garden of Ham House, Richmond-upon-Thames', in *Landscape Design*, 113 (February 1976), pp. 26–8.

51. Peter Mansfield, 'An 18th century landscape restored: the gardens of Claremont, Surrey', in *Country Life*, Vol. 165 (17 May 1979), pp. 1547–50.

52. Gordon Winter, 'Restoring a great landscape garden: Pains Hill, Cobham, Surrey', in *Country Life*, Vol. 169 (12 March 1981), pp. 638–40; progress is recorded in the *Painshill Park Newsletter*, published twice each year.

53. Mavis Batey, 'The conservation and restoration of historic gardens' in M. McGarvie, *Home is House and Garden*, 1984, pp. 8–9.

54. Hal Moggridge, 'Cadland, Hampshire: restoration of Capability Brown's landscape for Boarn Hill Cottage', in *Landscape Design*, 144 (August 1983), pp. 23–4.

55. Hal Moggridge, 'Blenheim Park: the restoration plan', in *Landscape Design*, 146 (1983), pp. 9–10, and Ralph Cobham, 'Brown in memoriam: Blenheim Park in perpetuity', ibid., pp. 11–12.

56. Paul Edwards, 'Warwick Castle – new landscapes for today's visitors', in *Landscape Design*, 151 (October 1984), pp. 45–6.

57. National Trust, *Conservation of the Garden at Stourhead*, Bath, 1978.

58. David Jacques and Michael Whitton, 'Computers in landscape practice', in *Landscape Design*, 152 (December 1984), pp. 49–50.

59. Landsman Bookshop, Hereford (n.d.).

60. Basilisk Press, 1976.

61. Hunt Botanical Library, 1966.

62. *Hortulus*, Toronto, 1980.

63. Anne Scott-James, 'A bibliophile's garden', in *The Garden*, Vol. 102, July 1977, pp. 281–8.

64. Mrs Batey was awarded the VMH in 1986 and the MBE in 1987 for 'services to the preservation and conservation of historic gardens'.

65. Roy Hay, *Gardening the Modern Way*, 1962, p. 30.

66. Alan Bloom, *Hardy Perennials*, 1957, p. 41.

67. Alan Bloom, 'Island beds of herbaceous perennials', in *Journal of the Royal Horticultural Society*, Vol. 89 (November 1964), pp. 457–60.

68. Adrian Bloom, 'Foggy Bottom', in *The Garden*, September 1985, pp. 410–14.

69. Beth Chatto, 'Plant grouping in an Essex garden', in *Journal of the Royal Horticultural Society*, Vol. 99,6 (June 1974), pp. 237–41.

70. Brent Elliott, 'The first table decoration competition', in *The Garden*, Vol. 112,2 (February 1987), pp. 78–80.

71. Elizabeth Coxhead, *Constance Spry*, 1975.

72. G. S. Thomas, *Old Shrub Roses*, 1955, p. 19.

73. G. S. Thomas, *Gardens of the National Trust*, pp. 175–6.

74. T. C. Wells *et al.*, *Creating Attractive Grasslands using Native Plant Species*, 1981.

75. Christopher Lloyd, *The Garden*, Vol. 101, June 1976, p. 322, July 1976, pp. 350–55.

76. Christopher Lloyd, *The Well-Tempered Garden*, 1970; revised edition, 1985, p. 9. In *Home and Garden* (p. 3), Gertrude Jekyll wrote: 'It takes more time, more trouble; it may even take a good deal of time and trouble, but then it is just right, and to see and know it is just right is a daily reward and a never-ending source of satisfaction.'

77. Stephen Rettig, 'The rise of the "Ecological Approach" to landscape design', in *Landscape Design*, June 1983, pp. 39–41.

78. Gertrude Jekyll, *Wood and Garden*, 1899, p. 219.

79. Josiah Conder, *Landscape Gardening in Japan*, 1882, pp. ix–x.

80. John O. Simonds, *Landscape Architecture*, 1961, p. 225.

81. Gertrude Jekyll, *Colour Schemes for the Flower Garden*, 6th edition, 1925, pp. 134–5 and illustration.

82. Gertrude Jekyll and Lawrence Weaver, *Gardens for Small Country Houses*, 4th edition, 1920, p. 45.

83. Geoffrey Jellicoe, 'Sutton Place, allegory and analogy in the garden', in *Landscape Design*, October 1983, pp. 8–9.

84. Marion Thompson, 'Sunset for Sutton Place?' in *Landscape Design*, December 1986, pp. 41–5.

Bibliography

General references:

Alicia Amherst, *A History of Gardening in England*, Quaritch, 1896.

Mavis Batey, *Oxford Gardens*, Avebury, 1982.

W. J. Bean, *Trees and Shrubs Hardy in the British Isles*, 8th edn, 4 vols., John Murray, 1970–80.

Janet Bord, *Mazes and Labyrinths of the World*, Latimer, 1976.

BBC, *Spirit of the Age: Eight Centuries of British Architecture*, BBC, 1975.

Derek Clifford, *A History of Garden Design*, Faber, 1962.

Alice M. Coats, *Flowers and Their Histories*, Hulton, 1956.

Alice M. Coats, *Garden Shrubs and Their Histories*, Vista, 1963.

Ray Desmond, *Bibliography of British Gardens*, St Paul's Bibliographies, 1984.

Ralph Dutton, *The English Garden*, Batsford, 1937.

Gardens of Britain series:

P. M. Synge, 1. *Devon and Cornwall*, Batsford, 1977.

A Paterson, 2. *Dorset, Hampshire and Isle of Wight*, Batsford 1978.

R. J. Bisgrove, 3. *Berkshire, Buckinghamshire, Oxfordshire, Hertfordshire and Bedfordshire*, Batsford, 1978.

T. J. W. Wright, 4. *Kent, East and West Sussex and Surrey*, Batsford, 1978.

K. Lemmon, 5. *Yorkshire and Humberside*, Batsford, 1978.

J. Anthony, 6. *Derbyshire, Leicestershire, Lincolnshire, Northamptonshire, Nottinghamshire*, Batsford 1979.

D. J. Sales, *West Country Gardens*, Sutton, 1980.

R. Sidwell, *West Midland Gardens*, Sutton, 1981.

Richard Gorer, *The Flower Garden in England*, Batsford, 1975.

Marie Luise Gothein, *A History of Garden Art*, trans. Laura Archer-Hind, 2 vols., Dent, 1928.

Miles Hadfield *et al., British Gardeners*, Zwemmer, 1980.

Miles Hadfield, *Gardening in Britain*, Hutchinson, 1960.

Hillier and Sons, *Hillier's Manual of Trees and Shrubs*, Hillier, 1971.

Peter Hunt (ed.), *The Shell Gardens Book*, Phoenix House, 1964.

George W. Johnson, *A History of English Gardening*, Baldwin & Cradock, 1829.

Barbara Jones, *Follies and Grottos*, Constable, 1953, 1974.

W. H. Matthews, *Mazes and Labyrinths*, Longmans Green, 1922; republished Dover, 1970.

Nikolaus Pevsner, *An Outline of European Architecture*, Penguin, 7th edn 1963.

Roy E. Shepherd, *History of the Rose*, Macmillan 1954; reprinted Heyden, 1978.

Christopher Thacker, *The History of Gardens*, Croom Helm, 1979.

Graham Stuart Thomas, *Gardens of the National Trust*, National Trust/Weidenfeld & Nicolson, 1979.

Chapter 2: The Medieval Garden (pp. 9–28)

Frank Crisp, *Mediaeval Gardens* (1924), reprinted by Hacker, 1966, 1979.

John Harvey, *Mediaeval Gardens*, Batsford, 1981.

Teresa McLean, *Medieval English Gardens*, Collins, 1981.

Walahfrid Strabo, *Hortulus*, Hunt, 1966.

Chapter 3: Tudor Gardens (pp. 29–50)
Chapter 4: Stuart Gardens (pp. 51–74)

Reginald Blomfield, *The Formal Garden in England*, Macmillan, 1892.

Isaac de Caus, *Wilton Garden*, c. 1645.

Isaac de Caus, *New and Rare inventions of Water-Works* 1659; reprinted by Garland, 1982.

Mary Palmer Kelley Cooper, *The Early English Kitchen Garden*, privately printed, 1983.

John Evelyn, *Sylva, or a discourse of forest trees, and the propagation of timber in His Majesties Dominions*, Martyn and Allestry, 1664; reprinted by Scolar, 1972.

Celia Fiennes, *The Journies of Celia Fiennes*, ed. C. Morris, 1949; reprinted by Macdonald, 1982.

John Gerard, *The Herball, or Generall Historie of Plantes*, 1597; enlarged edition of 1636 reprinted by Bracken, 1985.

David Green, *Gardener to Queen Anne: Henry Wise (1653–1738) and the Formal Garden*, Oxford University Press, 1956.

John Harris, *The Artist and the Country House*, Sotheby Parke Bernet, 1974.

Thomas Hill, *The Gardener's Labyrinth*, 1577; newly corrected and enlarged, Bell, 1652; reprinted by Oxford University Press, 1987.

Blanche Henrey, *British Botanical and Horticultural Literature before 1800*, Oxford University Press, 1975.

David Jacques and Arend Jan van der Horst, *The Gardens of William and Mary*, Helm, 1988.

William Lawson, *A New Orchard and Garden*, Alsop for Roger Jackson, 1618; reprinted by Garland, 1982.

Leonard Knyff and Jan Kip, *Britannia Illustrata*, Mortier, 1707; reprinted by Paradigm for National Trust, 1984.

Prudence Leith-Ross, *The John Tradescants*, Peter Owen, 1984.

Andre Mollet, *The Garden of Pleasure*, T. N. for John Martyn, 1670.

John Parkinson, *Paradisi in Sole, Paradisus Terrestris*, Lownes & Young, 1629; reprinted by Methuen, 1904, and W. J. Johnson, 1975.

J. M. Steane, *The Development of Tudor and Stuart Garden Design in Northamptonshire*, reprinted from *Northamptonshire Past and Present*, Vol V, No. 5.

Roy Strong, *The Renaissance Garden in England*, Thames & Hudson, 1979.

Christopher Taylor, *Archaeology of Gardens*, Shire, 1983.

Thomas Tusser, *Five Hundred Pointes of Good Husbandrie*, Denham 1580; reprinted by Oxford University Press, 1984.

Vitruvius Britannicus, reprinted in 3 vols., Blom 1967.

John Worlidge, *Systema horti-culturae: or, the art of gardening*, Burrel and Hensman, 1677; reprinted by Garland, 1982.

Chapter 5: The English Landscape Garden (pp. 75–105)

Jean Denis Attiret, *A Particular Account of the Emperor of China's Gardens near Pekin*, tran. Joseph Spence, Dodsley, 1752; reprinted by Garland, 1982.

Morris Brownell, *Alexander Pope and the Arts of Georgian England*, Oxford University Press, 1978.

Isabel W. U. Chase, *Horace Walpole: Gardenist*, Princeton University Press, 1943.

H. Frank Clark, *The English Landscape Garden*, Pleiades, 1948.

John Evelyn, *Sylva, or a discourse of forest trees, and the propagation of timber in His Majesties Dominions*, Martyn and Allestry, 1664; reprinted by Scolar, 1972.

John Harris, *The Artist and the Country House*, Sotheby Parke Bernet, 1974.

John Dixon Hunt and Peter Willis, *The Genius of the Place*, Elek, 1975.

Christopher Hussey, *English Gardens and Landscapes 1700–1750*, Country Life, 1967.

David Jacques, *Georgian Gardens*, Batsford, 1983.

Norman and Beryl Kitz, *Pains Hill Park*, Kitz, 1984.

Batty Langley, *New Principles of Gardening*, 1728; reprinted by Garland, 1982.

William Mason, *The English Garden: a Poem in Four Books*, 1783; reprinted by Gregg International, 1971, and Garland, 1982.

National Trust, *Conservation of the Garden at Stourhead*, Bath University Press, 1978.

Hugh Prince, *Parks in England*, Pinhorns, 1967.

John Serle, *A Plan of Mr Pope's Garden*, 1745; reprinted by Garland, 1982.

William Shenstone, *A Description of the Leasowes*, 1764; reprinted by Garland, 1982.

Dorothy Stroud, *Capability Brown*, Country Life, 1950; 2nd edn, 1975.

Stephen Switzer, *Ichnographia Rustica*, 1718; reprinted by Garland, 1982.

Stephen Switzer, *An Introduction to a General System of Hydrostaticks and Hydraulicks*, T. Astley, 1729; reprinted by Garland, 1982.

Vitruvius Britannicus, reprinted in 3 vols., Blom, 1967.

Horace Walpole, *The History of the Modern Taste in Gardening*, 1770; also included in Chase *q.v.*; 1827 edn reprinted by Garland, 1982.

Thomas Whately, *Observations on Modern Gardening*, Payne, 1770; reprinted by Garland, 1982.

Peter Willis, *Charles Bridgeman and the English Landscape Garden*, Zwemmer, 1977.

Peter Willis (ed.), *Furor Hortensis*, Elysium Press, 1974.

Kenneth Woodbridge, *Landscape in Antiquity: aspects of English culture at Stourhead 1718 to 1838*, Oxford University Press, 1970.

Thomas Wright, Arbours and Grottos: a facsimile of the two parts of *Universal Architecture* (1755 and 1758), ed. Eileen Harris, Scolar, 1979.

Chapter 6: Eighteenth-century Plant Introduction (pp. 106–19)

John Harvey, *Early Nurserymen*, Phillimore, 1974.

John Harvey, *Early Gardening Catalogues,* Phillimore, 1972.

Kenneth Lemmon, *The Golden Age of Plant Hunters,* Phoenix House, 1968.

Kenneth Lemmon, *The Covered Garden,* Museum Press, 1962.

Thomas Mawe and other gardeners (i.e. John Abercrombie), *Every Man his own Gardener,* W. Griffin, 1767.

Ronald Webber, *The Early Horticulturists,* David & Charles, 1968.

E. J. Willson, *James Lee and the Vineyard Nursery Hammersmith,* Hammersmith Local History Group, 1961.

Chapter 7: Into the Nineteenth Century (pp. 120–53)

Priscilla Boniface (ed.), *In Search of English Gardens: The Travels of John Claudius Loudon and his Wife Jane,* Lennard, 1987.

George Carter, Patrick Goode and Kedrun Laurie, *Humphry Repton Landscape Gardener 1752–1818,* Victoria and Albert Museum, 1982.

Sir William Chambers, *A Dissertation on Oriental Gardening,* Griffin, 1772.

William Gilpin, *Observations on the River Wye ...,* Blamire, 1789.

W. S. Gilpin, *Practical Hints upon Landscape Gardening,* Cadell, 1832.

John Harris, *Gardens of Delight: the Rococo English Landscape of Thomas Robins the Elder,* Basilisk, 1978.

Richard Payne Knight, *The Landscape: a didactic poem,* Bulmer, 1795.

J. C. Loudon, *An Encyclopaedia of Gardening,* Longman, Hurst, Rees, Orme and Brown, 1822.

J. C. Loudon, *The Suburban Gardener and Villa Companion,* 1838; republished as *The Villa Gardener,* 1850.

E. B. MacDougall (ed.), *John Claudius Loudon and the Early Nineteenth Century in Great Britain,* Dumbarton Oaks, 1980.

Edward Malins, *The Red Books of Humphry Repton,* Basilisk, 1976.

W. Marshall, *Planting and Ornamental Gardening,* Dodsley, 1785.

W. Marshall, *On Planting and Rural Ornament,* 3rd edn, Bulmer, 1803.

William Mavor, *A New Description of Blenheim,* 1793; reprinted by Garland, 1982.

Henry Phillips, *Flora Historica, or the Three Seasons of the British Parterre,* 2 vols., E. Lloyd, 1824.

Uvedale Price, *Essays on the Picturesque,* Mawman, 1810; reprinted by Gregg International, 1971.

[Humphry Repton], *The Landscape Gardening and Landscape Architecture of the Late Humphry Repton,* ed. J. C. Loudon, Longman, 1840.

Dorothy Stroud, *Humphry Repton,* Country Life, 1962.

Chapter 8: The High Victorian Garden (pp. 154–91)

David E. Allen, *The Victorian Fern Craze,* Hutchinson, 1969.

Alfred Barry, *The Life and Works of Sir Charles Barry,* Blom, 1972.

Nathaniel Cole, *The Royal Parks and Gardens of London,* Journal of Horticulture Press, 1877.

George F. Chadwick, *The Works of Sir Joseph Paxton,* Architectural Press, 1961.

John Davies (ed.), *Douglas of the Forests* (David Douglas's diaries 1825–33), Paul Harris, 1979.

Brent Elliott, *Victorian Gardens,* Batsford, 1986.

H. R. Fletcher, *The Story of the Royal Horticultural Society,* Oxford University Press, 1969.

John Fleming, *Spring and Winter Flower Gardening,* Journal of Horticulture Press, 1870.

Shirley Hibberd, *The Amateur's Flower Garden,* Groombridge, 1874.

Shirley Hibberd, *The Amateur's Rose Book,* Groombridge, 1874.

Shirley Hibberd, *The Fern Garden,* Groombridge, 2nd edn, 1869.

Shirley Hibberd, *New and Rare Beautiful Leaved Plants,* 1870.

Shirley Hibberd, *Rustic Adornments for Homes of Taste,* 1856; reprinted by Century/National Trust, 1987.

John Hix, *The Glass House,* Phaidon, 1974.

John Arthur Hughes, *Garden Architecture and Landscape Gardening,* Longmans Green, 1866.

Edward Kemp, *How to Lay Out a Garden,* 2nd edn. John Wiley, 1860.

Kenneth Lemmon, *The Covered Garden,* Museum Press, 1962.

C. McIntosh, *The Book of the Garden,* Wm Blackwood, 1853–5.

C. McIntosh, *The Flower Garden,* Wm S. Orr, 1838.

C. McIntosh, *The Orchard and Fruit Garden,* Wm S. Orr, 1839.

C. McIntosh, *The Practical Gardener and Modern Horticulturalist,* Thomas Kelly, 1828–9.

Joshua Major, *Theory and Practice of Landscape Gardening,* Longman Brown Green Longman, 1852.

Violet Markham, *Paxton and the Bachelor Duke,* Hodder & Stoughton, 1935.

William Paul, *The Rose Garden,* Kent & Co., 9th edn, 1888.

Geoffrey Taylor, *Some Nineteenth Century Gardeners,* Skeffington, 1951.

Geoffrey Taylor, *The Victorian Flower Garden,* Skeffington, 1952.

David Thomson, *Fruit Culture under Glass*, Blackwood, 2nd edn, 1881.

David Thomson, *Handy Book of the Flower Garden*, Blackwood, 1868.

J. H. Veitch, *A Traveller's Notes on a Tour Through India … during the Years 1891–3*, 1896.

Chapter 9: The Battle of the Styles (pp. 192–217)

Mea Allan, *William Robinson 1838–1935: Father of the English Flower Garden*, Faber, 1982.

Reginald Blomfield, *The Formal Garden in England*, Macmillan, 1892.

Henry Ernest Milner, *The Art and Practice of Landscape Gardening*, 1890.

William Robinson, *Alpine Flowers for Gardens*, John Murray, 1870.

William Robinson, *The English Flower Garden*, John Murray, 1883.

William Robinson, *Garden Design and Architects' Gardens*, John Murray, 1892.

William Robinson, *Gleanings from French Gardens*, Frederick Warne, 1868.

William Robinson, *The Parks, Promenades and Gardens of Paris*, John Murray, 1860.

William Robinson, *The Subtropical Garden*, John Murray, 1879.

William Robinson, *The Vegetable Garden*, John Murray, 1885.

William Robinson, *The Wild Garden*, John Murray, 1870; 4th edn of 1874 reprinted by Scolar, 1979.

John D. Sedding, *Garden Craft Old and New*, Kegan Paul, Trench, Trubner, 1891.

Chapter 10: The Edwardian and Neo-Georgian Garden (pp. 218–45)

Madelaine Agar, *Garden Design in Theory and Practice*, Sidgwick & Jackson, 1913.

Mea Allan, *E. A. Bowles and his Garden at Myddleton House*, Faber, 1973.

E. A. Bowles, *My Garden in Spring*, T. C. & E. C. Jack, 1914.

E. A. Bowles, *My Garden in Summer*, T. C. & E. C. Jack, 1914.

E. A. Bowles, *My Garden in Autumn and Winter*, T. C. & E. C. Jack, 1915; 3 vols, reprinted by David & Charles, 1972.

Jane Brown, *Gardens of a Golden Afternoon*, Allen Lane, 1982.

Jane Brown, *Vita's Other World*, Viking, 1985.

E. A. Bunyard, *Old Garden Roses*, Country Life, 1936.

Josiah Conder, *Landscape Gardening in Japan*, Kelly and Walsh, 1893; reprinted by Dover Books, 1964.

J. M. Cowan (ed.), *George Forrest VMH: Journeys and Plant Introductions*, Oxford University Press for RHS, 1952.

George Elgood and Gertrude Jekyll, *Some English Gardens*, Longmans, Green & Co., 1904.

Henry N. Ellacombe, *In a Gloucestershire Garden*, Edward Arnold, 1906.

A. M. Earle, *Sundials and Roses of Yesterday*, Macmillan, 1902.

C. W. Earle, *Pot Pourri from a Surrey Garden*, Smith Elder, 1897.

Reginald Farrer, *The English Rock Garden*, T. C. & E. C. Jack, 1918; reprinted by Thomas Nelson, 1955.

Reginald Farrer, *My Rock Garden*, Edward Arnold, 1907.

Mrs A. Gatty, *The Book of Sundials*, 1872; enlarged and re-edited by H. K. F. Eden and Eleanor Lloyd, George Bell, 1900.

S. Reynolds Hole, *Memories of Dean Hole*, Edward Arnold, 1892.

S. Reynolds Hole, *Our Gardens*, Dent, 1901.

S. Reynolds Hole, *A Book about the Garden*, Edward Arnold, 1892.

Christopher Hussey, *The Life of Sir Edwin Lutyens*, Country Life, 1950; reprinted by Antique Collectors' Club, 1984.

Gertrude Jekyll, *Colour in the Flower Garden*, Country Life, 1908; republished as *Colour Schemes for the Flower Garden*, Country Life, 1914 and Windward, Frances Lincoln, 1988.

Gertrude Jekyll, *Flower Decoration in the House*, Country Life, 1907.

Gertrude Jekyll, *Garden Ornament*, Country Life, 1918.

Gertrude Jekyll, *Home and Garden*, Longmans, Green & Co., 1900.

Gertrude Jekyll, *Old West Surrey*, Longmans, Green & Co., 1904.

Gertrude Jekyll, *Roses for English Gardens*, Country Life, 1902; republished with introduction by G. S. Thomas, Penguin, 1983.

Gertrude Jekyll, *Wall and Water Gardens*, Country Life, 1901.

Gertrude Jekyll, *Wood and Garden*, Longmans, Green & Co., 1899.

Gertrude Jekyll and Lawrence Weaver, *Gardens for Small Country Houses*, Country Life, 1912.

Francis Kingdon-Ward, *The Riddle of the Tsangpo Gorges*, Edward Arnold, 1926.

Francis Kingdon-Ward, *The Romance of Gardening*, Cape, 1935.

Audrey le Lievre, *Miss Willmott of Warley Place*, Faber, 1980.

Alice Martineau, *The Herbaceous Garden*, Williams & Northgate, 1913.

Betty Massingham, *Gertrude Jekyll*, Country Life, 1966.

Thomas H. Mawson and E. Prentice Mawson, *The Art and Craft of Garden Making*, 1900; 5th edn, Batsford, 1926.

Vita Sackville-West, *In Your Garden*, Michael Joseph, 1951.

Vita Sackville-West, *In Your Garden Again*, Michael Joseph, 1953.

Anne Scott-James, *Sissinghurst: The Making of a Garden*, Michael Joseph, 1975.

Sir George Sitwell, *On the Making of Gardens*, Duckworth, 1909.

V. N. Solly, *Gardens for Town and Suburb*, Ernest Benn, 1926.

B. H. B. Symons-Jeune, *Natural Rock Gardening*, Country Life, 1932.

George F. Tinley, Thomas Humphreys and Walter Irving, *Colour Planning of the Garden*, T. C. & E. C. Jack, 1924.

Michael Tooley (ed.), *Gertrude Jekyll: Artist, Gardener, Craftswoman*, Michaelmas, 1984.

H. Avray Tipping, *The Garden of Today*, Hopkinson, 1933.

John G. Veitch, *Hortus Veitchii*, Veitch, 1906.

Lawrence Weaver, *Houses and Gardens by Sir Edwin Lutyens, R. A.*, Country Life, 1925.

Ellen Willmott, *Warley Garden in Spring and Summer*, Quaritch, 1909.

Ernest H. Wilson, *China, Mother of Gardens*, 1929; reprinted by Blom, 1971.

Ernest H. Wilson, *A Naturalist in Western China*, Methuen, 1913.

Chapter 11: The Modern Garden (pp. 246–92)

Marjorie Allen and Susan Jellicoe, *The New Small Garden*, Architectural Press, 1956.

P. Bardi, *The Tropical Gardens of Burle Marx*, Architectural Press, 1964.

Alan Bloom, *Hardy Perennials*, Faber, 1957.

M. Hayworth Booth, *The Flowering Shrub Garden*, Country Life, 1938.

John Brookes, *Room Outside*, Thames & Hudson, 1969.

Jane Brown, *The English Garden in Our Time*, Antique Collectors Club, 1986.

Jane Brown, *Lanning Roper and His Gardens*, Weidenfeld, 1987.

Percy Cane, *The Creative Art of Garden Design*, Country Life, 1967.

Percy Cane, *The Earth is My Canvas*, Methuen, 1956.

Percy Cane, *Garden Design of Today*, Methuen, 1934.

Percy Cane, *Modern Gardens, British and Foreign*, Studio, 1926–7.

Thomas Church, *Gardens are for People*, Reinhold, 1955; 2nd edn, McGraw-Hill, 1983.

Elizabeth Coxhead, *Constance Spry*, William Luscombe, 1975.

Sylvia Crowe, *Garden Design*, Country Life, 1958; 2nd edn, Packard, 1981.

Margery Fish, *Ground Cover Plants*, Collingridge, 1964.

Margery Fish, *We Made a Garden*, Collingridge, 1956.

Roy Hay, *Gardening the Modern Way*, Penguin, 1962.

G. A. Jellicoe, *Studies in Landscape Design*, Oxford University Press, vol. I, 1960; vol. II, 1966; vol. III, 1970.

A. T. Johnson, *A Garden in Wales*, Edward Arnold, 1927.

A. T. Johnson, *The Garden Today*, My Garden, 1938.

A. T. Johnson, *The Mill Garden*, Collingridge, 1950.

A. T. Johnson, *A Woodland Garden*, Country Life, 1937.

M. E. Jones and H. F. Clark, *Indoor Plants and Gardens*, Architectural Press, 1952.

F. H. and J. L. Kranz, *Gardening Indoors under Light*, Viking, NY, 1957.

Christopher Lloyd, *The Well-Tempered Garden*, Collins, 1970; revised edn, Viking, 1985.

Kenneth Midgley, *Garden Design*, Penguin/RHS, 1966.

Russell Page, *The Education of a Gardener*, Collins, 1962.

J. M. Richards, *Modern Architecture*, Penguin, 1962.

Lanning Roper, *Hardy Herbaceous Plants*, Penguin, 1960.

Allan Ruff and Robert Tregay, *An Ecological Approach to Urban Landscape Design*, University of Manchester, 1982.

Peggie Schultz, *Growing Plants under Artificial Light*, Barrows, 1955.

John O. Simonds, *Landscape Architecture*, Iliffe, 1961.

Christopher Taylor, *Archaeology of Gardens*, Shire, 1983.

Graham Stuart Thomas, *The Old Shrub Roses*, Phoenix 1955.

Graham Stuart Thomas, *Plants for Ground Cover*, Dent, 1970.

Graham Stuart Thomas, *Three Gardens*, Newnes, 1983.

G. C. Taylor, *The Modern Garden*, Country Life, 1936.

Christopher Tunnard, *Gardens in the Modern Landscape*, Architectural Press, 1938.

Ronald Webber, *Percy Cane, Garden Designer*, John Bartholomew, 1975.

T. C. Wells *et al., Creating Attractive Grasslands Using Native Plant Species*, Nature Conservancy Council, 1981.

Illustration Sources and Acknowledgements

Black and white illustrations
(Numbers refer to pages)

Alinari, 7; the author, 125, 142, 206, 207, 237, 257, 289; The Rt Hon. the Earl of Aylesford (photo Alan Greeley), 97; Chris Baines, 286; Pietro Bardi, *Tropical Gardens of Roberto Burle-Marx* (1964), 268; Blenheim Palace, 98 (above); Alan Bloom, *Hardy Perennials* (1957), 279; E. Adveno Brooke, *Gardens of England* (1857), 180; Cambridge University, Collection of Air Photography, 47; Percy Cane, *Creative Art of Garden Design* (1967), 252; *Catalogus Plantarum* (1730), 118; Salomon de Caus, *Les raisons des forces mouvantes* (1659), 42; George Chadwick, *Works of Sir Joseph Paxton* (1961), 177; W. Chambers, *Plans, Elevations, Sections and Perspective Views of the Gardens at Kew* (1763), 108; Thomas Church, *Gardens are for People* (1955), 266, 267; K. J. Conant, *Carolingian and Romanesque Architecture*, 2nd edition (1966), 11; Country Life, 172, 204, 220, 240, 242, 250, 264; Frank Crisp, *Mediaeval Gardens* (1924), 18 25; Richard Einzig, 273; John Fleming, *Spring and Winter Gardening* (1864), 182; Fotomas Index, 13, 36, 59, 65, 71, 87, 92; *Gardeners' Chronicle* (1862), 159, 187; *Gardeners' Chronicle* (1870), 171; John Gerard, *Herball or General Historie of Plantes* (1597), 39; Alan Greeley (courtesy Ashford Hotels Ltd), 129; Thomas Hill, *Gardener's Labyrinth* (1586), 30, 44; Preben Jakobsen, 292; Gertrude Jekyll, *Colour Schemes for the Flower Garden*, 6th edition (1925), 223; Gertrude Jekyll, *Flower Decoration for the House* (1907), 281; Gertrude Jekyll and Lawrence Weaver, *Gardens for Small Country Houses* (1912), 219; Geoffrey Jellicoe, *Studies in Landscape Design*, Vol. 2 (1966), 270; Margaret Jourdain, *The Work of William Kent* (1948), 88; A. F. Kersting, 56, 61, 98 (below), 200, 202, 205, 216, 254, 276; R. W. King, 90; William Lawson, *New Orchard and Garden* (1618), 52; Loggon, *Oxonia Illustrata*, 57; Jane Loudon, *The Ladies Flower Garden of Ornamental Perennials* (1843), 163; John Loudon, *Hints on the Formation of Gardens* (1812), 147, 148, 149; John Loudon, *Landscape Gardening and Landscape Architecture of the Late Humphry Repton* (1840), 139; John Loudon, *The Villa Gardener* (1838), 175; Mansell Collection, 117 (below); Marlborough Picture Library, 113, 167, 189; Gervase Markham, *The Country Hous-Wife's Garden* (1617), 48; J. Martin (1817) (photo Simon Brookes), 136; Thomas Mawson, *Art and Practice of Garden Design*, 5th edition (1926), 226, 227; Philip Miller, *Gardeners Dictionary* (1730), 111; National Maritime Museum, 117 (above); National Trust, 49, 62, 63, 73, 78, 81, 83, 132, 188, 239, 241, 248, 249; National Trust (Waddesdon), 185; Painshill Park Trust, 277; John Parkinson, *Paradisi in Sole* (1629), 54; B. Platina, *Von der Eerlichte Zimlichen, auch erlaupten wolust des Leibs* (Augsburg, 1542, by Hans Weiditz), 24; Reef Point Collection, University of California, 221, 225; Humphry Repton, *Sheringham*, 133; William Robinson, *Garden Design and Architects' Gardens* (1892), 214, 215; William Robinson, *Parks, Promenades and Gardens of Paris* (1878), 186, 193, 194; William Robinson, *Wild Garden*, 2nd edition (1883), 195; Royal Horticultural Society, 144; RIBA Drawings Collection, 127, 135; Mrs L. Sales, 168; Steven Scrivens, 290; Ronald Sheridan, 6; Harry Smith Horticultural Collection, 121, 124, 233, 244, 285, 291; Dorothy Stroud, *Capability Brown*, 2nd edition (1975), 96; Victoria and Albert Museum, 72; Ellen Willmott, *Warley Garden in Spring and Summer* (1905), 235.

Colour illustrations
(Numbers refer to colour plates)

Bridgeman Art Library, 1, 6, 9, 23, 24, 26, 30; National Trust, 2, 3, 5, 7, 10, 11, 13, 14, 22, 29; reproduced by gracious permission of Her Majesty The Queen, 4; A. F. Kersting, 8, 15, 17, 19, 20, 28, 31; Michael Holman, 12; Harry Smith Horticultural Collection, 16, 21, 34; National Trust (Waddesdon Manor), 18; Iris Hardwick Library, 25; Picture Point, 27; Richard Bisgrove, 32, 33; Graham Thomas, 35; Michael Laurie, 36; John Brookes, 37; Valerie Finnis, 38; Jerry Harpur, 39, 42, 44; Museum of Garden History, 40; David Austin, 41; Adrian Bloom, 43.

Index

Page numbers of black and white illustrations are given in **bold** type.
Colour illustrations are indexed by plate number.